INSUFFICIENT FUNDS

INSUFFICIENT FUNDS

The Culture of Money

in Low-Wage Transnational Families

Hung Cam Thai

Stanford University Press
Stanford, California

Stanford University Press
Stanford, California

Printed in the United States of America

Library of Congress Cataloging-in-Publication Data

Thai, Hung Cam, author.
 Insufficient funds : the culture of money in low-wage transnational families /
Hung Cam Thai.
     pages cm
 Includes bibliographical references and index.
 ISBN 978-0-8047-7731-5 (cloth : alk. paper) --
 ISBN 978-0-8047-7732-2 (pbk.   )
 1. Vietnamese--United States--Economic conditions. 2. Vietnamese--United
States--Social conditions. 3. Immigrants--Family relationships--United States.
4. Immigrants--Family relationships--Vietnam. 5. Money--Social aspects--United
States. 6. Money--Social aspects--Vietnam. 7. Families--Economic aspects--United
States. 8. Families--Economic aspects--Vietnam. 9. Transnationalism--Social
aspects--United States. 10. Transnationalism--Social aspects--Vietnam. I. Title.
 E184.V53.T45 2014
 305.8959'22073--dc23
                          2013042134

ISBN 978-0-8047-9056-7 (electronic)

Typeset by Bruce Lundquist in 10.5/15 Adobe Garamond

To my students and teachers

TABLE OF CONTENTS

ACKNOWLEDGMENTS

My first gratitude is reserved for the more than 120 men and women who spent time sharing with me stories about their lives. Some of them may disagree with my analysis, but I hope they recognize the importance of their stories in helping the world understand dilemmas associated with the culture of money among transnational families.

My second thanks go to the institutions that provided financial support: the Pacific Rim Fellowship, the Hewlett Foundation, the Freeman Foundation, the John Randolph Haynes and Dora Haynes Foundation, the Senior Research Fellowship in the Asia Research Institute at the National University of Singapore, and the Faculty Residential Fellowship at the Institute of East Asian Studies at Berkeley. Many thanks to former dean Cecilia Conrad at Pomona College for providing generous research funds for fieldwork and for time off to write, and to Associate Dean Jonathan Wright for approving the earmarking of such funding, even when the earmarking seemed unconventional.

A team of research assistants from the United States and Vietnam was involved in different phases of the project: from the United States, my students Dani Carillo, Christopher Fiorello, Kyla Johnson, and Nicole Runge came to Vietnam to help me collect data; and from Vietnam, Loc Mai Do, Nhat Minh,

Bich Nguyen, Hanh Nguyen, Nga Nguyen, Tuan Nguyen, and Tuyet Phan helped with fieldwork and data analysis. Bich and Nhat worked tirelessly for more than three years managing the research team, recruiting respondents, helping to oversee the transcription of data, and summarizing interviews. On campus at Pomona, Ciera Divens, Laura Enriquez, and Delilah Garcia helped collect and verify hard facts. Howard Chang and Jordan Pedraza organized relevant readings, created the bibliography, and provided various other forms of research support. Notably, Jordan spent an entire year digitizing all the materials in my office on one USB disk so I could be globally portable. The input of these sixteen research assistants was vital to the core work that went into the book.

The chapters of this book contain ideas developed over a decade, during which time I benefited greatly from conversations with many more people than I can name. In various contexts, I am grateful to Sherry Apostol, Ingrid Banks, Daniele Belanger, Huong Bui, Richard Bui, Jorgen Carling, Nicole Constable, Bui The Cuong, Mary Danico, Ajay Deshmukh, Pawan Dhingra, Joanna Dreby, Mach Duong, Lai Ah Eng, Yen Le Espiritu, Sarah Fenstermaker, Evelyn Nakano Glenn, Patrick Harms, Kimberly Kay Hoang, Lan Anh Hoang, Arlie Hochschild, Adi Hovav, Evelyn Hu-Dehart, Sallie Hughes, Sergey Ioffe, Gavin Jones, Miliann Kang, Nazli Kibria, Nadia Kim, Jaime Kurtz, Vivian Louie, Edward Necaise, Sinh Nguyen, Eileen Otis, Rhacel Parrenas, Allison Pugh, Karen Pyke, Kitsana Salyphone, Leah Schmalzbauer, Celine Shimizu, Rachel Silvey, Joe Singh, Lok Siu, Jinnhua Su, Barrie Thorne, Mika Toyota, Kim Xuyen Tran, Allison Truitt, Kim Chuyen Truong, Takeyuki Tsuda, Linda Trinh Vo, Biao Xiang, Brenda Yeoh, Jean Yeung, and Peter Zinoman.

During the final stage of this book, I unexpectedly received a writing fellowship that allowed me to spend nine months at the Institute of East Asian Studies at UC Berkeley. I am thankful to members of the faculty group there who met regularly to discuss our work, including You-tien Hsing, John Lie, Xin Liu, and Qing Zhou. Special thanks to the director, Wen-hsin Yeh, who provided skillful moderation for our group meetings, and to Rochelle Halperin and Charlotte Cowden for cheerfully administering all our events.

I am indebted to Bryan DeWitt, Jason Gonzalez, Gilda Ochoa, Patrick Snyder, Whitney Snyder, Khoi Tran, My Huynh Tran, and Linus Yamane for reading the entire book and giving valuable feedback. David Hinson and Patricia McDonald, two friends from my undergraduate years, also read the entire book and gave editorial advice about reframing materials for readability and analytical rigor. The final person who read the manuscript and to whom I am most indebted is Jude Berman, whom I met while on the fellowship in Berkeley. Jude read countless drafts, and the book would be sloppier and much less readable without her critical feedback.

I am also grateful for the feedback I received from audience members at universities, conferences, bookstores, and community organizations where I delivered lectures, including in Tel Aviv, Beirut, Paris, Bucharest, Rome, Prague, Singapore, Beppu, Kyoto, Tokyo, Lund, Saigon, Hanoi, Da Nang, Beijing, Penang, Hong Kong, Kunming, Kuala Lumpur, Montréal, Seoul, Miami, Blacksburg, East Lansing, Sacramento, Berkeley, Denver, Atlanta, Portland, San Francisco, San Diego, Los Angeles, Boston, Tucson, New Orleans, Santa Barbara, Pomona, and Claremont.

In Claremont and Los Angeles, friends and colleagues provided support that made the balance of teaching, writing, and fun achievable. They include Eileen Cheng, David Elliott, Peter Flueckiger, Dru Gladney, Elizabeth Glater, Bryan Gobin, Sharon Goto, Eric Hurley, Eysha Hurley, Shelva Hurley, Pardis Mahdavi, Lynn Miyake, Hoang Nguyen, Gilda Ochoa, Rhacel Parrenas, Ben Rosenberg, Heather Williams, and Sam Yamashita. Most importantly, I am indebted to Lynn Rapaport for her support as a colleague and friend, and to Sheila Pinkel for her wisdom and humor. Gail Orozco and Kayo Yoshikawa provided administrative support on a daily basis and made it possible for me to serve concurrently as chair of the Department of Sociology and director of the Pacific Basin Institute while working on the book. Sheri Sardinas recently joined the Department of Sociology and has been a terrific staff member. Madeline Gosiaco has provided administrative support in the Intercollegiate Department of Asian American Studies, for which I am thankful. Michele Levers and Cindy Snyder from the Honnold Library were incredibly helpful in gathering materials whenever I needed a source, sending them to me at lightning speed when I requested them. Anna Ratana and Theresa Alvarez made sure everything in my personal life was in order so I could flourish in my professional life.

I am extremely grateful to Kate Wahl, editor-in-chief at Stanford University Press, who acquired my book and then served as my editor. Kate's feedback helped sharpen the arguments and clarify many points. Kate was always encouraging, yet straightforward, honest, and professional; she truly lives up to her national reputation as a dream editor. I am also indebted to the two anonymous reviewers who read the entire manuscript and provided constructive and helpful comments, as well as to Jan McInroy for the incredible work on meticulously copyediting the book. At the press, Frances Malcolm provided critical and speedy administrative support, while Emily Smith, the production editor, shepherded the book through the final phase of getting it into print.

My personal thanks come last for the people whose friendships enriched my life while I worked on this book. In Vietnam, My Chau, Jonathan Gordon, Thanh Kim Hue, Dam Vinh Hung, Huong Lan, Ut Bach Lan, Tin Le, Daniel Logan, Nga Nguyen, Thuc Nguyen, Kieu Oanh, My Tam, Le Thuy, Kim Chuyen Truong, Linh Truong, and Bach Tuyet provided companionship whenever I needed, and especially when I needed help in recruiting respondents. My friendships with Richard Bui, Huong Bui, and Chanh Phan in Vietnam provided a sturdy anchor for a wonderful life there and enabled me to thrive in my work. Richard and Huong opened their homes to me generously whenever I needed to be in Vietnam, and I am grateful for their friendship, generosity, and interest in my work. In France, my dear friend Mary Boyington provided constant support from afar via Skype, as well as a haven during my visits to her home in Aix-en-Provence when I needed a break from life outside the Vietnam–U.S. corridor.

In Berkeley during the final stage of writing this book, a number of friends were integral to the daily, nonstop task of writing; without them, I am confident I would not have been motivated to complete the task. Anjelica Randall urged me to learn the art of taking walks, which I am convinced was the ultimate trick in getting the writing done. Neetha Iyer stepped in at the perfect moment to cheer me on to the finish line. Sherry Apostol provided intimate labor in many forms, most important of which was the daily and often unplanned companionship so essential for my well-being. At Berkeley, the proximity to a few of my lifelong friends meant I was able to call on them whenever I needed to get away from the treacherous mental work of writing. Ajay Deshmukh and Jinnhua Su made themselves available whenever I asked to do anything that got me away from writing. Matthew Nemethy knew just the right moment to disrupt my writing. All these friends came to my house when I needed the disruption, but also respected the times I had to be alone to get the work done. Finally, Sergey Ioffe never fails to be a reliable ear to listen to any dilemma I face, as well as to celebrate with me anything that needs celebration, no matter how far apart we may be at the time. I am most fortunate to have found a best friend in adulthood with whom social equivalence, anomaly, idiosyncrasy, loyalty, reliability, trust, brilliance, and humor are entangled in such a complex and fun way. It is through Sergey that I learned that friendships do not naturally develop, but are made through focused effort and intent. And yet, paradoxically, true friendship is achieved effortlessly over time.

Victoria and Clive Elppa made sure I was on task each and every day, calling me every hour in the last six months of writing, and cheerleading with a daily report on my progress when I sometimes felt I could not write another word. Claudia Rucaa made sure I never got lost wherever I went, and happily joins me on every single journey I make.

NOTE ON TRANSLATIONS

Vietnamese is a tonal language with varying regional dialects that requires the use of diacritic marks. I have chosen not to employ diacritic marks in order to facilitate smooth reading. In addition, as with any research involving translations, some words do not have exact translations, and some words lose their complexity once translated. When translations seriously lose intended meanings, I have provided the original Vietnamese words in parentheses without diacritic marks. In complicated cases, I have provided additional explanations in the endnotes.

INSUFFICIENT FUNDS

CHAPTER I

SIX TALES OF
MIGRANT MONEY

THIS BOOK tells the story of money and migration among
transnational families in the Vietnamese diaspora, with a
specific focus on families of low-wage immigrants living in the United States
and their left-behind non-migrant relatives in Vietnam.[1] It is about the culture
of money, as experienced by those who give, those who receive, and those who
spend, as well as about those who left and those who stayed put. This nearly
forty-year narrative begins with the mass exodus of Vietnamese emigrants after
the Vietnam War ended in 1975, picks up again with the post-1986 reentry of
Vietnam into the world economy after a decade hiatus of economic progress,
and picks up yet again in 1995, when the United States and Vietnam resumed
diplomatic relations after a twenty-year suspension.[2]

The people you are about to meet include members of transnational families whom I met and interviewed in Vietnam. Their stories give us a sense of
how migrants sacrifice for their left-behind relatives back home, as well as why
they are compelled to give and spend money. At the same time, these stories tell
us about a global culture of relative consumption that has prevailed in many
economies of the developing world, owing to increasing numbers of transnational migrants making return visits and spending money there.[3] The ways

in which different members of these low-wage transnational families interpret giving, receiving, and spending money—all of which are embedded in classical sociological concerns about obligation, reciprocity, status, and economic behavior in family life—carry significant implications for understanding the contemporary intersection of social class and migration under global capitalism. I first introduce three immigrant individuals now living in the United States; in the following section, we meet their respective non-migrant relatives living in Vietnam.

THE MIGRANTS

Cam Bui lives in southwestern Philadelphia in a small rented apartment, less than a ten-minute drive from the city's Vietnamese enclave, where she goes to work and socialize.[4] Now thirty-eight years old, she came to the United States with one of her older brothers in the early 1990s at the age of nineteen. Her parents and four other siblings live in and around Thu Duc, a suburb seventeen miles outside Saigon's city center.[5] Last year, Cam married another Vietnamese immigrant, whom she met at the Catholic church she attends in the Philadelphia community. She returns to Vietnam to visit her family more often than her brother does because she is able to take off more easily from her job as a cashier at a supermarket owned by a co-ethnic friend. Both she and her brother, however, regularly send money to support the entire family in Thu Duc.

The two began sending money after Cam returned to Vietnam in 1999, her first visit in about a decade. Their father had had a heart attack, but it would have been too expensive for both siblings to make the trip. When she arrived, Cam was relieved to find her father had recovered; however, her month-long stay showed her the extent to which she had forgotten the reality of Vietnam. She explains: "I knew, of course, people don't have a lot, but I did not know the severity of poverty, on the street, in my parents' neighborhood. Everywhere you go, it was a different world from America. When you get older, you see things differently." That initial visit led Cam to reexamine her life in America:

Up to that point, I think I always felt that I did not do so well in America. I always compared myself to all my friends who went on to college and got professional jobs. But that first visit really forced me to think about how lucky I am to live in America, how I have so much more than my family. I always know that at a minimum, I can find a job, no matter how low-paying. My siblings cannot say the same in Thu Duc because there are absolutely no jobs there.[6]

When Cam returned to Philadelphia, she acted on her new transnational view by telling her brother she thought they should regularly send money back home. Previously, they typically sent money only when an emergency arose. At first, her brother resisted Cam's proposal, claiming they should continue to send money only when someone needed it. Cam says her brother "did not think we could afford to send money regularly and he did not want people in Vietnam to expect it from us on a regular basis." Even though her brother was worried about adding to their financial burden, Cam was willing to work longer hours for extra pay, as long as her brother could contribute some money. Eventually she convinced him to give $300 a month. Cam herself decided to put in about $500 per month. This amount is about a third of her monthly pay, if she includes pay for the ten overtime hours she added weekly. As she says, "My heart aches every time I think about one of my sisters, who is married with two children and they all live in a house that has a dirt floor."

Cam and her brother now have a system for managing how much and how often they send money to family members. "We have a separate bank account for *gui tien* [sending money] to our family so we can keep track of the money. We try hard, no matter what, to send money on a regular basis," Cam explains. "Our family cannot support themselves no matter what they do in Vietnam. All our siblings work, but none of them makes more than $150 per month, and they all have children. So we decided that because we were lucky to come to America, we would help them out."

Cam cares deeply for her left-behind family members in Vietnam, a few of whom helped to fund the passage for her and her brother to come to the United States as boat refugees among thousands of "unaccompanied minors."[7] She feels indebted to her family for the passage, but perhaps even more important, Cam's perspective about economic privilege and her own financial status—however limited it might be by her $12-per-hour job—is rooted in her dual frame of reference for life in Philadelphia and in Thu Duc. She feels extremely lucky, for example, that she does not live in a house with a dirt floor, and that she can drink water directly from the tap. When I met her, Cam had made six visits back to Vietnam, staying more than one month each time. Her goal in each subsequent visit was to make life even better for her family there. "I wanted to do everything I could to help my family," she says. "I got extra work. I started working on weekends. I started spending less money. In addition, every penny I saved I would send back to my parents, brothers, and sisters. I began to see them as my only responsibility in life."

.   .   .

Dinh Le is a thirty-six-year-old man who rents a room from a Vietnamese immigrant family in San Jose, California. He and his parents came to the United States when Dinh was eighteen, under the sponsorship of Dinh's older brother and his brother's wife. Dinh lived with them in Orlando, Florida, before he decided to move to California to attend a community college. Although he did not know anyone there, he went by himself because he had always dreamed of going to California, which has the largest Vietnamese immigrant population in the United States (i.e., in San Jose, Orange County, and San Diego). He has been going to school part-time at the community college, but does not think he will finish. He explains, "I've never liked school and I am not sure if it is going to get me a good job. If I transfer to the university, I think the best I could do is study accounting, but that is so boring." He is now working in San Jose as a carpenter, a job he says he enjoys because he is always on the move. Dinh is one of the highest-paid immigrants I interviewed for this book, making nearly $20 per hour. He describes himself as very hardworking and hopes to own a business one day.

Dinh returned to Vietnam for the first time shortly after he moved to California. Of that first return trip, he says, "It was the time of my life. It was like California on steroids! I always wanted to live in California because of the large Vietnamese population, but I should have thought about coming back to Vietnam and living here for some period. It is like I found a sense of myself that I could never describe before." Although he has entertained the thought of living in Vietnam, he plans to stay in the United States because he says he could not find a job in Saigon that would pay him anywhere near his wages in San Jose.

When I met Dinh for the first time in Saigon, I assumed from his spending habits alone that he had a lot of money. One summer evening, for example, Dinh invited me out with his cousins, two uncles, and some other relatives. We went to Monaco,[8] a large and fancy nightclub that had just opened. As a gracious guest, I ordered only one bottle of beer for the night, but was quickly astonished that Dinh had ordered for the table three bottles of Hennessy cognac, the very expensive, but most preferred, drink because of the status it conveys at nightclubs in the city. When it was time to pay the check, it came to nearly $400.[9] I must have looked astonished, so Dinh quickly said, "Don't worry, my friend, I got it covered. It's a night out with my family. We are having a good time."

During our interview the next day, as I treat Dinh to some much cheaper coffee, I broach the topic of money and ask why he did not split the bill with me or the other family members, including his two uncles who came with us. Without hesitation, and as if he thinks this was my first visit to Vietnam, Dinh explains:

When you go to nightclubs in Saigon, you have to remember that the prices are not local prices.[10] Everything here is catered to overseas people, especially to us Viet Kieu.[11] All the businesses here, they know that white foreigners living in the city won't spend $100 on a bottle of Hennessy. As Vietnamese men, we know how to play it right. We know how to spend money. As for my uncles, I would never ask them to pay for anything when we go out. It's my treat when we go anywhere. We make much more money than they can ever make in Saigon, so it's only right that we pay for everything.

In contrast with Cam, Dinh rarely sends money back to his family in Vietnam. Rather, he freely spends it on them when he makes return visits. In addition to lavish nights out, he has bought them pricey gifts, such as fancy picture frames and expensive clothes from the United States. He says he likes to spend money on his family because he wants them to know he loves them and he is willing to pay for them "to have the best time in the city." Dinh explains that he knows each bottle of cognac he buys costs more than the monthly income of one of his uncles. That does not matter. The important thing, Dinh says, is that "they know I am able to spend money like a foreigner. They have to know that we are doing well in America and that we have the cash to play." There is no question that Dinh is a big spender when he returns to Saigon.

· · ·

Quang Tran is a young-looking forty-two-year-old man who lives in a Vietnamese enclave of about six thousand people in northeast Atlanta, Gwinnett County, Georgia. He is married and his three children attend the Gwinnett public schools. He and his wife take a daily ninety-mile round-trip to the Atlanta International

Airport, where they work as airplane cabin cleaners. They moved to Gwinnett to be near its small Vietnamese community, where housing is cheaper and nicer than what is available near their workplace. Quang says his job is good because it is stable, unionized, and provides full health benefits as well as paid vacation time. Almost none of the immigrants featured in this book reported receiving these benefits from their work.

Quang is from a well-to-do family in Vietnam, and in many ways, migrating to the United States more than two decades ago as a boat refugee was an experience of downward mobility. Yet he says he and his wife "have a good life in Atlanta. We have good friends. Not a lot of money, but we have more than many of our friends and family in Vietnam. We could do something else, like open up a business, but we would have to work a lot more hours and probably have to force our children to work in the business with us, like so many other Vietnamese families." Both Quang and his wife have a sturdy network of family in Vietnam, where they try to go every two or three years. On three occasions over the past decade, Quang went by himself because they could not afford to bring the entire family. Quang says they make sure the children grow up with a strong sense of their Vietnamese identity and attachment to their family in Vietnam.

Unlike Cam's family, Quang's family in Vietnam is not poor by the local standards. For example, he has one brother who works at the post office and another who owns a jewelry store; although his one sister is unemployed, her husband makes a steady income driving taxis in the city. By local measures, his left-behind family is middle class in their cultural context, even if each of them has a monthly income in Saigon of less than $300. The biggest financial difference between them and Quang, however, is that his siblings in Vietnam all own the modest houses in which they live, whereas Quang and his wife have more than twenty-five years left on the $900-per-month mortgage for their three-bedroom suburban house in Gwinnett. Like Dinh, it is important to Quang that his family knows he is doing well in the United States and has "a good life." He explains:

I do have a good life in Atlanta. When I look at my brothers and sisters in Saigon, even among the successful ones who own their businesses, I feel they have less security in their lives. They don't have insurance, and they do not have the future of social security in retirement that we have in America. I think life is better in America, even if it's lonely. It's fun in Vietnam and you have more family there, more community, but you can't really have a future there.

One clear way that Quang shows his family he has a good life in the United States is to give them money on a regular basis: "We make sure to send everyone some money on New Year's, but also when they need it. The truth is that if you live in America, you have to show your family you can give them money on special occasions. If you don't give them money, they think you are failing."

Quang explains that he controls most of the money in his household, especially when it comes to sending money to family in Vietnam. His wife, although not entirely happy with the arrangement, does not object because she has a brother, also living in Atlanta, who supports her family in Vietnam. Quang and his wife earn nearly $43,000 in combined yearly income and they estimate they send about 10 to 15 percent of that to Vietnam every year. In contrast to Cam, Quang says he does not think his family really needs the money he regularly sends back: "I think they would be fine if we don't send them money, but as a family member living in America, you have to send money back home regularly." Whereas Cam sends money because she feels an immense sense of responsibility for her family, some of whom live in abject poverty, Quang's motivation for sending money is to make a symbolic gesture to convey that he has achieved the American Dream.

· · ·

Cam, Dinh, and Quang live in diverse places across the American landscape: a small apartment in an ethnic enclave of Philadelphia, a rented room in San Jose, and a suburban house on the outskirts of Atlanta. They are all Vietnamese low-wage immigrants with no college degrees, which means their prospects for stable employment in the American economy are relatively limited. Although it is difficult to quantify the experience and identity of being poor,[12] demographers define low-wage workers as those who earn up to 200 percent of the prevailing minimum wage, which in 2012 was $7.25 per hour.[13] Thus, anyone earning $14.50 per hour or less in 2012 was demographically a member of the low-wage labor force.[14] Nearly half of all immigrant workers in the United States belong to this labor force, compared with one-third of all native workers.[15] This low-wage labor force is the backbone of American society because its members do most of the hard physical labor that helps the world's strongest economy flourish. The forty-six Vietnamese immigrants interviewed for this study have very few resources and scant savings. Their jobs barely allow them to make ends meet, yet they do not rely on government assistance for their daily expenditures. Most rent their homes, with about a quarter sharing a home with multiple families. Furthermore, and importantly, most manage to economize in such a way that they can make return visits as well as give and spend money on a regular basis in Vietnam. Most fit the classification that Katherine S. Newman and Victor Tan Chen term the "missing class" or the "near poor," because for the most part, the migrant respondents in this study do not face the same problems as do those living below the poverty line, which in 2012 was $23,050 for a family of four.[16] For example, the migrants in this study do not live in socially isolated neighborhoods, nor are they seen standing in welfare lines.[17]

These three individuals are similar because all have sturdy transnational family ties in Vietnam that compel them to make regular return visits, despite having very limited means to do so.[18] More important, their return visits to Vietnam have compelled them in myriad ways to give and spend money, as well as to continue giving upon their return to the United States. Cam is extremely concerned about her family's welfare in Saigon: her gratitude and her sense of being lucky to be in the United States, along with her guilt, have motivated her to commit a huge portion of her wages to her family. Dinh, on the other hand, *spends*, rather than *gives*, money when he makes return visits. This spending behavior allows him to demonstrate his relative success in the United States. He participates in consumption behavior that he would not take part in at home in San Jose. And for Quang, like Dinh, it is very important to show his family in Vietnam that he has a good life in America, according to the definition he has developed. However, unlike Dinh, Quang *gives* money when he returns to Vietnam as well as while he is back in the United States.

THE LEFT-BEHIND

Lan Bui is one of Cam's four younger siblings, the sister Cam identified as the least privileged. Lan is a tailor who works in a small shop in District 12 of Saigon, where she earns a little more than 2 million VND a month, the equivalent of about $100. She first left the family home in Thu Duc to work in a foreign-owned garment factory, where she agreed to live in a dormitory the company built for workers. Later, through the introduction of a friend, she was able to get a job in a small shop in the city making twice the amount she earned at the factory. A twenty-seven-year-old woman with a soft smile but an assertive personality, Lan met her husband at the factory where she worked. They have two children, who are too young to go to school, so Lan leaves them in Thu Duc with her parents while she and her husband work at the tailor shop.

Lan says she and her husband wish to open their own tailor shop in the city, but that would require more capital than they have. She says her sister Cam has been helpful to her family but cannot help with Lan's goal of opening a tailor shop: "Even though she had been away for so long, Cam came back and saw our living standards, and she has been helping us over the past few years. She promised that she will help pay for the educational fees for my children to go to school. Even though it's a public school, we still have to pay fees that my husband and I cannot afford."

Lan and her husband own a tiny plot of land on the outskirts of Saigon, where they are slowly building a modest home. As is the case for many young couples in Vietnam, they had the financial help of their parents, who gave them $4,200, which, along with their savings, allowed them to buy the plot outright. After two years, however, the house still has only a roof, basic furnishings, and dirt floors. When their children visit, they sleep in a loft built of cheap wood bought from construction companies that sell leftover materials in the urban communities springing up around the new Saigon. Instead of a bathroom with plumbing, they use an outhouse. "We hope to slowly save more money and build up our house," Lan says, "but land is all we need for now, and we are fine with the roof over our head. One of my brothers did the same, and within two years he was able to put concrete floors in his house." Lan and her husband make a joint income of about 5 million VND per month, which is slightly more than the average income of people living in the city's outskirts.[19] Through careful spending habits, they are able to save about 20 percent of their income monthly. All they need is about 12 million VND to put concrete floors in the house, which Lan says they should easily be able to save within two years.

Lan and her husband used to ride their bicycles six miles each way to and from the tailor shop. The trip took about thirty minutes each way, and along the picturesque ride, they would stop at the market, visit friends, and run errands. When Cam bought them a motorbike, they were the first among their coworkers at the tailor shop to own one. Their lives were transformed because they could travel long distances for leisure and to shop. Nevertheless, as Lan explains, the gift was not accompanied by the expected boost in status:

To be honest, I have been embarrassed for many years to tell people that I have a brother and a sister living in America. Because we have nothing to show for it. I was afraid that people would say, "You have the reputation, but not the goods." I don't know why but it took them a long time to return home. Over the years, we saw so many other people with family members from abroad come back, bringing back gifts, building homes for their families, and people's lives were changed much better than ours. When my sister came back, we only got the motorbike, so even though I know my coworkers wondered how we got the money to buy the motorbike, we did not tell everyone that my sister gave it to us.

·   ·   ·

Dinh's uncle, Son, is a forty-eight-year-old shop owner in District 3, the district located adjacent to the bustling center of Saigon. Son sells a wide assortment of household supplies, with a focus on simple and cheap health and beauty items, such as shampoo, toothpaste, and lotion. He got into the business when his wife's family in Vietnam helped make the initial investment. When I met him, he had owned the shop for more than fifteen years. Ten years ago, with savings and a steady income from their business, Son and his wife were able to buy the upstairs unit of their shop, and they live there now. Son explains that together they make nearly $1,000 per month, which is a handsome amount considering that the average monthly salary in Saigon is about $150. This small-scale mercantilism generates enough income that Son and his wife can take their five children on annual vacations along the Vietnamese central coast, where they go to a seaside hotel and eat plenty of seafood "at least two weeks a year," Son says. He has a large network of relatives living abroad, including his nephew.

Son was one of the uncles who came along on that expensive night out at the Monaco nightclub, a topic I raise with him. Son is quick to say, "Dinh does that each time he comes back here. We can't stop him. Since he lives abroad, he must have money to play with. But anyways, it's only once in a while that he comes back, so I think it's good that he tries to have some fun." When asked if he ever feels obligated to pay on these outings, Son provides a nuanced explanation: "Sometimes I feel uncomfortable that he spends so much money, like when he bought those expensive bottles of cognac. You know, many Viet Kieu, when they come here, spend a lot of money," he says. "I think some of them pay for everything, which is not always good. In my case, I am his uncle, an elder to him, so I should pay sometimes. But my wife and I have been talking about how very costly it is for us when Dinh or any of the other overseas family members visit." Son continues:

We have to spend more when they visit, even if they are paying for us to go to expensive places. Most of the time, to be honest with you, they take us to places that we normally would never go to, and we think it's a waste. But we have to be polite and pretend we enjoy those activities. Then, we have to return the favor by doing something nice for them. Of course, we can't pay as much as they spend, but we have to do something more than just take them for a bowl of noodles. My wife and I have become very careful about how we plan to spend money when they are in town.

Son is a frugal man who believes he has a good life in Vietnam as a small shop owner. He and his wife have tremendous freedom in their work lives. They live in urban Saigon, with plenty of attractive amenities around them; they have no debt, take regular vacations, live near relatives, and are able to afford to send their children to relatively good schools. By most local and global measures of quality of life, they have peaceful and privileged lifestyles. Their nephew, Dinh, however, thinks that they are poor because they live in a modest apartment above their shop and sell cheap household supplies, none of which costs more than $3. They also do not own a car, although Dinh on one occasion promised to buy them one. At the moment, Son and his wife drive a modest motorbike that they bought eight years ago.

The family's household income of $1,000 per month is not half of what Dinh makes in San Jose, but it allows them much stronger purchasing power, given the disparate cost of living between Saigon and San Jose. Son says:

I can't just sit in Vietnam expecting my family to send me money. I know many people here are like that—they sit around, never work, and wait for their monthly money delivery. But my wife and I are not like that. We are healthy and we can work. We have never been dependent on anyone, and not on anyone living abroad. The only time my wife and I have been dependent on family was when we borrowed some money from her parents to buy the shop that we now own.

Unlike Lan, Son does not feel pressured to tell his neighbors and friends that he has family living abroad. This is because Son himself is economically self-sufficient. If anything, Son sometimes feels burdened when his nephew returns to Vietnam, because even if Dinh spends lavish amounts of money on them at frivolous places, Son says he has to return those favors by spending more than he wants on his nephew.

.   .   .

Quang's sister, Truc Tran, is a cheerful fifty-four-year-old woman who speaks with a quick pace, often interrupting others before they finish their sentences. She has a twenty-one-year-old son and a fourteen-year-old daughter. Until five years ago, Truc earned 2.5 million VND a month working at a department store as an invoice collector for the food court, where shoppers buy coupons in exchange for food at one of the many kiosks. The only income she and her husband currently generate is from his work as a taxi driver in the city. He earns about 6 million VND a month, the equivalent of about $300. Her husband started this job two years ago when Quang gave them $3,000 to "buy" a taxi license on the black market. They spent $2,000 on the license and used the rest of the money to buy a large TV for the small apartment they occupy in a dilapidated building about twelve miles from the city center.

With quick steps in her walk, Truc is friendly and inviting. She offers me coffee and lunch when I visit, even though it is only 10 a.m. At our first meeting, Truc is conspicuously curious about life in America. She shoots a barrage of questions: "You know Quang lives in Atlanta. Are you far from him? Will you visit him in Atlanta? Do you know where he works? Is it a good job? Do you know if his house in Gwinnett is in a nice community?" Truc is also direct, like many local Vietnamese, about the topic of money: "How much money do you make it America? Is it easy to get a job there? Does the government really support you if you are unemployed?"

It does not take long to figure out that Truc has limited knowledge of her brother's economic life in Atlanta, or of life in the United States generally. It is also quickly apparent that she evaluates people based on how much money they have. Thus, economic standing is an important measuring stick for social status in her view. For example, instead of asking about what I teach, Truc says, "You teach at a university, you must make so much money," with a smile of approval and admiration. When I turn the tables and ask about her general view of life in the United States, Truc says, "I think it is very comfortable. Everyone knows that. My brother sent us pictures of his house, and it looks beautiful. You see where I'm living now—this small apartment we rent here is not even five hundred square feet, and four of us live here. It's very crowded." Referring to the pictures Quang sent her, Truc continues:

Quang's house in Atlanta is five times bigger and he and his wife each own a car. Both he and his wife have good jobs, and their children go to beautiful schools. They sent us pictures of their cars, house, and schools, so we know they are very comfortable over there. We also heard that if you are unemployed and you have young children, the government would take care of you. That's a great country. It's very modern. You are very lucky to live there, too.

To be fair, however, one reason Truc does not fully know about the economic reality of life in the United States is because Quang has been generous to her and her family. The measuring stick she uses to evaluate success is based partly on how much money Quang distributes to her and her family. He does not explicitly convey to Truc his economic standing in the United States.

On two occasions, Truc asked Quang for relatively large amounts of money, and he sent them to her. The first sum was the $3,000 Quang sent her husband to acquire a taxi license, an amount that would have taken her husband a year to earn. The second sum was $1,600, which Quang sent so her son could pay the initial tuition to attend an English-language school in the city. Quang not only sent the money but also agreed to pay the $120 monthly tuition required for Truc's son to maintain the English classes. Of her brother, Quang, Truc says, "He's always been a generous person, always giving to his family. When my parents were still living, Quang made sure to send money every month to support them. He's also been the most successful in the family. That's why he got to America and none of us were able to go. He was willing to take the risk and to spend all of his life savings in the 1980s. I tried to escape by boat, too, but each time I did not succeed."

Truc plans to send her son to Australia so he can study computer engineering. "I hope he can get a good job there," she says. "And then, if he gets a good job, he can live there and eventually sponsor us to live in Australia with him. It would be better to live in a Western country, modern, and with good amenities."

Truc has no savings to execute the plan to send her son to study abroad. She says her son will probably not get a scholarship because "those are for the best students, and my son did not go to the best schools, so he can't compete for those scholarships." Yet Truc is optimistic because she believes Quang will help her son financially. She says, "Quang loves his nephew very much. And he also knows that I want to leave the country and probably the only way for us is to go to Australia because it is very hard for Quang to sponsor us to America." She says the total cost to study in Australia is about $18,000 per year. "I don't think that will be a big problem for Quang," she quickly says when asked if that amount is reasonable to expect from Quang. "If he can't give it to us, I will just ask him for a loan."

Truc's main reference point for a better life—in particular, for going abroad— is anchored in the streams of money her brother has been sending over the past few years. These funds convey to her the enormous possibilities that would exist if she could leave the country. She takes heart from the fact that when Quang sent $3,000 for the taxi license, he did not hesitate or ask any questions. In addition to the money her brother sends, Truc is guided by what her friends and neighbors have achieved in the past decade in Vietnam, especially those who have strong family networks abroad. "Many people have gotten rich in Vietnam because their overseas families help them so much," she says, speaking more slowly to make her point:

There are many, many families who have gotten rich here because of Viet Kieu money. They have bought properties, sent their children abroad, taken luxury vacations. There was a woman who used to live in the apartment next door to me, and then her sister came back to visit and saw her conditions, and now she owns two houses in the central business district. She rents one out and lives in the other, and has done nothing for the past several years, except count the money she receives from rent.

· · ·

Non-migrants' conceptions of money are guided by the economic behavior of their overseas relatives, whether those relatives send money to the homeland or spend money during their regular return visits. In addition, their views of money have been transformed in recent years due to the dramatic increase in consumption behavior in Vietnam, starting in the mid-1980s when foreign influences became more visible, especially in urban centers of the country. Lan feels somewhat embarrassed that she does not have the material possessions to warrant showing her friends and coworkers that she has relatives living abroad. By extension, having relatives abroad means that many Vietnamese citizens have redefined their standards of living. Son, on the other hand, feels burdened by the new standards about how much to spend to have a good time in Saigon that his nephew, Dinh, has imposed on him and his family. He feels that he must reciprocate to his overseas relatives when they spend money on him, even in unnecessarily lavish ways. In some ways like Lan, but very different from Son, Truc has come to expect future sources of money from her Atlanta-based brother, rather than relying on earnings from her husband or her own employment in Vietnam.

THE STUDY OF MONEY IN LOW-WAGE TRANSNATIONAL FAMILIES

What are the cultural and personal meanings of giving, receiving, and spending money among families divided across borders? With a few notable exceptions,[20] the meanings associated with migrant money have been too personal or too mysterious for scholars to tackle, unless they deal with "development" issues, such as household expenditures and poverty alleviation, or with the numerical and economic outcomes of financial flows in the new global economy.[21] *Insufficient Funds* applies the case of the Vietnam–United States migration corridor to unravel the personal and emotional antecedents and consequences of what I call *monetary circulation* within low-wage transnational families[22]—that is, the interconnected but distinct activities of giving, receiving, and spending money.[23] Monetary circulation in transnational families is much more than solely a financial matter; it is embedded in complex systems of cultural expectations, self-worth, and emotional economies. Attending to these issues will render visible the hidden relational economic activities of low-wage transnational families in order to spotlight migrant money as an important macro-actor in the global economy of finance.

As both refugees and family-sponsored migrants, the overseas family members in this study have experienced some relative upward mobility despite the fact that, as low-wage workers, they live at the margins of their host societies and often work at precarious or tedious jobs. Paradoxically, in the meantime, their families back home have experienced a tremendous improvement in living standards and lifestyles—owing not entirely, but mostly, to money the migrants regularly have sent from a distance as well as brought to the homeland over the past two decades. At the core of these transnational families, therefore, are tensions and contradictions surrounding the paradox of mobility among those who give, those who receive, and those who spend money, raising important questions about economic obligations and social equivalence among those who live transnational lives. We will see that migrants endure great sacrifice to give money to their non-migrant family members, and to save money to spend when they make return visits. However, this sacrifice is not simply a story of altruism; instead, it is embedded in complex notions of kinship and an assemblage of social obligations, social worth, and social comparisons across transnational social fields.

Insufficient Funds focuses on the experiences of low-wage workers because of the precariousness such workers face in their jobs while trying to provide for non-migrant relatives back home. Significantly, except for a few anomalous cases involving large purchases,[24] 90 percent of the migrants in this study allocate between $1,200 and $3,600 annually to their non-migrant families.[25] These seemingly small amounts constitute a consequential economic output for low-wage workers, generally accounting for between 10 and 25 percent of their incomes. Thus, low-wage migrants economize in myriad ways to accumulate revenue for the transnational monetary circulation they enable.[26] These small amounts from low-wage migrant workers, whom the economist Michele Wucker dubs "heroes of the developing world,"[27] are a powerful global force, and the reason that we must view migrant money as an international financial institution.[28] Feminist economists Maliha Safri and Julie Graham estimate that at least 12 percent of the world's population lives in transnational families with consistent monetary flows.[29] The annual monetary gross value of these transnational families is nearly $5 trillion,[30] an amount that goes beyond the money sent from a distance by migrants via formal banking institutions and includes informal transfers and other kinds of money circulated by migrants, as well as the productive outputs migrant money can have for their non-migrant family members.

The different positions migrant workers in the low-wage labor force occupy across transnational social fields have been the focus of a number of studies in recent years,[31] but most of what we know is about the spending habits of the non-migrant relatives in transnational families.[32] Much less is known about the ways in which migrants affect consumption patterns in the homeland, especially when they make return visits there and spend their money.[33] Existing evidence suggests that low-wage immigrants are increasingly turning to the homeland, as one response to their postcolonial predicaments of racial and economic exclusion,[34] in order to valorize status at a time when global capitalism has diminished their economic and social worth in core nations of the world.[35] As Mary Waters succinctly states, some migrants' "sense of self is tied to the status system in the home country."[36] This transnational focus is particularly important because, although immigrant workers constitute only about 10 percent of the U.S. population, they make up more than 20 percent of the low-wage labor market.[37]

Migrant money within low-wage transnational families is, to borrow an analytic from Viviana Zelizer, "special money."[38] It is special money for two primary reasons. First, the people who give and spend it usually earmark the money for specific expenditures. Second, and more significantly, money in low-wage transnational families is special money because it offers migrants the ability to return to the homeland to participate in the sphere of consumption, which is one of the few avenues open to them for asserting competence, social worth, and status. Given the persistent restricted and blocked mobility as well as the undignified working conditions that low-wage migrants face in the new economy, the affection, love, respect, and esteem gained from giving and spending money are not only highly seductive but frequently necessary to maintain a sense of personal dignity.

To capture monetary circulation within the Vietnam-United States migration corridor, and to avoid the problem of methodological nationalism that pervades many transnational studies,[39] I anchored this research in the homeland of low-wage Vietnamese immigrants.[40] The significance of the homeland is underscored for low-wage migrants when we see the powerful relational dynamics within the confluence of their visible capital set against the invisibility of their labor. I chose Ho Chi Minh City as the primary research site for virtually all the data collection. I echo my respondents' frame of reference to the city by calling it "Saigon."[41] Furthermore, at times, I refer to it as the "the new Saigon," conceptualizing it as the city that emerged after 1986 when Vietnam launched Doi Moi,[42] a political and economic renewal campaign that moved the country from a centrally planned economy to a socialist-oriented market economy. As Ashley Carruthers asserts, "Using the name 'Saigon' in place of Ho Chi Minh City is now common practice in Vietnam and conveys no marked political meaning."[43]

Saigon is a strategic site for this study for two prominent reasons. First, with a population of nearly nine million people, making it the largest city in the country,[44] Saigon is where the vast majority of Vietnamese immigrants from the United States have family ties. This is because the exodus of Vietnamese migration over the past nearly four decades originated mostly from the South, with Saigon accounting for the largest proportion of those migrants.[45] Second, Saigon is the economic heartbeat of the entire country. More than 50 percent of all foreign direct investments within the country pass through or stay in Saigon,[46] and more migrant money arrives in Saigon than in any other city or province in the country.[47] Recent data indicate that at least 15 percent of all households in Saigon receive money from abroad.[48]

Over a period of more than seven years,[49] I spent thirty-five discontinuous months conducting fieldwork and in-depth interviews. I conducted two long phases of fieldwork, one for ten months and one for seven months.[50] In addition, except for one winter and one summer, I spent every summer and every winter during this period in Saigon.[51] The analysis for this present study draws primarily on ethnographic data and multiple in-depth interviews with 121 individuals in Vietnam whom I met during these various stints of fieldwork.[52] These included 98 members of transnational families, 46 of whom were low-wage migrants from the United States and 52 of whom were their non-migrant relatives living in Vietnam. I interviewed all respondents—the migrants and their non-migrant relatives—during the migrants' regular return visits to the city. As well, I conducted a set of exploratory interviews with 23 "locals" in Vietnam to shed light on the perspectives of those individuals who have no transnational associations with the overseas population, either in the United States or elsewhere.

The migrant respondents are all low-wage workers who returned to Vietnam to visit at least five times within a ten-year period.[53] They are all first-generation immigrants; four came to the United States prior to the age of twelve.[54] None has a college degree and virtually all work in jobs that pay hourly wages. They work in occupations such as furniture deliverer, supermarket butcher, cashier, nail salon worker, hairstylist, factory worker, hotel maintenance worker, and airplane cabin cleaner. I met men who regularly work seven days of fifteen-hour shifts as furniture deliverymen and women who toil every day in thirteen-hour shifts as manicurists in nail salons. For many of these workers, taking one day off a month is considered a luxury. The average reported annual income of the migrant respondents is about $26,000; more than a quarter of them make less than $20,000.[55] Yet these incomes put all the respondents above the minimum wage and above the federally defined poverty level. The precariousness of their lives is often exacerbated not only by the lack of health care benefits and of institutionalized vacation time, but also by treacherous working conditions. Their non-migrant families hold similar jobs in Saigon, except that wages are fifteen to twenty times *less* than those of the migrant interviewees. Notably, nearly 40 percent (n = 20) of the fifty-two non-migrant relatives are unemployed—many of them by choice, usually after their migrant relatives began giving them monthly stipends that match or exceed their wages, which are all less than $200 per month.

Although I focus on low-wage migrants, the socioeconomic makeup of the Vietnamese diaspora is highly diverse, reflecting different waves of migratory flows over the past nearly four decades as well as the contexts of reception that migrants face in different geographical spaces.[56] Students of migration and diaspora are well aware that more than three million Vietnamese refugees and immigrants have settled in more than 110 countries worldwide,[57] with about 80 percent concentrated in ten core countries and more than half living in the United States. The first mass out-migration began as a refugee exodus days before April 30, 1975, with the imminent fall of Saigon, when U.S. troops pulled out of Vietnam,[58] although sporadic migration from the country occurred before this period.[59] Thus, the Vietnamese diaspora has been mostly understood in the context of the mass postwar refugee migration. In recent years, Vietnamese emigrants have exited the country to various parts of the diaspora mainly through family reunification sponsorships,[60] but also through marriage migration[61] and labor flows.[62] By now, copious research has reported on the flight, settlement, and life outcomes of Vietnamese refugees, especially from the era of the boat refugees' exodus.[63] Picking up as well as departing from the analysis of the "refugee figure" in Vietnamese immigration history,[64] this book is part of the slow but growing collective effort among a number of scholars seeking to analyze the global, transnational, and diasporic forces embedded in the intensifying market economy of Vietnam.[65]

I do not attempt to document the experiences of transnational families involving migrants residing in multiple zones of this diaspora.[66] The focus in this work is on only the transnational families of the Vietnam–United States migration corridor, specifically the permanent residents and citizens of the United States and their non-migrant relatives in Vietnam. Although the tendency in the migration literature is to characterize racial and ethnic groups as minimally heterogeneous,[67] this study expands on what Lisa Lowe calls "multiplicity" within Asian America by examining the conditions of a specific group of low-wage immigrants.[68] To this end, I focus on the dynamics of social class and immigration for low-wage transnational families and do not put much weight on the internal heterogeneity of the group. For instance, except for a chapter focusing on gender relations, I do not look at variability in the marital or parental status, age, year of migration, or geographical diversity of the migrant respondents. Indeed, as the first book-length study on money and migration in Vietnamese transnational families, this work suggests many opportunities to extend the comparative analyses of social class and immigration.

Isolating the experiences of people in the Vietnam–United States migration corridor is justified for several reasons. First, immigrants in the United States, compared with those in other parts of the globe, confront distinct economic opportunity structures, welfare states, and histories of migration. Second, the United States is home to more than half of the total overseas Vietnamese population. It is the largest source of money received by Vietnamese annually from relatives living abroad, as well as the largest source of migrants who return to visit the country. Survey data reveal that more than two-thirds of remittances to Vietnam come from the United States.[69] The focus on the Vietnam–United States migration corridor, however, is justified most of all because of the unique social position Vietnamese immigrants occupy in the opportunity structure of the American economy, resulting in a distinct sociological paradox. Compared with the other five major Asian American groups,[70] the Vietnamese are the least successful[71] and the least educated, and make the least amount of money.[72] Yet, a recent survey of a nationally representative sample of the Asian American population reveals that compared with their Asian American peers, Vietnamese Americans are the *most* likely to say they send money to someone in their home country. Nearly 60 percent of Vietnamese Americans reported sending money to the homeland in the past year.[73] This work investigates both the reasons for this surprising fact and its consequences for family members on both sides of the migration corridor.

CHAPTER 2

THE MAKING OF
A TRANSNATIONAL
EXPENDITURE CASCADE

A CROSS THE GLOBE, more than 215 million people live outside their country of birth.[1] These migrants send more than $500 billion annually to family members in their countries of origin,[2] benefiting about one-tenth of the world's population; more than 80 percent of this amount goes to developing countries.[3] For many of these developing countries, migrant money represents more than 10 percent of the gross domestic product (GDP). Annually, this migrant money is close to three times the amount of foreign aid flowing into the developing world, and is almost as much as the amount of foreign direct investment.[4] In some countries, migrant money exceeds the amount of foreign aid and foreign investment put together.[5]

These macroeconomic indicators do not include the substantial amounts of pocket money that migrants bring back to give and spend during their return visits. Such pocket transfers, or "informal remittances," are estimated to supplement the recorded remittances by at least 50 percent,[6] and experts speculate that in Asia, the informal money may increase the reported remittances by anywhere from 15 to 80 percent.[7] Whether sent through formal or informal channels, migrant money is a private economic transfer and resource. Therefore, and significantly, such money is mediated by the personal and emotional transnational links of family and kinship. This chapter presents a brief overview of recent socioeconomic changes in Vietnam to contextualize the political economy of private money in relation to transnational families within the U.S.–Vietnam migration corridor. In Chapter 3, we pick up once again with personal stories, illustrating how these private economic transfers are interpreted by different members within transnational families.

THE RISE OF TRANSNATIONAL FAMILIES

The growth trend among transnational families is well established.[8] These families are defined as those whose "members of the nuclear unit (mother, father, and children) live in two different countries."[9] The migration literature reflects this definition, with most studies focusing on the links between temporary and contractual migrant workers and their left-behind children and spouses.[10] I do two things differently in my contribution to this body of work. First, I spotlight the situations of permanent residents and citizens of the United States with their left-behind, non-migrant relatives.[11] Second, I broaden the definition of transnational families to include immediate family members, as well as siblings and other relatives (e.g., grandparents, aunts, uncles, and cousins).[12] This broad definition of transnational families reflects the development of what Roger Rouse calls "migrant circuits" under global capitalism,[13] a formulation that captures the multidimensional and multidirectional flows of migrant kinship. The inclusion of extended kinship in studies of transnational families is employed in a number of other recent studies,[14] and responds to standing critiques by feminist scholars about the hegemonic definitions of the family,[15] and especially to the pioneering work of feminists of color who cite the importance of including class and race when theorizing about families.[16]

I did not initially anticipate studying monetary flows among extended families, but serendipitously stumbled upon this pattern in the course of doing research on the return activities—the occasional or recurring sojourns made by members of migrant communities to their homeland. In this study, 10 percent of monetary circulations occurred between adult children and their elderly parents in Vietnam;[17] nearly 70 percent were between adult siblings; and 20 percent were between other relatives, such as aunts, uncles, grandparents, and cousins. This project excluded the situations of labor migrants; thus, there are no cases of money given or spent by parents who were separated from their children.[18] In this work, I suggest that bonds of emotional depth and closeness may not correspond to biological kinship ties in typically assumed ways.[19] For instance, the widespread practice of living in extended households means some members of the Vietnamese diaspora might be closer to their grandparents or aunts and uncles than to their own parents.[20] Likewise, some migrants distribute more money to cousins than to their own siblings.

Transnational families began to form across the Vietnam–United States migration corridor in 1975,[21] when the first mass exodus of Vietnamese immigrants landed on American soil after Saigon fell to Northern Vietnamese troops at the end of a long and devastating war.[22] The intensification of transnational family activities, the increase in opportunities for migrant relatives from the United States to return to visit,[23] and the accordant escalation of monetary circulation did not occur until after 1995,[24] when President Bill Clinton reestablished diplomatic relations with Vietnam,[25] thus ending a twenty-year hiatus. The international renewal of diplomatic relations followed the 1986 macrostructural reforms,[26] when the Vietnamese government reopened its economy after having closed it to most of the world for more than a decade.[27]

Among transnational families worldwide, two types of migrants circulate money to their countries of origin.[28] The first are diasporic subjects who live and are permanently settled outside their countries of birth. These settlers have gained either permanent residency or citizenship in their destination country. The second are contract and temporary migrants, who make up the pool of workers for most of the world's migrant labor market.[29] Because Vietnamese temporary and contractual labor migrants are a recent addition to the global workforce,[30] they are much less significant to the circulation of money into Vietnam than are citizens and permanent residents, who make up the largest portion of the diaspora.[31] Although more than 3 million Vietnamese immigrants living in the diaspora are permanent residents or citizens of their destination countries, only about 500,000 are labor migrants.[32] The most recent comparative data reveal that about two-thirds of migrant money comes to Vietnam from individuals who have gained permanent residency or citizenship in their countries of destination,[33] with the remaining amount coming from contractual and temporary labor migrants.[34] By 2010, more than half the money sent through formal channels came from Vietnamese-origin permanent residents or citizens living in the

United States, and most of that amount came from low-wage workers who sent money to their left-behind extended family members.[35] It is also important to note that of the $51 billion sent in 2010 by all immigrants in the United States to their home countries throughout the world, approximately 10 percent went to Vietnam from U.S.-based Vietnamese immigrants.[36]

TRANSNATIONAL MOBILITY OF CONSUMPTION

The increasing significance of migrant money to the current Vietnamese economy must be considered within the context of macroeconomic changes in the country over the past two decades. In 1990, Vietnam was the poorest country in the world, with a per capita GDP of $98.[37] In that same year, the countries with the second- and third-lowest per capita GDP were Somalia at $139 and Sierra Leone at $163.[38] For the ten years following reunification in 1975, virtually no economic progress occurred in the country;[39] however, despite this decade of inactivity, Vietnam emerged in the early 1990s as one of the fastest-growing countries in Asia. Between 1990 and 2010, the economy grew at an annual average of 7.3 percent, and per capita income almost quintupled.[40] This economic growth sharply reduced the national poverty rate, which fell from 58 percent in 1993 to only 14.5 percent in 2008. In the relatively brief period between 1994 and 2010, the country lifted more than 30 million people, or 40 percent of the total population, out of poverty.[41] Thus, from the standpoint of economic analysis and macroeconomic indicators (e.g., poverty alleviation and GNP), Vietnam moved from being one of the poorest economies in the world to being perhaps one of the most successful with respect to GDP growth.[42] Vietnam has emerged as one of Asia's "tiger" economies.[43]

Migrant money has been one of the biggest contributors to this economic growth.[44] The share of remittances in the GDP increased from a mere 0.5 percent in 1991 to more than 5 percent in 2000, with its peak at 9 percent in 2008, which was more than the actual GDP growth.[45] Since 2000, remittances from overseas have been higher than foreign aid; they also surpassed foreign direct investments from 2003 to 2006. Remittances grew dramatically, from only $35 million in 1991 to more than $9 billion in 2012.[46] By late 2012, Vietnam was the ninth-highest remittance-recipient country in the world.[47] These statistics include only money sent through formal channels and do not account for "pocket transfers"[48] (i.e., money that migrants bring back to the homeland to give to or spend on family members), which constitute the largest portion of money flowing among transnational families in this study.[49]

The rapidity of monetary flows by overseas family members has shifted norms of consumption and the personal market rates of material and monetary gift giving. We will see that because non-migrant relatives generally do not know what life is like "on the other side," their expectations for financial support can seem unreasonable. At the same time, the situation is more complex when we encounter migrants who spend beyond their means when they make return visits, making it appear as if they have more money than they actually do. It is important to consider these new norms, because none of the non-migrants in this study has ever been abroad, so this group's views of money and of monetary circulation in relation to family life are based solely on their national experience.

By the late 1990s, the growth of a global commercial culture and the intensification of a global supply of goods and services in the new Saigon meant that urbanites had the opportunity and the aspiration to buy in ways that were impossible before free-market reform. Among those with transnational families, many continue to engage in upward comparative consumption by relying on the financial support of foreign capital—namely, that of their overseas relatives. In this context, the visible presence of migrants in the new Saigon is even more significant because of the potential flows of capital they bring back to the country. These overseas relatives are returning to a homeland now free from the postcolonial power dynamics that they confront in the United States, yet they bring these dynamics with them and exercise them at the family level through monetary circulation. We will see how these complex power dynamics arise out of and perpetuate misunderstandings and perceptions about the misuse of money, as well as unrealistic promises made to non-migrant relatives who have limited knowledge about the financial lives of their families abroad.

THE RISING ECONOMY OF NEEDS

The recently developed complex social dynamics relating to monetary circulation in the new Saigon are embedded in what I call a *transnational expenditure cascade*. In the United States, research in economics points to an expenditure cascade, whereby increases in spending among those in high-income brackets pressure those below them to also spend more, even when the incomes of those "on the bottom" have not increased.[50] When relative spending travels down the levels of the cascade, any savings that lower-income people have are spent on keeping up with those above them. Thus, expenditure cascades are triggered by people's perceptions about the rewards of relative spending and about comparative notions of what constitutes adequacy, and whether "adequate" is enough.[51] Some of this relative spending is precipitated by redefinitions of "needs" prompted by changes in the availability of particular goods or services; however, in many cases it is triggered by social comparisons or envy, because needs are defined in the context of who takes ownership of new goods and services.[52] In short, what pushes people to spend is a status orientation achieved through the personal and symbolic meanings they gain from the purchases they make, in comparison with the purchases made by others.[53]

Cornell economist Robert H. Frank argues that relative spending sometimes occurs out of necessity rather than out of a consumerist status orientation.[54] When families buy homes in expensive neighborhoods, for example, they may not simply be "keeping up with the Joneses." They may choose more expensive neighborhoods because better schools are available there for their children, while families who spend less on housing may have to send their children to lower-quality schools.[55] Yet in most circumstances,[56] an expenditure cascade has to do with *comparative spending*, which derives from how consumerism is anchored in status orientations.[57] The spending behaviors of those at the top of an economic cascade shift the frame of reference for people with lower incomes, leading the latter group to spend more than necessary, for whatever reasons, on a wide variety of goods and services. For instance, we will encounter some non-migrant respondents who lived for decades without air conditioners in their homes, but suddenly required one when their neighbors and friends began to acquire that household item, which was previously considered a luxury.

This sort of expenditure cascade has been in the making in the new Saigon ever since Vietnam went through its 1986 market reform campaign. It is a transnational expenditure cascade because of the impact that giving and spending money among migrant members of transnational families have had on the spending habits of other migrants, their non-migrant relatives, and Vietnamese society in general. For example, the introduction of a plasma TV into a neighborhood by a migrant family making a return visit could be all that is needed to prompt an entire social network to base their next TV purchase on this new social standard. This kind of comparative spending has unquestionably affected families and individuals at all income levels in the new Saigon, and has the potential to significantly affect the psychological and social fabric of those least able to compete in the new consumption practices of the city. The transnational expenditure cascade results from the comparative spending behavior and aspirations through processes of giving, spending, and receiving money among transnational families. This cascade is both an antecedent and a consequence of monetary circulation that has gained momentum over the past two decades. Furthermore, and consequentially, given the relative newness of the material landscape of the country, there is every indication that the transnational expenditure cascade will accelerate spending behaviors in different regions of the country for years to come.[58]

Sometimes it is difficult to determine who belongs where in the Vietnamese transnational expenditure cascade. One reason for this is that the culture of consumerism in the new Saigon since market reform exhibits a complex interplay among global culture, migrant return visits, non-Vietnamese foreign influences, the rise of a local wealthy consumerist class, and a mass working-class population eager to take part in consumptive practices. For example, most people in Saigon in the 1990s did not have a washer and dryer in their home; they did their laundry by hand. This was true of both the rich and the poor. The difference was that wealthier families had maids to do their laundry for them, while the vast majority did the work themselves. Soon after the South Korean consumer durables company LG launched its brand in Saigon in the late 1990s, every family felt the need for a washer and dryer, and many went out to buy them. The same process occurred in subsequent years for air conditioners, flat-screen TVs, and more recently, smartphones. In short, people in the new Saigon redefined what constitutes a "need."

But the popularization of global commodities resulted in a new type of poor people that perhaps had not existed beforehand: the washing-machine-less, the air-conditioner-less, the flat-screen-TV-less, the smartphone-less. A new category of rich people also was created when the overseas population began to make return visits. Suddenly, as macrostructural changes allowed for easier travel back to the homeland, members of the overseas Vietnamese low-wage labor force began to attach new economic and social meanings to their overseas low-wage and low-status jobs. Strikingly, many non-migrant members of transnational families engage in consumption with money sent and given by overseas family members who, while barely eking out a living in the United States, thought the money they were sending would help their non-migrant relatives buy basic necessities, such as food and medicine. This consequent mobility in the new transnational expenditure cascade is full of contradictions: the position of the poor cannot easily be determined, and neither can the position of the rich. What is poor here might not be poor elsewhere. The same can be said of what is rich.

The ability of migrants to convert low incomes in the United States to high incomes in Vietnam exacerbates the confusion over status and social class. This confusion frequently is amplified by the confluence of cheap labor and expensive (often imported) goods, such that sometimes the valuations of material and labor seem inconsistent. For example, one non-migrant started a sizable business, hiring ten employees with $4,000 given to him by his sister; another non-migrant supports a family of four on a $200 monthly income, yet spent the $7,000 given to him by his nephew on a Japanese-model motorbike. This kind of disparate valuation and pricing could not exist in the United States (and in the industrialized world generally) because labor costs are regulated and because the cost of goods and labor are not highly variable within the same market.[59] Finally, confusion over status and class is aggravated by the fact that people from the same family work in similar low-wage, low-status jobs in their respective local contexts, but their incomes are differentiated by a factor of 15 to 20 simply because of the transnational divide between their locations.

This transnational expenditure cascade introduces new living standards, extinguishes old ones, and in the process shapes and invents new lifestyles, permitting some to increase their sense of competence, esteem, worth, and status, while simultaneously diminishing economic security. The conceptual lens of a transnational expenditure cascade thus points to the powerful effects arising from the giving, spending, and receiving of money in the homeland by a diasporic group for whom comparative spending is a recently developed phenomenon. Such new patterns of consumption in the developing world by members of transnational families provide an important analytical frame for understanding status and social class on a global scale, but much of how we understand class and status in the West is nation-specific.[60] For instance, the

Weberian theoretical tradition of class divisions tends to compare social groups and individuals along class lines within the same national economy and society.[61] In contrast, the Marxist tradition within "development studies" tends to view international differences between macro- and micro-level class experiences in the dichotomous terms of "first and third world," "developed and undeveloped," and "core and periphery" countries.[62] In this approach, as noted by Smitha Radhakrishnan, "class divisions within a nation-state remained crucial, but the binary categorization *between* countries obscured the possibility of analyzing class divisions *across* national states."[63]

The analytic of social class on a transnational scale is particularly imperative to the lives of low-wage immigrants whose income, without question, takes on different social and economic meanings when they visit the developing homeland. This is perhaps most vivid when we consider that Vietnam remains one of the poorest countries in the world, with an annual per capita income of just a little more than $1,000,[64] while its largest emigrant stock resides in the richest country of the world.[65] So we will see, for example, how truck drivers, restaurant workers, and food preparers who make minimum wages can return to Saigon and buy their non-migrant families luxury items such as motorcycles, air conditioners, and fancy refrigerators—commodities that with the return of migrants are becoming part of the norms of consumption, and in some sense, are framed as necessities.

. . .

The transnational expenditure cascade has gained momentum since it has become a mundane matter for members of the Vietnamese diaspora to return home for family visits, tourism, and other social and economic activities. The Vietnamese government estimates that in 2008, more than 500,000 migrants returned to visit, a dramatic increase from 87,000 in 1992 and just 8,000 in 1988.[66] Yet, except for some cursory media attention and the work of three scholars,[67] virtually no research has examined return migration or return visits by the overseas population from the United States, and especially how this group has altered standards of consumption and hierarchy in the country.[68]

The impact of monetary circulation with respect to consumer behavior from the standpoint of the homeland is a strategic site of inquiry for a number of reasons. The relatively rapid movement in Vietnam's transitional economy

toward a free market has provided consumers with the motivation and opportunity to engage in kinds of consumer behavior that did not exist before the
transition. Similar patterns have been observed since the 1970s, when the world
began to witness major economic reformations in a number of nation-states.
In the 1970s, China started its economic transition to a market economy, followed by Vietnam in 1986, and then the former Soviet Union and Central and
Eastern Europe (the former Comecon bloc) throughout the 1980s and 1990s.[69]

As these nations moved from a centrally planned system of economic governance to a market-based one, consumers were introduced to new goods and
services that had not previously existed. These "transitional economies" suddenly
created a class of citizens who were "free to pursue their acquisition fantasies."[70]
Ownership of goods in transition economies, as noted by Lascu, Manrai, and
Manrai, "plays a significant role in status definition."[71] And as Shultz and his
colleagues note, "Goods, brands, and symbols associated with popular culture
and conspicuous consumption are very much part of Vietnam now and their
popularity is increasing exponentially."[72] Such new acquisitive ability is mostly
concentrated in urban areas, where global commodities seduce a growing middle
class. This emerging consumer class, however, accounts for only about 10 percent of the entire population of Vietnam. Survey data show that only about
one-third of the urban population of Saigon and Hanoi, and about 5 percent
of rural citizens, totaling altogether no more than nine million people, make
more than $350 per month. Nonetheless, global capitalists have turned to such
transitional economies and the new affluent of the developing world for their
business. As one report notes,[73] the future for Louis Vuitton, a major French
luxury brand, is not in Madrid or Lyons but in Hanoi and Guangzhou. A quick
stroll down either Le Loi Boulevard or Dong Khoi Street, the two main cor-
ridors in the new Saigon, allows even the casual tourist to observe displays of
every major global luxury brand, from Gucci to Prada to Louis Vuitton.

Although Vietnam shares characteristics with other transitional economies,
its uniqueness stems from its turbulent history of military engagement with
France, Japan, and the United States, which produced one of the most sizeable
emigrant stocks worldwide.[74] The emergence of new affluence and decadence
in the new Saigon drives some left-behind members of transnational families
to turn to potential funds from this emigrant stock in order to take part in
the new material landscape of the city. Equally important is the fact that the

homeland serves as a crucial social space for the low-wage migrants, who upon their return are able to engage in modalities of consumption from which they often are excluded in the United States. The visibility of migrant capital in the homeland set against their invisible labor has powerfully launched the transnational expenditure cascade. The following chapters examine different meanings attached to money, as well as different kinds of consumptive practices that account for the making of this transnational expenditure cascade. We first look at what money means to the left-behind members of transnational families.

CHAPTER 3

MONEY AS
A CURRENCY OF CARE

L INH TRAN is a neatly dressed third-grade teacher who lives on the outskirts of Saigon, in District 11. Barely in her thirties, she speaks about life as if she has gone through all its stages, giving advice about everything and anything that comes up in our initial three-hour interview amidst the hubbub of customers' laughter and the clacking sounds of many servers moving quickly back and forth at a hip, tiny café in the central business district. As we sit by a window looking out onto Mac Dinh Chi, a small, busy street of quaint cafés and shops, Linh tells me she and her family moved to Saigon ten years ago from a provincial town in central Vietnam. Even though her manners continue to reveal traces of a provincial woman, she makes a point of articulating her sense of urban and global sophistication. For example, she describes the prestige that comes from her teaching job the way many young Vietnamese urbanites talk about their jobs with foreign companies—the prime source of status among young, modern city dwellers. Linh also constantly refers to her membership in a transnational family, a source of status for many non-migrant relatives in the new Saigon.

Linh begins our conversation by telling me about her two female cousins living in Orange County, California. One of these relatives, Gloria, has been back to Saigon almost every year since 2001. On each return visit, Linh says, "I am always with her. I go everywhere with her. We are two very close friends. We understand each other like none of our other family members. When she goes back to America, we talk on Skype or Yahoo almost every day." Gloria's mother is the elder sister of Linh's mother, and in some ways, Linh talks about Gloria as if she is her own sister. Linh's description makes it clear her relatives in Vietnam hold Gloria in high esteem:

She is a hardworking person and everyone respects her. She knows how to treat her family well and takes care of them [*lo lang*].[1] She is the kind of person who sticks to her words; she does not let people down. When she says she will do something, she will do it. She does not lie, and she does not like to trick people. She also gives her fullest when she is committed to something. That's why everyone respects her here. We admire her very much because even though she works hard and she has money, she knows how to have fun.

When non-migrant family members in this study describe their overseas relatives, they speak repeatedly about the relative as a "good person," a "respectable person," a person of "moral principles [*dao duc*]," or simply "a good family member." These labels, which are similar to Linh's description of her cousin, typically portray individuals who stick to their word, who will do something when they say they will, and who give their fullest when they commit to something. But most importantly, almost every time I ask non-migrants what they value and honor most about their relatives, they say it is knowing how to "treat their families well" and knowing how "to take care of" their families. Non-migrants often use these descriptions to talk about overseas family members, who command a presence in left-behind households even if they are absent from the homeland for long periods, or in some instances, if they have not returned at all. The left-behind family members rarely talk about the "funniest" relative or the "most athletic" or the "smartest" or the "most successful." Early on in my data collection, it became clear that no matter how smart, funny, successful, or athletic they might be, overseas relatives rarely are held in high esteem among family members unless they "take good care" of those left behind. "Taking good care" is, simply put, about giving money. Thus, economic distribution within the transnational family is a crucial, if not the most important, measuring stick for conferring affection and emotional depths. Giving money to family members in the homeland is the key to fulfilling and maintaining one's status in a transnational family. When Linh describes how her Orange County–based cousin Gloria "takes good care" of those left behind, her comments are typical of those given by non-migrant respondents. "She sends us money whenever we need it and she always makes sure to ask if we need money for anything. With her, I do not ever need to ask for money," Linh explains. "She knows that I do not make a lot of money as a teacher here. I make in a month what she makes in a day as a nail salon worker in Orange County. I do not have to explain it to her." In elaborating on the importance of maintaining tacit codes of familial obligations, Linh says:

You know, it is not easy for us to ask for money. We have to keep some dignity and self-respect to not ask every time something comes up and we need to pay for something. They know that we cannot earn a lot of money in Vietnam, unless we open up a big business, which requires a lot of money to do. Gloria is truly a good person and she knows how to take care of her family when we do not have to ask her for money. [*Can you tell me one way she took care of you?*] When I was going to the university, she came with me to see my living situation, and she decided to pay for all of my schooling because she saw that my living situation was not good. When I graduated, she bought me a motorcycle so I could use it to travel to work.

Focusing on the non-migrant relatives in the sample, this chapter examines how virtually all non-migrant respondents report that a central way to care for one's family is to give them money, and that overseas relatives are obligated to distribute monetary support. This is especially salient in a country without a reliable credit market for the majority of the population, where most people recognize there are only three ways of procuring large amounts of cash: corruption, gambling, and overseas relatives.[2] I discuss the role monetary circulation plays in transnational families as it pertains to stigma and status; I also examine social comparisons that individuals make about what others receive from their overseas relatives.

Recent influential research on the qualitative aspects of money, such as *The Purchase of Intimacy* and *The Social Meanings of Money* by Viviana Zelizer, provides the basis for understanding money in non-economic, social, and emotive terms.[3] When we move away from thinking about money as only a market phenomenon, we can challenge the conventional approach to money as an "ideal of numerical calculability, which necessarily blunted personal, social, and moral distinctiveness."[4] Underscoring the social, personal, and relational dynamics of money can open up the perspective that money is not simply an instrument of rational exchange, but part of an economy of exchange based on norms, values, and specific networks.

MONEY AS A CURRENCY OF CARE

In classical sociological theory, from Karl Marx and Friedrich Engels to Georg Simmel and Max Weber,[5] money has typically been identified with the market, entirely separate from intimate and family relationships.[6] Because it was attached to the market, money was seen as impersonal and depersonalizing. According to this quantitative view, money was distinguished only by its utility value of exchange; if different currencies were used, for example, exchange rates could easily be created for equivalence. Consequently, classical theorists saw the power of calculation and calculability as the defining characteristic of money and markets. As Weber argued, the impersonal nature of money made it "the most perfect means of economic calculation."[7] For the most part, although they evaluated the consequences of money on the economy and on the macro determinants of society, classical theorists did not adequately consider money as a social and personal matter. Instead, money was generally defined in terms of its three basic functions in the market: as a medium of exchange, a store of value, and a unit of account.[8]

Beginning in the 1980s, the efforts of a number of scholars across disciplines questioned calculability as the only feature of money.[9] They asserted that, contrary to the classical view of money as solely a function of utilitarian value in the market, money has a wide range of social meanings for users. Jonathan Parry and Maurice Bloch succinctly point out that "what money means is not only situationally defined but also constantly re-negotiated."[10] The separation of money from the market became a central research agenda for Zelizer, who shows that money, in fact, shapes and is shaped by personal agendas, social relations, and cultural practices.[11] More recently, Kevin J. Delaney analyzes the diverse cognitive, emotional, and temporal ways that workers in different labor niches, including priests, poker players, and hedge fund traders, approach the use of money.[12] In his formulation of a *cognitive economic sociology of money*, Delaney argues that the way individuals interpret money is frequently related to the kind of work they do, and that such interpretations often are integrated into personal life outside the workplace.[13] In light of the research on the qualitative, symbolic, and social meanings of money that emerged in the 1980s, money in transnational families can be best understood by looking at the seemingly discrepant views and interpretations of non-migrants and their migrant relatives on the circulation of money.

Respondents were generally up-front about the circulation of money in family life. This is reflected in their everyday public and private discussions of money, which show no evidence of problems with disclosing money matters, such as how much one makes, how much one owes, and how much one gives to or receives from family members. The novelty of the relatively large flows of capital and commodities engenders a certain kind of curiosity that frequently makes discussions about money a matter of leisure and entertainment. It is not out of the ordinary in Vietnam, for example, for people to ask each other upon first meeting how much money they make. It is also not out of the ordinary for people to openly disclose what they have bought for their house or for their families, or how much they pay for commodities, services, and leisure. Not only do people share stories about what they buy, but they almost always disclose the cost of purchases. These patterns reflect the transitional nature of the Vietnamese economy, whereby people recently have had the opportunity to consume goods that did not exist in Vietnam before market reform.

A similar pattern was identified in a study about China which found that after the Chinese government opened its market, citizens began to wear name-brand clothes with price tags and labels left on for the simple reason that they wanted to display how much they paid for their merchandise.[14] Given that money is a common topic for open discussion, non-migrants talk consistently and with bluntness about three dimensions of monetary circulation: the importance and expectation of giving money to family across the life course as a form of care, the status or stigma of receiving (or not receiving) money from overseas relatives, and social comparisons with other non-migrants who have overseas relatives.

PEOPLE ARE RICH OVER THERE, AND PEOPLE ARE POOR OVER HERE

Kieu is a gregarious woman with a skill for commanding people's attention whenever she enters a room. Although she is outgoing, Kieu easily switches to a serious demeanor when the topic is appropriate. In her mid-fifties, she is proud of her fair skin, something she elaborates on when our conversation turns to vacation spots in Vietnam. She mentions that her thirty-seven-year-old son, Kevin, who lives in upstate New York, likes to go to Phu Quoc Island, in the far south, when he visits and that she and her husband go with him every year, even though she prefers the mountains of Dalat because she does not like sun exposure. According to Kieu, she and her husband had a business selling lightbulbs on a busy street in central Saigon. They made about $200 a month, and with help from Kevin, had no problem supporting themselves over the years. However, five years ago, a buyer asked to purchase their business. They decided to accept the offer after Kevin promised to provide a monthly stipend of $500 if they retired. Kieu takes great pride in her son's financial responsibility for the family:

He is truly devoted [*that co hieu*] to his parents. Over the years, he has helped us with anything that we needed. He has also helped his younger brother and younger sister with their lives here. He does have responsibilities with his family in New York, but he has done his duty as a son and an older brother for his family in Vietnam. Even after he got married eight years ago, he continued to help us, to send us money regularly. It has never been a question or a problem for him to help us.

Although non-migrant communities differ with respect to the intricate ways individuals interpret how their migrant relatives express care and affection for one another, the expectation that migrant relatives will financially support family in the homeland is not specific to Vietnamese transnational families. Researchers have found cases around the world (e.g., in the Philippines,[15] Honduras,[16] Ghana,[17] Cape Verde,[18] and Congo[19]) that demonstrate the importance of money as a significant aspect of expressing devotion and affection in transnational families. The money non-migrants receive from their families often represents "the expression of profound emotional bonds between relatives separated by geography and borders."[20] Non-migrant relatives often consider migrant relatives who give or spend money to be better family members than those who stay put and are poorer.[21] Non-migrants hold this view because they do not perceive the work undertaken by their migrant relatives as being arduous, or at least not as arduous as their own labor. This view severely alters non-migrants' perceptions of currency values, despite the fact that family members on both ends of the transnational social field do similar kinds of low-wage work within their local contexts.

Thus, non-migrant individuals find ways to attach themselves to relatives from abroad for the very reason that love, affection, and care have been signaled by those living abroad through the distribution of material resources, namely money. Anthropologist Cati Coe calls this phenomenon the "materiality of care."[22] Coe complicates the prevailing discussions about transnational care by pointing out that care among migrant families tends to depend upon a "discursive and cognitive split of emotions and material resources that is particularly salient in the West."[23] In Ghana, she reports, "the materiality of care is important in and of itself as well as its signal of emotional depth and closeness," and non-migrant family members "understand material care as a sign of love and tend to praise or criticize a relationship on the basis of economic exchanges."[24] Whereas Coe focuses mostly on parents and their left-behind children, the idea of materiality of care also resonates with other members of Vietnamese transnational families. This is also particularly important in the context of Vietnamese cultural repertoires about money, in which monetary support serves to maintain civil relations among adult children and elderly parents, as well as among adult siblings and extended kin, among whom the well-to-do are expected to provide more for the collective needs of the family system.[25] This "common purse" approach to income sharing within households is prevalent in a number of countries.[26] My research shows that non-migrant relatives tend to view monetary support as a signal that their migrant family members care for and love them.[27] At a minimum, such monetary support maintains civil relations within this culture of obligation and engenders emotional depth and closeness. The materiality of care is especially salient when a non-migrant needs capital to invest in a business, renovate a house, or pay for educational expenses.

The centrality of the materiality of care to the formation of strong emotional bonds in Vietnamese transnational families is clear from the moment migrants arrive on Vietnamese soil for a return visit, and can be gauged by the welcome that non-migrant relatives give them. Put simply, non-migrants put more value on migrants' expression of care and love through money than on other aspects of love and care, such as bringing back sentimental gifts from the United States or even keeping in close touch. When non-migrants gather to welcome home multiple migrant members of transnational networks, it is easy to qualitatively distinguish between the relationships they form with those who give money and the relationships they form with those who do not. The migrants they treat with the most attention, care, and affection tend to be those who have given the most money to the non-migrant household.

A case in point: I attended a large family gathering not far from the central business district to welcome two migrant sisters, Tuyet and Han, who have arrived in Saigon for a two-week trip. Tuyet and Han, who live in Orlando, Florida, are in their forties, are married, and have children. They are visiting a wide network of relatives, including nieces, nephews, two brothers, uncles, and their seventy-year-old father. Eleven of these relatives live in one house, owned by their father. Although the house is more expensive than the average home and is located in an extremely desirable part of the city, the family members are for the most part cash poor. Few of the adults are working, and they have scant savings. Tuyet and Han have kept the family afloat for the past fifteen years.

Because they are married and have children, and because their husbands have no remaining relatives in Vietnam, Tuyet and Han make fewer return visits than do most of the migrants interviewed for this study. On each visit, they returned together, and on two of the visits, they were unaccompanied by their husbands and children, all of whom have returned to Vietnam only once. The children for the most part have little to do with life here, as one of the sisters explains: "They are fully Americans. It's also too expensive to bring the whole family back every time we come, because we want to save money to give to the family here in Vietnam." To express their overseas status, these two women return wearing similar jewelry and clothes, such as distinctly Western jeans and T-shirts, and name-brand sunglasses, whereas none of their non-migrant female relatives except the teenage girls wear jeans.

The returning migrants generally pay for their own welcome-home parties. The extent of cooking and decor and number of guests vary widely, depending on how much money the migrants spend. Tuyet paid for the largest portion of this party, which was especially elaborate. Her non-migrant nephew Trong, a talkative twenty-two-year-old man, later makes this clear. As we wait in line for our food, he says, "Tuyet bought all the food and all the drinks. She's very cheerful [*vui vẻ*] and generous."

Trong proudly discloses that he is a third-year business student at RMIT in Saigon, a branch of Australia's Royal Melbourne Institute of Technology. This university is marketed to Vietnamese families who cannot afford or do not want to send their children abroad for a university degree. At $7,000 per year, tuition is not cheap, though it is much less expensive than studying abroad, especially considering that many RMIT students, such as Trong, live at home with their families in Saigon. Attending RMIT is a notable expression of class distinction because it places families among the elite who can afford the tuition. Even though those who study abroad actually pay more money, they are largely invisible in the daily life of the Saigonese.

This distinction, of course, does not go unquestioned by the local population because students in Saigon represent a cross-section of Vietnamese contemporary moneymakers and global aspirants: they are the children or relatives of political elites, nouveau riche business owners, foreign expats working in the city, and the overseas population. The non-migrant relatives of the overseas population in particular have an internal hierarchy that reflects the diverse class composition of the diaspora. Those, like Trong, who can afford to attend RMIT vie for rank among other global aspirants within the social order of the new Saigon. But that system of social ranking relies on a certain kind of capital. Trong talks about how he has managed to pay for his tuition over the years:

My aunt, Tuyet, three years ago proposed that I try to go to Florida and study there, and I could live with her family. But it was too difficult for me to get the visa. It's also more expensive to go study abroad, even if I got the opportunity to live with Aunt Tuyet and her family. So when I did the research, RMIT was a good option. It's expensive for a local citizen, but much cheaper than going abroad, especially to America. Aunt Tuyet then promised me that if I studied hard, she would pay for my tuition. Each year she sends me the money and it goes straight to the payment for tuition. Without her, I could never go to school like this, and I know that the education at RMIT is better than any school in Saigon.

Trong's comparison of his two aunts demarcates the standards for caretakers. Han gives her family money, but not as much as Tuyet; thus Han is not thought of as highly by her relatives, as Trong makes clear:

Aunt Han is nice and funny, but she does not care as much about the family back here. Everyone knows that Tuyet takes care of the family. She takes care of Grandfather more than Han and her family do. Aunt Tuyet sends money every month, but Aunt Han only sends it during New Year's and on special occasions, and she only sends small amounts, just to say that she remembered the holidays, like the Vietnamese New Year. Like for this party, Aunt Tuyet gave my mother all the money to buy all the food and drinks. Han did not give anything, except whenever she comes back, she brings gifts from America, especially for the children.

Anthropologists Mandy Thomas and Allison Truitt found that monetary gift giving is a mundane matter in Vietnamese society, and that when transnational gift giving takes place, recipients overwhelmingly prefer money to commodities as gifts.[28] For example, when Thomas conducted research among transnational families in Hanoi, she often brought material goods from her respondents in Australia to their Vietnamese families in Vietnam. Thomas writes, "As the recipients came forward and opened their gifts, I was surprised that they seemed somewhat disappointed. I heard a young woman mutter that money would have been better than presents."[29] Many of her respondents expressed that non-monetary gifts were useless and wasteful, and some indicated that they sold gifts sent from abroad or exchanged them for goods they would otherwise purchase with money.[30]

Thus, because of non-migrants' strong belief in expressing filial affection and love through material distributions, and especially monetarily, respondents frequently evaluate relatives abroad in terms of their ability to "know how to care [*biet lo lang*]." Non-migrants applaud those who maintain traditional views of family sacrifice and obligations, which they view as central features of Vietnamese kinship.[31] "They know how to take care of their families," a male respondent in his mid-fifties explains. "It impresses me that when someone has been away for so long, they remember the homeland, they remember their family, and they know how to take care of their relatives back home."

Being a good caretaker to their family primarily means that migrants give money on a regular basis, preferably without being asked, following tacit codes of kinship. It is therefore common for non-migrant relatives to socially and emotionally dismiss those from abroad who make return visits with no cash in hand, or who leave to go back overseas without giving family members departure cash gifts. "What is the purpose of living in such a rich country without giving and helping your family?" asks one middle-aged female respondent. Some non-migrants explain that when their overseas relatives tell stories of economic difficulties abroad, they feel the migrants are simply trying to hide their success in order to avoid giving money. One respondent says it succinctly: "Every time my brother comes back, he complains about his life in America. If he doesn't want to take care of us, it's fine, but he doesn't have to exaggerate about how harsh [*kho khan*] life is in America." Other non-migrants expect those who make sacrifices in the name of family to do so by living frugally, working longer hours, depriving themselves of luxuries (e.g., buying smaller homes and more modest cars), or even going into debt. These characteristics gain special attention from non-migrant family members. As the beneficiaries of sacrifices, non-migrants see the distribution of material care, notably money, as an inherent aspect of having overseas status, and sacrificing for the financial well-being of the family as a form of care and love.[32] Khoi, a thirty-two-year-old café owner, explains this logic while discussing his sister, Siu, who lives in New Mexico:

My sister is very devoted to our family. She works extra hours at her job at night and on weekends so she can save money to send to our parents. She said she never bought a new car in America. Even though everyone she knows has a new car, she decided to save her money to send it back to the family in Saigon. She knows how to save and take care of the family. I think it's a sacrifice on her part, but she is also lucky to be in a country where she makes good money. She has the option of working longer hours for extra money.

Financial support within the family is important in Vietnamese society generally, but it is not valued to the same degree by left-behind family members who give money to each other as it is by migrants who give money to those left-behind, particularly in instances when the kind of wage disparities that typify transnational ties are not present. For example, elsewhere I argue that while adult daughters in Vietnamese families rarely are expected to provide financially for their elderly parents, adult *migrant* daughters are expected to provide because migration brings economic power, which non-migrants expect to be passed on to the left-behind.[33] When Lien, a woman in her sixties who sells textiles at the main market in town, is asked how she differentiates between the financial responsibility of migrant and non-migrant family members, she is amused by the question:

Why do you make me want to laugh? It is easy to understand. Everyone knows that you can make so much more money over there [pointing her finger to the door, referring to any place overseas]. You can work like a dog here in Vietnam all your life and you can never make as much as the people over there. That's it [*vay thoi*]. There is nothing difficult to understand about this fact. People are rich over there, and people are poor over here. And that's it. Nothing hard to understand. If you have money, you have to help your family. You have to know how to take care of people who don't have as much money as you.

Simply put, non-migrant members of transnational families see money as a currency of care from their migrant relatives. They feel that those who left the country ought to financially support those left behind, which is the primary signal of taking good care of one's family. For non-migrant relatives, then, overseas relatives who fail to take on the financial responsibility for those left behind are seen as selfish [*ich ky*], or more commonly, they are seen as fake Viet Kieu [Viet Kieu *gia/dom*]. "There are some Viet Kieu who come back here and they never give even a coin to anyone," a female non-migrant interviewee in her late forties says:

They come and they spend money right in front of your face, and they never give anyone anything. Some of them come and stay at your house and eat your food, and when they leave they give you nothing. They are the most selfish Viet Kieu. We call them the fake Viet Kieu because they don't act like Viet Kieu. You never see money come out of their pockets into someone's pocket. They only spend it on themselves.

STATUS OR STIGMA OF THE OVERSEAS RELATIVES

At around 10 p.m. in a crowded alleyway in an area of District 4 known for its high crime rates and drug dealings, I follow Lam to his narrow townhouse, which he inherited from his parents. Lam is a shy, handsome man in his late forties. I spent the day with him and his family to observe their work lives at their small noodle stand, which is similar to any of the ubiquitous street hawker stands one sees in the developing world of Asia. Lam's noodle stand has a high volume of loyal customers, and on any given evening, one can see his team of ten young workers from the Mekong Delta, all making about $50 a month, run around frantically to make sure customers get their orders correctly.

Lam and his wife run this business, which they were able to acquire only because his sister from Texas gave him $4,000 two years ago to buy all the equipment. Although he is thankful to his sister for the money, Lam speaks about it with some ambivalence. "Without my sister's help, I could work for a lifetime and never even save $1,000. How can I save $4,000? It was finally a time that my sister could rescue us from poverty by helping us to buy equipment for the noodle stand," Lam explains. "We were lucky because my wife was already working for a noodle shop for many years, so we knew how to make good noodles for customers, but we didn't have the money to start our own business earlier. I feel very lucky that my sister gave us the money to do this." But as Lam elaborates, he notes that money has not always been forthcoming from his sister:

It was a long time already since she helped us with this much money. [*Did she help you before with a large amount?*] About five years ago, she gave me $1,200 so I could buy a motorbike. At that time, everyone had a motorbike, and I was one of the last people in the city to ride around in a bicycle. After she got us that motorbike, she did not mention money for a long time. We never talked about it, and it's sometimes difficult to ask her for money because I am shy about it. I have to have some self-respect, too. She knew that I had some financial problems and did not have good work here, but she never asked us. I think if she had given us money years ago, I would be doing better financially.

For many non-migrants, the initial return visits from overseas relatives in the local scene have contributed to a tremendous increase in monetary circulation. Foreign investments and other forms of global capital also spurred this increase in the 1990s and into the early twenty-first century. Yet, even more than broader economic forces, the intensification of migrant return visits during this period has made visible and vivid the potential benefits of having overseas relatives, many of whom were bringing back an enormous amount of capital either to invest independently or to give to their non-migrant family members.

Over time, and in this atmosphere, many non-migrant members of transnational families make social comparisons about the market rate of monetary circulation that they hear others receive from overseas relatives. Some feel embarrassed if they have overseas relatives and very little to show for the status of being in a transnational family. Thang, a mid-forties construction worker, explains this candidly. Thang is married and has two small children. His wife works as a hairstylist and manicurist in a small beauty shop, where she earns less than $100 per month. Their combined monthly income is about 5 million VND per month, equivalent to $250. This amount was more than the average household income in Saigon at the time I met Thang. He had been trying to save money so he could become the business partner of a friend who does flooring for new residential and commercial properties in the city. To enter this business, Thang needs $10,000 in start-up capital, an amount that would take him a lifetime to save with his current income. When he and I first talk about money, he begins by saying that the monthly income he and his wife generate "can sustain us on a month-to-month basis because we are not very materialistic people. My wife is very careful with money, so we try to spend what we have." This statement is striking because in the same conversation, Thang reveals that he hopes his younger brother in Florida will help him with the $10,000 he needs to enter the flooring business with his friend. How can Thang claim to be so frugal and to spend only "what we have," but expect such a large amount of capital (relative to his income) from someone else? He explains:

I never really depended on my brother for anything, so it is only a one-time request that I will ask him. He has been sending us money once every six months, but the amount he sends is very little. He never sent more than $200 at a time, and normally it's just a small gift that he sends during the holidays. You know, in Vietnam, people stare at you if you have family overseas and you have nothing to show for it. If you have relatives abroad, and you are living like my wife and me, it is embarrassing at times to go out on the street and have nothing to show that you have family living abroad. You know, in Vietnamese, we call it *"co tieng, ma khong co mieng"* [a good reputation without the goods].

Like most non-migrant family members, Thang says the shame he feels sometimes keeps him from conveying to his neighbors and friends that he has a brother living in the "richest country in the world." Nearly a third of the non-migrant interviewees shared similar feelings, claiming that they were not receiving material distributions that reflected their membership in a transnational family network. For instance, Ha, a humble woman in her late thirties who works as a cashier in a pharmacy near the central post office of the city, underscored the importance of honor in having a relative living abroad. In a ninety-minute interview in the back room of the pharmacy, after she finished a shift in the late afternoon, and during a quiet and deliberate moment, Ha explains:

For many people in Vietnam, it is an honor [*danh du*] to have a family member living abroad. It can mean a lot for people. If your family is poor here and if you have someone "over there" [*ben kia*] who can support the family here, people feel very special for it. Just one person can keep the honor for an entire family, for so many people. People here, in Vietnam, you know, especially now since everyone cares about clothes and material stuff, judge you if you have material stuff. People worship money here, and it's the overseas family who can provide that. They judge you if you have family overseas. It can be good but it can also be bad if you don't get any money from them. If you have good family overseas who can take care of you, it can bring you status and honor. But if your family does not take care of you, it can be embarrassing.

Ha elaborates on the notion of feeling embarrassed by relating an example from her neighborhood:

There is this old couple in my alley in a modest house, they have a son living in America, and when the son came back, the wife was so happy. She talked to the whole neighborhood to tell everyone that she has a son living in America. It was like she was bragging. When her son came back, everyone thought that he will rebuild the house for his parents or his parents will have so much more to show for his return. But after he left, nothing about them changed for years. After three years, every time we saw the couple, they would try to avoid people in the neighborhood. [*Why?*] I think they were ashamed and afraid that people might ask them about their son. Everyone knows they have a son living in America. But really, they had nothing to show for it.

Both Thang and Ha reveal how embarrassing it can be when one has nothing to show materially for being a member of a transnational family network. How do these feelings of shame and embarrassment come about? And, more important, how do new standards of living manifest in transnational family relationships? In an atmosphere of dramatic economic changes with the potential for a range of sensorial effects through new commodities, it would be unusual if non-migrant members of transnational families did not probe, let alone scrutinize, each other on a regular basis about monetary circulation. Inevitably, gossip proliferates in the homeland, feeding everyday understandings or fantasies of earning potential and monetary circulation. In her research on Mexican transnational families, Joanne Dreby reports that for many families living across international borders, gossip plays a central role in how people come to understand the realities of migrant lives.[34] One important purpose of gossip is that it serves as an informal means of passing on information to members of a community. However, as Dreby observes, because "migration gives some family members access to wealth which may or may not be passed on to non-migrant family members, gossip may draw attention to the inequalities family members experience while apart."[35] In addition, in the Vietnamese case of transnational families, gossip about money often involves exaggeration of what migrants can buy or give to family at home, which then potentially alters people's perceptions about the financial capability of the overseas population.

Indeed, when we talk about Thang's business plan, I ask him if he thinks the $10,000 he hopes to receive from his brother is unreasonable, and how he came to feel it was acceptable to ask his brother for such a large amount. He explains:

I have a friend whose sister gave him $25,000 last year so he can buy a van to use as a transport business. My friend told me that his sister does not make more money than my brother, so I think my brother probably has more money. My brother knows many people in Saigon with relatives abroad, and I think he knows that people receive money from their family to open businesses or to build houses. It would be odd if he does not want to help me out because it would look embarrassing to our friends.

On one occasion, I join Thang and four of his male friends for beer at a street café, an occasion that illustrates how gossip and fantasies about migrant money can produce undue expectations among non-migrant members of transnational families, as well as in Vietnamese society in general. Early in the evening, one of Thang's friends asks me if we ever drink on the streets in the United States. I reply that it is unusual, but some cities do have outdoor cafés, although these do not resemble the street cafés of Saigon because they do not have miniature seats and tables where people sit very close to the ground. When I explain this, a second man chimes in, "Yeah, of course you will never sit outside on the ground like this. America is too rich and beautiful to sit outside on the streets!"

As they cheer and clang their glasses, a third man announces that his sister has just bought a Lexus in Atlanta for more than $70,000, to give an example of how wealthy he hears people can be in America. His statement is surprising, since this man rode a very old, dilapidated bicycle to the gathering, whereas everyone else got to the scene via motorbike. In contemporary Vietnam, rarely do you see anyone riding a bicycle if that person has an overseas relative (especially a sibling). The new consumer culture has compelled most locals to make their financial status obvious through external attributes, such as clothing, motorbikes, and various sorts of personal objects. It is also common for people to exaggerate the cost of goods that they buy, either because they want to signal status or because they simply do not know the valuation of commodities, especially goods from overseas. This exaggeration reflects the reality of an economy undergoing transition, with no frame of reference for individuals about the new commodity frontier.[36]

When asked what his sister does for a living in Atlanta, this man says, "She works as a seamstress for a large clothing factory." I am surprised by this detail, and given the other men's doubtful expressions, surmise that they are as well, so I change the subject. To save embarrassment for all involved, I quickly say I think buying such an expensive car is unusual even for rich people; however, it is possible to buy expensive cars in the United States thanks to the financing system that is available (an economic reality about which most Vietnamese know). When I mention this, the man proudly and loudly replies, "She paid for the whole thing in cash!" It is clear that either this man and his sister are exaggerating the price of the car she bought or she went into debt to buy it without telling him.

In either case, this man's loud proclamation at this streetside café sheds light on the many ways in which gossip helps to engender ideas about the possibility that a low-wage factory worker in the United States could pay cash for a $70,000 car. It is now common, in fact, to hear how the inflated valuation of goods, prices, and buying power can easily be misunderstood through the circulation of everyday gossip. Gossip about money, who gets it, and who has it, whether real or imagined, allows non-migrant members of transnational families and Vietnamese society generally to construct expectations, obligations, and norms for migrant families based abroad.[37] This is especially true in the context of transnational networks with members from the United States, where buying is heavily linked to a credit system that does not exist to the same magnitude in other countries of the developed world.[38] Part of producing gossip, especially when one inflates the buying power of migrant relatives, involves calling critical attention to the success of migrant relatives, whether or not the buying power actually translates into purchases. This, of course, often goes unquestioned because the temporal and spatial distance means that large segments of Vietnamese society are either unaware of or unsuspecting of people's claims to buying power.

When asked an open-ended question about how they "feel" when their overseas relatives give them money, more than 80 percent of the fifty-two non-migrants noted first and foremost that they felt "proud" [*hanh dien*] when they received money from their migrant family members. Strikingly, only 10 percent mentioned "grateful" [*biet on*] as their first feeling. In fact, when asked to elaborate, only about half of respondents mentioned gratitude as one of the feelings they have when receiving money from overseas. What do these feelings mean for non-migrants? First, non-migrant relatives come to understand the success of their migrant relatives when their migrant families distribute material care, especially money, providing the consequent pride. Second, individuals in both transnational and non-transnational families have come to understand that material distributions by migrants, especially money, is a signal of love and affection to non-migrant families.

The pride of receiving money was most vividly displayed by Hai and Tien, a couple in their early fifties, who live in a typical townhouse in Saigon's District 10. I met them through their thirty-two-year-old daughter, Ngoc, who knew one of my research assistants. Ngoc makes nearly $35,000 as an assistant manager of a chain hair salon in Knoxville, Tennessee, an amount that put her near the top of income earners in my sample of migrant respondents. She has returned to Saigon each year for the past seven years. Her parents are probably in the middle class in their cultural context in Saigon. Hai and Tien tell me they could easily quit working as merchants selling children's clothes in the informal open-air market nearby if Ngoc were to give them $300 per month. However, Tien insists they should keep their business so they do not get bored and lazy over time, even though Hai says, "Our daughter would be happy to support us."

During each return trip in the summer over a seven-year period, I visited with Ngoc and her parents regularly, and each time I saw gradual improvements in the house Hai and Tien have owned for more than thirty years. On one occasion, just two days after I return to Saigon, Hai calls to invite me for dinner. On this particular evening, he greets me outside with an unusual sense of excitement. Before I have time to get out of my taxi, he has already opened the gate to their townhouse. I cannot help but behold a gigantic TV, flaring like a huge fire through the open door of their residence. With an even more cheerful smile than normal, Hai shakes my hand through the taxi door window and quickly exclaims, as if I have not yet seen the obvious TV, "Oh, you just missed Ngoc by a few days. She just flew back to Knoxville a few nights ago. You should have been here last week to see her take her mother on a shopping spree at the new electronics plaza. Come inside, take a look!" I reciprocate with my own sense of excitement for him: "Is that right? Let's take a look!" Before we make it to the front door, Tien greets me with similar excitement. As we walk into the house, they both say in unison, "You see it? You see it?" referring, of course, to the new fifty-two-inch Hitachi plasma TV. Directed by Hai, we sit in the dining area, not far from the TV, and I begin to ask Hai questions about Ngoc, while Tien goes into the kitchen to prepare coffee.

Sensing their happiness, I comment that they are lucky because Ngoc must have gotten a promotion recently and wanted to show her love, respect, and filial piety [*hieu*] to them. As Hai begins to talk about their recent vacation to Hanoi, Tien abruptly comes out and asks me to follow her upstairs to the rooftop, where she shows me the new washing machine and dryer Ngoc just bought for them. Then we walk back downstairs and she leads me into the kitchen to show me the new stove, microwave, and refrigerator Ngoc just bought. I begin to calculate in my head how much Ngoc must have spent, especially knowing that appliances typically cost more in Saigon than in the West. Then I bluntly ask Hai how much Ngoc has spent on them in the span of a month. In response, Tien starts a long soliloquy:

Oh, Ngoc is such a dutiful daughter [*co hieu*]! We are so proud to see her succeed in America and for her to take care of her parents like this! I see other families' children are not dutiful, and so they are unfortunate that the children don't take good care of them like Ngoc takes care of us. On this trip, we didn't ask for all this stuff, but she insisted on buying everything for us, especially the large TV for her father. We said to her we don't really need these things, we just want her to visit us regularly and that's enough. But she said she had been saving for a year to make sure she had $7,000 to buy us all this stuff.

With a sense of incredible pride on the new centerpiece of their house, Hai looks at me and exclaims, "You see, that TV is more than $3,000!"

Ngoc's story provides an extreme example of how relatives (in this case, non-migrant parents of an adult child living abroad) interpret large amounts of spending as a signal of love and affection. Importantly, this pattern emerged across different types of relationships among respondents. In many instances, siblings, uncles, aunts, and cousins revere those who buy them large items or who simply express their love through hard cash, which is, in fact, most preferred. Scholars have found that in advanced capitalist countries, money often is considered an inferior gift object because it implies that gift givers do not take time to think about the gift. As David Cheal notes, "It is generally felt that there should be 'a little bit more behind' (the act of giving) than just simply taking money out of your wallet."[39] Although in some cases money is seen as a gift, money can be symbolically and materially represented in a range of care practices in Vietnamese society. Therefore, money is seldom articulated as a gift within the family, which is likely a primary reason that so few non-migrants report that gratitude is the first feeling they have when they receive money from relatives abroad.

. . .

In Western societies, money generally flows *only* within the nuclear family. Parents typically give money to children, but not vice versa; furthermore, little or no monetary circulation occurs between adult children, parents, and other adult kin.[40] In contrast, one of the most important features of Vietnamese society is that money holds families together and maintains bonds of intimacy and care across generations.[41] The exchange of money in the forms of gifts, loans, and favors is a reflection of a larger system of kinship practices based on obligations and reciprocity. Truitt notes that as Vietnam expanded its market economy, money became a medium of sociality in a country where the vast majority operates on a cash economy. "At least momentarily," she writes, "the credibility of the note itself is no longer invested in its abstract value in the marketplace, but in the personalized exchanges that constitute social reproduction."[42] As a result, the exchange value of money offered to relatives is less significant than the value of the amount in relation to "previous obligations, the nature of the relation, and the perceptions of status."[43] In some instances, monetary support maintains civil relations among adult children and elderly parents, or among adult siblings; in all cases, the well-to-do migrant members are expected to provide more than are their poorer non-migrant relatives for the collective needs of the family. Thus, despite the conventional unacceptability of money as a caring object in Western societies,[44] the non-migrant respondents in this study frequently talked about the warmth of hard, cold cash as a currency of care.

To make sense of the global impact of monetary circulation throughout the world, it is necessary to take into account specific cultural practices and symbolic meanings that different members of transnational families attach to material and monetary distribution. This chapter has offered an understanding

of how non-migrant members of transnational families interpret the relationship between monetary support, care, affection, and even emotional depth.
Most non-migrant relative interviewees expressed candid views about material
distribution: giving money to the left-behind is a central avenue for how migrants express love and affection to their non-migrant relatives. For this reason,
most respondents attach status and/or stigma to patterns of monetary circulation. On the one hand, the absence of monetary circulation poses tremendous
stigma for non-migrant members of transnational families because it signals
that their migrant relatives are indifferent to their well-being. On the other
hand, non-migrant recipients of money say they feel proud more often than
grateful for the money they receive, a clear reflection of how they interpret
material distribution. Their sense of pride is embedded in how they view their
migrant relatives' success abroad, as well as how they interpret the love and affection they get from their migrant relatives through the distribution of money.

CHAPTER 4

THE MIGRANT
PROVIDER ROLE

IN AN ARTSY CAFÉ off the corner of Le Loi and Dong Khoi, two of the most expensive boulevards in the new Saigon, forty-one-year-old Quy Le from Houston reveals he has worked as an electrical maintenance technician for the past fifteen years. His job, which pays $17 per hour, is to maintain the printing needs for more than five hundred cubicle workers in a data processing company. On his second espresso, Quy says that nowadays it is very difficult for people to get full-time work at his company, so he feels lucky to have a stable position. From his income and savings, he consistently helps his brother and sister with money. A third sibling, a sister, is married into a rich family, so she does not need his financial support. Although he has other extended family members still living in Vietnam, he has only committed to giving money to his two younger siblings. Giving money to them has become a mundane matter for Quy. "I started to send them money probably five years ago, after my parents stopped working in Houston, so I wanted my parents to stop taking the responsibility for them," Quy explains. He describes his first return visit, and what motivated him to support his family:

When I came back for the first time, I really loved it here. My brother and sisters were wonderful. The only thing was that they had very little then, and you can see that they had nothing for so long. You can see it in the way they looked; my brother was about half my size. He was going to school to learn how to fix elevators, and I thought it was a good job for him. Everyone needed elevators in the city at the time. And my sister wanted to learn English so she could get a job at a high-end hotel in the business district. For both of them, I thought it was a good idea to give them money so they can try to better their lives with skills. I bought them both motorbikes so they could ride them to school, because the bicycles seem so hard to ride to me. Back then, it was the cheap kind of motorbike that I bought for them; it was only about $1,000 for each one. I wanted to make sure they had what they needed . . . I felt sorry for them [*toi nghiep*]. I did not want my brother and sisters to be like everyone else, like the rest of the poor people here.

Besides buying motorbikes and paying for his siblings to acquire job skills, Quy also regularly sends them money. He says, "I want to make sure they don't worry too much about their day-to-day expenses, so I give them each about $150 per month. I figure that is almost twice the amount most people their age earn with full-time jobs. Basically, I spend about $300 a month supporting them." When I ask if this has been difficult for him financially, he says he does not see it as "a huge problem." However, he explains, "I had to cut back on my living expenses. Even though it's $300 a month, something extra always comes up, and that's when I sometimes worry about money. I'm lucky because I don't have a car payment, so that isn't an additional cost. My wife and I also are not big spenders. We also occasionally give money to her family, but not monthly like I give to my siblings."

Money received from overseas relatives has become an institutionalized dimension of contemporary Vietnamese society, especially in Saigon, where consumption and remittances are the highest in the country.[1] In this chapter, I establish that migrants view their non-migrant relatives' lives and living conditions through a transnational optic. It is from this vantage that migrants develop strategies for helping their relatives improve their standard of living. Migrant respondents express deep concern about their family members' health and well-being. They report that when they first returned to visit Vietnam, they instantly compared the economically deprived lives of their non-migrant relatives with their own lives in the United States. "When we first came in the late 1990s, the power was cut off every two hours, and it was in the middle of the city," recalls Quang, the airplane cabin cleaner from Atlanta. Another fact of life in Vietnam until recently was the extremely short supply of essential commodities, such as food and medicine. "I remember when we first came back, I was worried about getting medicine when we needed it, so we always brought back bulk supplies of over-the-counter medicine for our families," recounts Cam, the cashier from Philadelphia. Another migrant respondent notes quite dramatically, "When we came in 1997, it was unbelievable how hard it was to find clean, healthy food. For one, you could never drink water, and I had to brush my teeth with bottled water. And the meat supply was disgusting when you go to the markets. I made sure that my family got the best meat supply when I was visiting."

In the early phase of return visits, most migrant respondents brought medicine and other essentials that were too expensive or unavailable in Vietnam. Others gave their relatives money to buy essential supplies in Saigon; yet others began to send money from a distance before they even made their first return visit. Tuyet, a woman in her mid-forties from Orlando, describes how she first sent money:

When we first got to Florida in the early 1980s, like everyone else we were struggling financially. Most people were on food stamps and welfare, and so no one really thought about the people left in Vietnam. It was also difficult to send money back home because we could not communicate with our families in Vietnam. Both my husband and I had family back there, and we still do because we could not sponsor our brothers and sisters to America. When we heard of services to send money, or when we first had friends who returned to Vietnam, we sent money to our brothers and sisters. Sometimes, if someone got sick, we would send money right away, but most of the time, normally, we just sent money so people can live day to day.

Most migrant interviewees report that they calculate the typical expenditures for local citizens in Vietnam, and based on that amount, send their relatives money on a regular basis. When they do this calculation, they often compare their wages transnationally, as Chi, a fifty-two-year-old restaurant worker from New York, explains:

When I go back to Saigon, I see many poor people like my brother and two sisters. One of my sisters makes only about $40 a month working as a cleaner in a hotel, and my brother makes only $70 a month as a security guard. So every month I send them each about double their monthly incomes, which they say helps them out a lot. When something big comes along, like if someone gets sick, I would help more. Last year, for example, my niece needed some money because she was trying to enter a school to learn English, and I gave her about $800 for the tuition fees. How can we complain to them when they are making only $40 or $70 a month? Even though I make only about $1,600 a month working at a restaurant, it is still much more than they can ever make in Vietnam.

Migrant respondents see their relatively privileged economic situation in the West, no matter how precarious their work condition, as a compelling reason to provide for the non-migrants. As one female factory worker from Los Angeles, in her late twenties, explains, "I wanted to help them as much as possible because I saw with my own eyes how pre-modern life was in Saigon at the time, and it was not that long ago. After that first trip, I came back to America, I immediately made sure that I did not spend money on stupid things like expensive clothes or restaurants like I used to; any money I saved I would put away to give to my sister in Saigon."

ALTRUISTIC BEHAVIOR AND MONETARY CIRCULATION

The homeland is a crucial reference point from which migrants develop economic strategies. Migrants deliberately economize their lives in the United States to save and accumulate capital for their non-migrant relatives' necessary daily expenses. A transnational optic makes this kind of economizing feasible for migrants because of the enormous disparity in earning power between the developing world and the United States, which sometimes makes the expenditures from the homeland seem inconsequential, especially if their relatives' expenses are kept to the necessities.[2] This disparity is evident when we consider that in 2010 the annual per capita income of Vietnamese citizens barely exceeded $1,000, whereas the average income for Americans in the same year was $39,791.[3] Moreover, because of this international disparity, Vietnamese low-wage migrant members of transnational families inhabit contradictory social positions through the forces of globalization and through their dual frame of reference, by living in the United States and having family in Vietnam.[4] On the one hand, they work long hours in jobs that pay low wages in the United States; on the other hand, they strive to support homeland family members who they believe carry only inconsequential expenditures. Thus, while the migrant respondents are at or near the bottom of the American economic pyramid, their incomes take on different economic and social meanings when they return home.[5]

Until the late 1970s, scholars for the most part pointed to altruism as a key motivation for migrants who send money to their non-migrant relatives in the homeland.[6] Since then, analyses of the motivations for sending material remittances (i.e., both monetary and non-monetary) to the homeland have yielded mixed results.[7] Some scholars conclude that motivations for sending to the homeland are more complex than straightforward altruism. For example, self-interested migrants may give money to their non-migrant relatives because they seek long-term benefits to support their continued return visits to the homeland or for possible return settlement.[8] Another reason to send money, some scholars argue, is that it generates tremendous deference and respect among families back home, not entirely because such money supports non-migrants' daily expenditures,[9] but also because it conveys the success of the migrants.[10]

Focusing mostly on money sent from a distance (i.e., remittances) scholars currently divide their analytical focus into two dominant models that help explain the effects of money on the homeland.[11] On the one hand, those adhering to the *dependency model* argue that remittances increase inequality and generate a culture of migration as a result of the implied encouragement and pressure to spend money on goods that are not necessary for daily life—in short, to engage in unnecessary consumption.[12] On the other hand, those adhering to the *development model* argue that remittances help poor countries with economic growth by raising household incomes to a level that otherwise could not be earned in the home country.[13] This latter perspective points to how monetary flows into the homeland help alleviate repressed economies, thereby potentially solving economic and social problems associated with underemployment, unemployment, and population density.[14] Critical of the dichotomous views on migrant money, Jeffrey Cohen proposes that a transnational approach to analyzing remittance allows us to "break down the contradictions of dependency and development and defines the outcomes of migration and remittance use as rooted in a series of interdependencies that emphasize production and consumption, class and ethnicity, and the individual and the community while transcending localities and national boundaries."[15] Following Cohen, I underscore the interactive nature of transnationality with respect to analyzing monetary circulation, and its potential implication in the development of the transnational expenditure cascade in the homeland.

On the one hand, migrants in this study view monetary support as a form of economic assistance, resembling what has been documented in the literature about altruistic behaviors in remittance patterns among migrants.[16] On the other hand, their non-migrant relatives perceive material distribution as a family duty, which is frequently linked to moral principles, raised expectations, and perceptions of migrants' success. As some scholars note,[17] significant asymmetries of information and power are evident in relation to the ways money is perceived and used by those who give and spend it and those who receive it. When asked why they give money to relatives, most migrants express a transnational view, citing the comparative economic deprivation of their non-migrant relatives, and point to the feasibility of supporting necessity-driven consumption. Loi, a convenience store clerk in his mid-thirties who makes $11 per hour in Tampa, Florida, illustrates aspects of this point:

When you think about the history of us Viet people who got lucky to leave Vietnam, you have to think about so many people who wanted to leave during that time and could not. Even though I was only ten years old when my family came to America, I can still remember how hard life was back then in Vietnam. When I came back the first two times to visit all my parents' brothers, sisters, and my cousins, everything was still the same. I saw how hard life is for my relatives there. One of my mom's sisters wakes up every day at 3 a.m. to make these sweet rice cakes so she can sell to schoolchildren by 8 a.m. She makes no more than $5 each day, and when you think about the amount of work they do just to make those dollars, it's really heartbreaking.

Similarly, Luu, a thirty-four-year-old from Houston who makes $9 per hour preparing food at a small restaurant, talks about her brother's job in Saigon's port:

Whenever I come back, I go see my brother work at the port for several hours, and it changes my entire way of looking at my life. In America, you can get a job easily working in an air-conditioned room, and the hours are always fair. You are not treated like a servant. But in Saigon, if you are working for a company, a big company like the Saigon port system, you are like a slave. They control your time, there are no regular hours, and they boss you around all day. It is depressing to go there because I feel like it is like a prison for my brother. He works in the hot sun all day, with breaks only to use the restroom. And it's physically hard work for about twelve to fifteen hours a day.

I told him he can quit his job and I will give him his $200 monthly income, but he refuses to quit.

Significantly, while many migrants' occupations (i.e., predominantly jobs in the service sector and/or manual labor) in the United States are similar to their relatives' jobs in Saigon, the migrants often view their jobs as better than the jobs of their relatives. This difference can be attributed to the fact that workers in the United States have certain government-enforced rights that Vietnamese workers do not have, that working conditions in the United States are generally superior to conditions in Vietnam, and that dramatic wage disparities exist between the two countries.[18] Most migrants' incomes were generally fifteen to twenty times greater than their non-migrant relatives' incomes, even for the same job. Consider, for instance, that the lowest-earning non-migrant in this study made about $600 in 2004, whereas the lowest-earning migrant made nearly $15,000 in the same year[19]; both of them work in restaurants.[20]

Thus, it is striking that, like Luu, more than half the migrant respondents said they asked their relatives to quit their jobs and offered to give them wages on a monthly basis. Because most non-migrant members of transnational families make less than $200 per month, migrants did not view their proposed contribution as an excessive amount.[21] This was the case even though, for many, sending a $200 monthly "stipend" to a relative in Vietnam accounted for as much as 10 to 20 percent of their own income. When migrant respondents who sent money on a regular basis to their non-migrant relatives were asked if they felt it was a duty, most said they did not feel it was a duty, unless it was to their parents. Notably, only 10 percent of the migrant respondents circulated money to their parents. Rather, migrant respondents framed their monetary giving in terms of "helping" their relatives with life essentials. An, a forty-six-year-old cook at a Vietnamese restaurant in Northern California, contrasts the help she provides for her left-behind siblings in Vietnam with her obligation to her parents, who live in the United States: "It's not an obligation like I feel an obligation to my parents. If my parents need anything, I will make sure they have what they need so they are healthy." She elaborates:

For my relatives here [in Saigon], especially for my siblings, I think it's mostly I feel I want to help them [giup do] have a better life. I want to be sure they have necessary things. Everyone everywhere will have to work for a living. So no one can sit around doing nothing and expect others to be obligated to them fully. My job in California is not as difficult as it is for my two brothers and one sister here, but I still have to work very hard. I still have to work every day about ten hours a day, so it's not easy for me. I have to remind my family of that. Sometimes it's just difficult for them to remember that because they also know that I make in one hour what they make in two days here.

Mach, a thirty-eight-year-old maintenance worker at a large hotel in Boston, offers a similar description; like An, he compares the economic assistance he provides for his left-behind relatives with his obligation to his parents in the United States. He emphasizes that he is especially careful to let relatives know he is willing to help them with—and only with—necessary expenses to maintain a decent standard of living. "I say calling it a duty [*bon phan*] would be incorrect. I don't feel an obligation to my relatives in Saigon," Mach explains. "I mean that I feel I want to help them, that I do have a role to help them [*vai giup do*], but not a duty like I would have to my parents." He expands on this perspective in relation to the rise of a remittance reliance culture in Saigon:

I think for many people in Saigon, having a family overseas can make a big difference in their lives. For many of them, it can mean whether they eat meat regularly or not. I think having meat, for example, is a necessity for good health. But I think many locals here have unreasonable expectations of their overseas families. That can be a problem for everyone because when you talk about money, it can never be enough. How much is enough for anyone? I think that's why I always tell my two sisters here that they have to remember that my wife and I work very hard in America and we have children to raise. If they need things, we can help them, but we can't support them with things they want, especially if the things they want are just wasteful.

Though most migrant respondents said they want to help their relatives with essentials and daily expenditures, their definitions of what constitutes a good standard of living ranged widely, depending on each one's reference point(s), and directly affects their level of monetary circulation. Many of the migrants referred to standards of comfort that can be considered truly global and/or Western. For example, a few migrants indicated they aspire to buy cars for their non-migrant family members, despite the fact that only a small percentage of elites, most of whom are concentrated in urban areas, own cars in Vietnam. Cars are, of course, ubiquitous in the United States, a point of reference some migrants turn to when they think about necessities for their migrant relatives. However, the clear contrast between standards of living in the United States and Vietnam, as exemplified by such amenities as basic running water and proper plumbing, appears to have profoundly affected how other migrants are compelled to economically assist their non-migrant relatives.

We see this in the case of Cam, the cashier from Philadelphia. Cam's sister lives a seventy-five-minute drive from Saigon in a house she owns, which has a dirt floor. Cam describes the emotionality of her visits: "Every time I go back to Saigon, and then when I have to leave, I cry and cry for days before I leave. And on the day of departure, it's like a funeral in my parents' house in Saigon. I cry uncontrollably. But when I cry, I hold inside the reason I cry. I don't let them know why I cry because I don't want them to think that I am afraid of being separated from them." She expands on the cause of her emotions as she begins to cry during this interview:

I don't cry because I am afraid that I won't see them again or that we won't have communication when I get back to Philadelphia. I cry mainly because the thought of leaving my sister in that dirt-floor house hurts me. The thought of it is like a needle puncturing me through my stomach. And then when I get on the long flight home back to Philadelphia, I cry from the time I get on the plane to the time I get to my apartment in Philadelphia. And even though my apartment in Philadelphia is tiny with my husband and me, I know that I can drink the water from the faucet, that I have a toilet to sit on, and that I don't get my feet dirty when I walk on the carpet inside my apartment. Nothing really compares to living in a house with a dirt floor.

Even when they work for wages as low as $5 per hour (e.g., waiting tables at restaurants with set wages),[22] migrant respondents consistently compare themselves favorably to their non-migrant relatives in terms of economic opportunity structures, especially labor conditions. Their structural positions in the United States are often compared transnationally. This transnational comparison is highly significant because half of the migrant interviewees said they had very little or no savings and were living paycheck to paycheck.[23] And yet, the issue of housing complicates their comparative economic circumstances. When asked about their housing in the United States, only a little more than 20 percent ($n = 10$) of migrant respondents indicate that they own their residences. In contrast, more than 40 percent ($n = 21$) of the non-migrant respondents own their own house in Vietnam.[24] Despite these differences, the migrants see themselves as economically better off. These patterns reflect previous research, reported by scholars such as Mary Waters,[25] Luin Goldring,[26] Robert Courtney Smith,[27] and Yen Le Espiritu,[28] that suggests migrants turn to the homeland for a relative comparison of economic status even when they work in low-paid menial jobs. This dual frame of reference is evident during their visits to the homeland when the migrants' invisible labor is accentuated by their visible capital through the clothes and jewelry they wear, which are clearly more fashionable, expensive, and flashy than the clothes and jewelry of their non-migrant relatives.

In short, many immigrants use a transnational status system to view their position in the global economic opportunity structure. In her groundbreaking study of Filipino/a transnational communities, Espiritu suggests that class status and identity can be ambiguous when viewed transnationally because some immigrants who struggle economically in the United States view themselves as part of the upper class when they are back in the homeland.[29] It is thus not always meaningful to use standard measures of class, such as income or education, when speaking about migrants who live transnational lives.[30] In general, migrant respondents have widely varying views of their own and their non-migrant relatives' living standards, but these evaluations of adequate standards are more often than not entangled in the wide disparity of valuations that migrants attach to the outcomes of giving and spending money.

TRANSNATIONAL ECONOMIC STRATEGIES

Vietnamese low-wage migrants aspire to become transnational providers and to raise the standard of living for their non-migrant families by providing money to cover daily expenditures. Migrant respondents can be classified as different types of providers. A first group is composed of what I call *total providers*. These migrants generally view non-migrant relatives' households in Vietnam as part of their permanent household budget. They take a "transnational household" approach to their family economy.[31] Migrants in this group are total providers because they strive for their non-migrant relatives to have a minimal standard of living that includes the coverage of necessities, such as housing, medicine, and food. In addition to providing for general daily expenditures, they spend money on relatives when they return, such as taking people out to eat lavish meals and going on vacations with relatives. The second group of respondents, *non-spending providers*, generally provide basic necessities for their relatives, as do those in the first group; however, they differ from the first group because they generally abstain from spending money on relatives when they return to Vietnam. Finally, members of a third group, *non-providing spenders*, tend to spend money on their families when they make return visits, but do not provide money regularly for their relatives. These three groups help contextualize the range of provider roles taken on by migrant respondents. These are Weberian ideal types,[32] so it is likely that some respondents change their approach to being a transnational provider over time or due to shifting circumstances in terms of resources, expectations, and relationships.

A stock clerk at a major supermarket chain in Arizona, whose job consists of unpacking cartons and putting products on display, offers a revealing account of the total provider. Migrants of this type regularly reorganize expenditures in almost all facets of their lives in the United States so they can give money to their non-migrant relatives in Vietnam. From an economic standpoint, these migrant respondents view their non-migrant relatives as part of their transnational households. Migration scholars have questioned the use of household analytics as a primary unit of analysis because not all households act as a collective,[33] nor are such households inherently altruistic.[34]

Notwithstanding these observations, the early work of Nazli Kibria on Vietnamese refugees in the United States maintains the importance of households as units of analysis.[35] Writing about changes in family relations and economic strategies among Vietnamese refugee arrivals in the mid 1980s, Kibria points out that up to that point, many discussions of immigrant family life had ignored household structures and family ideologies when analyzing economic behaviors of immigrants.[36] Her ethnographic data on Vietnamese refugees suggest that "one of the most basic ways in which households differ is in their composition—who is included in the boundaries of the household."[37] She found that households with greater differentiation in their age and gender composition were better able than households with less differentiation to pool resources in order to widen their structures of opportunities and support systems. Kibria calls this process "patchworking," or the pooling of diverse resources into the household economy "by emphasizing the unity of household interests and the economic significance of kinship ties."[38]

The term *patchworking*, she argues, better conveys Vietnamese economic strategies than does the term *pooling* because patchworking "conjures up an image of jagged pieces of assorted material stitched together in some haphazard fashion."[39] This notion of patchworking is fruitful to consider in the context of contemporary Vietnamese migrants, who make economic decisions according to a transnational household strategy that includes some variant of patchworking. Their strategies differ from the economic strategies and adaptations that Kibria found with the early arrivals among Vietnamese immigrants, but there are crucial resemblances, including the reliance on extended kin for material support.

I met Phuc in the Tan Binh district of Saigon on a popular, busy street of recently renovated houses, many of which were funded by migrant money. Because streets in Saigon are now visibly segregated on the basis of the kinds of capital that circulate into them, it is easy to recognize the hierarchy and heterogeneity of migrant money on particular streets in the urban landscape. Tan Binh, for example, is unlike Districts 2 and 7, the wealthiest suburbs of Saigon, where one sees many foreigners building new houses. Few of the homes in Districts 2 and 7 belong to Vietnamese migrants, except the superrich; instead they are owned by other global actors, such as foreigners who work for multinational companies and regional Asian capitalists from Japan, Hong Kong, South Korea, and Taiwan. Phuc gave a sizable amount of money to a relative in Vietnam for renovating a house, a situation that is rare among other migrants. Phuc says he gave his brother $27,000 six years ago, and at that time Phuc's only request was that his brother either start a business or renovate the house Phuc's parents left to him when they came to the United States (sponsored by Phuc) more than a decade earlier. The brother decided to renovate the house, which is where I met Phuc for our interview.

Phuc exemplifies the total provider. He enumerates the tangible ways in which he restructures his finances to help his left-behind family members. "Everyone knows that America is the best place to live in the world," he begins. "We have freedom and we have things that people elsewhere don't have. I have family in Germany, and they say it's very hard to start a business because their country is very small. In Vietnam, it's so crowded everywhere you go. There is no space for you to breathe, and you would be lucky if you just have a safe place to live." Phuc expands on why he helps his family in Vietnam:

It's hard to do anything here unless you have money and help from family overseas. I see this in my brother's friends: many of them can try to save for the rest of their lives and they can never renovate their house like my brother did with the money I gave him six years ago. [*Was it difficult for you to give away that much money?*] Well, that amount of money was all that I saved after twelve years in America, but I think once I saw how hard my brother had it in Vietnam, I had to make decisions about my finances. My wife and I both decided to work a few extra hours a week to save and get the money back. We also try to reduce spending in ways that we can, but I think that just working more hours will help us get back the $25,000 within four years.

In addition to asking for more night and weekend shifts in order to work longer hours and recoup the money he gave his brother, Phuc talks about cutting back on expenses so he can send $250 monthly to his brother. This time, he draws on his experience as an immigrant when he first arrived in the United States. "I don't think it was hard for us to go back to where we were when we first landed in America. You know, when we first got there, we had nothing," Phuc explains. "My wife and I were living with relatives in Phoenix at first. We started to save money to rent our own house, and later bought a car. We saw our lives improving very much. That's what's great about America—you can work hard and save easily as long as you are willing to put in the time." He elaborates on how this perspective compelled him to economically assist the left-behind:

When I came back to Saigon and saw my brother and his family still living in the dilapidated house I grew up in, in Tan Binh, I convinced my wife to reduce some of our expenses. We sold our second car, and now we are used to using one car. And we stopped eating out, which we did a lot before we went back to Vietnam. I remember calculating how many days we could support a family in Saigon each time we ate at a restaurant in Phoenix.

As total providers, in addition to giving his brother's family a monthly income of $250 and giving his brother a large sum to renovate the house, Phuc and his wife spend money on his brother when they visit Vietnam:

When we come back to visit, we like to treat them well, so we take care of the expenses when we go around town, try new restaurants in Saigon, and things like that. We also like to take an out-of-town vacation with them somewhere in Vietnam, usually in the mountains near Dalat. It's expensive to take my family and my brother's family, but since it's only once a year, we try to save up and can manage it.

When asked whether his brother shares some of the expenses when he makes return visits, Phuc explains:

No, we are very careful not to have them spend money when we visit because he and his wife make about $300 combined, so if they paid for anything that we do in the city, it would be a burden on them. If we eat at home, my wife gives his wife money so she can go buy groceries. We understand they don't have the funds to host us, so when we come to Vietnam, we plan for all of these things. We plan for daily expenses like food not just for us, but also for his family because it would be weird if we ate separately in his house.

In contrast with total providers, such as Phuc, non-spending providers give their relatives monthly incomes to pay for daily expenses, but make a point of not spending money when they return to visit. The primary reason they cite for not spending money during their visits is fear that their relatives will have unrealistic expectations about monetary circulation. As one respondent succinctly puts it, "If you give them the image that you have a lot of money, they think you can print it!" This is similar to what Supriya Singh and her colleagues found among Indian migrants in Australia, a phenomenon that she calls the "money tree syndrome,"[40] whereby remittance recipients assume that it is easy to earn money in a foreign country and that such money is plentiful.[41]

Similar studies have also documented unreasonable expectations among recipients of migrant money, who sometimes request luxury goods that their migrant relatives cannot afford for themselves.[42] Thus, respondents who take on the role of non-spending providers are careful to prevent their families from having unreasonable expectations. Han, a woman in her early forties who lives in Orlando, Florida, and works in a nail salon, explains, "Some people can really get out of control with giving their relatives money, so a lot of local Vietnamese here [in Vietnam] think we can print money or that money grows on trees in America. They have no idea how hard we work, and even though we can easily send $200 or $300 a month, it's money that we can do something else with." She elaborates on her specific strategy of being a non-spending provider:

I don't give my relatives any extra money besides their monthly expenses, and I am careful about not giving more than they need. When I am here in Saigon, I try to not spend lavishly in front of them because they will have the impression that you have money. It's sometimes difficult because, you know, we are on vacation, and we work so hard that sometimes we want to treat ourselves nicely, but we don't want to let them think we have a ton of money to spend. I prefer to give gifts, but they don't care about gifts. All they want is the money.

Sang, a thirty-seven-year-old retail clerk from Dallas, became careful about his spending after his non-migrant brother spent his money on a lavish purchase. "Four years ago when I got a big bonus at work, I sent money back to my younger brother and asked him to buy a TV to put in my parents' house," he explains. "At that time, they were selling big flat-screen TVs in Saigon, and I knew my parents really wanted it because I had made a visit and they told me to bring one back to them." He expands on how his trust in his brother changed as a result of this transaction:

I figured I could just give my brother money to buy it for them. I thought it was good to buy it since my brother and my sisters were living with my parents and they all could watch the TV. When I came back the following year, I found out my brother sold his old bike and used the $1,500 I sent him to upgrade to a fancier bike. He tried to convince me the bike was better for the whole family! [He laughs.] So I knew then that I had to be very careful with how much money I send so they don't think money grows on trees in America. I was careful to just give them enough money to spend on necessities, and if there was an emergency, I would help.

Non-spending providers report that they send a fixed amount of money every month, and that when they return to Vietnam, they try to avoid spending on activities such as eating out and vacations. "Sometimes money is a very sensitive topic, even though you are right that we are very up-front about money in our culture," Cam, the cashier from Philadelphia, says when asked about attitudes toward money in her family. "But I think that sometimes families in Vietnam don't really know how hard we work in America." She elaborates on her strategy of being a non-spending provider:

If you just want to provide for them so they can take care of their daily expenses, they think you have unlimited amounts of money. I don't take them out to eat or anything like that in Saigon because it can get expensive. It's also a problem sometimes because if you take them out to eat, and you don't take them to a very nice place, they think you are cheap and you don't want to treat them well. It's always a problem, so I try to avoid these uncomfortable situations by just giving them money for essentials, without spending money on wasteful stuff when I visit.

In contrast, a smaller group of migrants generally do not give regular amounts of money to their relatives to maintain daily expenditures, but rather spend money on their relatives when they make return visits, including buying them what they need. Among these non-providing spenders, levels of spending behavior vary widely between men and women; this is the topic of Chapter 6, but here I underscore the various reasons these non-providing spenders convey for not giving regular amounts of money. Interview data suggest that they do not want to create a culture of reliance among their relatives. Whereas non-spending providers feel the same, non-providing spenders say they prefer to buy their relatives goods to avoid the discomfort of suspecting that their non-migrant relatives spend frivolously the money they send. Thus, they avoid sending regular amounts. Chinh, a thirty-eight-year-old car mechanic from Northern California, comments:

I don't want to be responsible for my uncle here [in Vietnam], so at the beginning, I was careful to not let him think I would be willing to support him. I see many people who all of sudden, when they come to Vietnam, just because they see people here with a different standard of living, automatically start to send regular amounts of money to their relatives. It's like they become a welfare system. I don't think that's good for anyone. If they start to think you can support them, even if it's only $100 or $200 per month, they will want to quit their jobs and just sit around and depend on your money.

Similarly, Trinh, a forty-two-year-old nail salon worker from Southern California, says the following:

Sometimes it's difficult when it comes to money. I want to help them [her two brothers] and spend money on them when I go there. Whenever I come to Vietnam, I try to see if they need anything and sometimes I will buy them what they need. Like, I bought my brother a motorbike a few years ago, and then when my youngest brother got married, I furnished his whole house for him. I try to give to them in that way, but I don't want them to think I can grow money in America. So that's why I don't want to send them money regularly. If there is an emergency, I might help them, but so far there has not been any emergency.

Besides not wanting to create a culture of reliance among their relatives, non-providing spenders also worry that if they send or give money directly to their relatives, the relatives will spend it on goods and services that the migrants deem frivolous, a topic I cover in Chapter 8. Their worry is not completely unfounded. Some migrants found that the money they gave, especially when it was sent from a distance, was used for goods and services they would not have approved, and might have labeled as luxuries. These migrants frequently mandated that receivers spend funds on daily needs, such as food and health care. As a case in point, thirty-six-year-old Trai, a department store worker from Southern California, was surprised and disappointed when he found out on his first visit to Vietnam how one of his sisters spent the money he had sent:

There is no question that I have to help my two sisters out in Vietnam because I am the only one who got to migrate to America. Because I could not sponsor them to America, since they were older than twenty-one,[43] I feel sorry for them, so I just send them money every month for their expenses. A few years ago, I sent them each $2,500 so they could renovate two of the bedrooms in the house my parents left them when I sponsored my parents to America. When I came back, I found out that one of my sisters was using her money on fancy clothes and stuff that rich kids in Saigon are buying. She was not using the money to upgrade the house, or even for necessities. After I came back, I decided I would not send her money from America anymore, and definitely I would not send her large amounts.

Hien, a forty-three-year-old nail salon worker from North Carolina who had made annual return visits for six consecutive years, remarks:

Every year when I go back, I see that people in Saigon are spending much more money and buying a lot more stuff. I have so many nieces and nephews in Saigon, and I could not believe how much they were spending on things. I don't understand how they make only $100 per month, but they can buy a $500 cell phone. I know many people in Saigon have Viet Kieu money, but I can't afford to support my family that much! When I returned two years ago, I remember my brother asking me for a big flat-screen TV. I told him, "No way! I can't even afford to have one for myself in America!"

As Hien explains, many respondents point to "Viet Kieu money" (i.e., money from overseas Vietnamese) as the source of a rise in material culture in Vietnam. Long, a thirty-seven-year-old mechanic from Florida, explains, "Of course, it is all about Viet Kieu money. How else could such a poor city open up name-brand stores like Gucci and Versace? I know so many locals who use their Viet Kieu money to buy luxury items." Long describes a personal experience with an overspending non-migrant family member that illustrates his point:

I discovered this the bad way when I came back and I saw my cousin with a Gucci bag. She wrote me when I was in America asking for money so she could take English classes in order to get a job at a five-star hotel, and I thought it was a good job for her. But when I came back, I tested her English. I knew right away she did not take English classes, so I asked her what she had spent the money on. She kept telling me she saved the money and was waiting for the right time to take English classes. And that was like eighteen months ago that I gave her the money. So one day I saw her carrying a Gucci bag, and I knew that thing was real. I was like, "Damn, let me see that bag!" It was real, definitely. I knew she had taken my money to buy that bag. I was pissed!

Thus, non-providing spenders say that instead of sending their non-migrant relatives money directly, they spend money on them when they make return visits, a pattern that has been documented in other studies.[44] Long elaborates upon this tactic:

I don't want to deal with the uncomfortable situation of asking them all the time how they spend the money I give them, so I decided after learning from mistakes that I will wait and buy them stuff when I visit. And if they need anything like money for English classes, I go directly to the school and pay for them. This way I don't have to worry or suspect that they waste my hard-earned money. [*What if they need money while you are not in the country?*] They will have to wait. There is really nothing urgent I can see in their lives. I mean, if it is an emergency, like a health care issue, then I will send money. Other than that, anything can wait for me to return because I come back often enough.

·   ·   ·

Migrant members of transnational families see the giving and spending of money on their non-migrant relatives as a form of care. Non-migrants similarly interpret monetary circulation as a form of care. However, whereas non-migrants view the giving of money (even by siblings and other extended kin) as a duty and obligation, the migrants themselves do *not* view material and monetary distribution as an obligation. Migrant members of transnational families take on a transnational optic, meaning that they actively compare their position within the American economic landscape to their relatives' economic position in Vietnam. This transnational optic compels migrants to financially assist their families in Vietnam. In doing so, some migrants economize in their U.S. households in order to save and accumulate for their relatives. They do so with the intention of providing essentials and necessities for their family members.

The three types of providers among migrant respondents foreground key variations among migrants with respect to how they give, send, and spend money. Total providers not only routinely provide for the daily expenditures of their relatives, but also spend money on the relatives when they make visits. Non-spending providers do not tend to spend money on relatives when they visit; instead, they prefer to give a fixed, routine amount to support their relatives' daily expenditures. Finally, non-providing spenders spend money on their relatives only when they make return visits, and opt to avoid giving routine amounts because they fear the money they give will be spent on frivolous goods. This typology of transnational providers is an early attempt at categorizing and explaining the flow of money among transnational families and allows us, at a minimum,[45] to understand how profoundly the personal and social differences that senders, spenders, and receivers assign to monetary circulation within transnational families (i.e., even those who originate from the same cultural pecuniary repertoires) affect familial relationships. These differences generate tensions, inconsistencies, and dilemmas as those on both sides of the oceanic divide take part in the transnational expenditure cascade.

CHAPTER 5

THE AMERICAN DREAM
IN VIETNAM

DAO NGUYEN is a fifty-one-year-old single mother of two who works in a nail salon in Charlotte, North Carolina. She recently bought a two-bedroom house with the help of her nineteen-year-old daughter, Kristy, who, when she turned sixteen, asked her mother for permission to work at a fast-food restaurant so she could help the family financially.[1] Dao agreed because Kristy's wages provide an important source of income to supplement their mortgage payment. Together, the mother-daughter team takes care of Kevin, Dao's twelve-year-old son. The family came to the United States when Kevin was barely two years old. They lived in Sacramento, California, until Dao's husband left her for another woman. She then moved with the two children to Arizona to work at her friend's nail salon. Dao saved enough money to move again, this time to Florida, where she lived with a man she had met through mutual friends. Four years later, after that relationship failed, she had saved enough money to move a fourth time. This time, Dao moved to Charlotte to be near her only brother. As a manicurist at the nail salon, Dao earns from $1,500 to $3,000 a month, an amount that fluctuates depending on the tips she gets from customers. Her co-ethnic employer guarantees Dao a minimum income of $1,500 a month, and gives her some flexibility in working hours. The salon is open from 9 a.m. to 9 p.m. daily, and Dao can choose any six of the seven days to work, as long as she works ten hours on each of her six workdays.

Dao's boss lets her take time off each year so she can make return visits to Vietnam. She says her children do not enjoy the trips as much as she does. "They don't really understand life there," Dao says. "I think it's too dirty and too loud for them. They are too American, so I let them choose if they want to go with me." Each year, she pressures them to go with her because she wants them to spend time with family in Vietnam; when they choose not to go, they stay with their father in California or with their Charlotte-based uncle. These trips are expensive, so Dao is extremely frugal when she is in the United States so she can save money for her return visits. As was the case in California, Arizona, and Florida, Dao says she rarely goes shopping in Charlotte, and if she does, it is only for the children. She also never goes out to eat at restaurants. "I let my son have a little money so he can go places with his friends," Dao explains, "but all our food we can eat at home, and I always have something cooked and ready to eat in the kitchen." Dao has never been to the movies and does not subscribe to cable TV, saying she would do so only "for the Vietnamese channels." Finally, Dao never takes vacations in the United States.

The story of Dao illustrates how low-wage immigrants who occupy multiple social spaces across transnational social fields strive to make sense of their low-wage conditions by turning to the material reality of their lives across the oceanic divide.[2] Dao functions like a migrant laborer and has virtually no interface with the public life of Charlotte, except for her food supply and her workplace. Nonetheless, she says she enjoys living in the United States. "I am very happy with my life in America," she says. "My children are healthy. They are good children and they study hard. I have supportive friends in Charlotte, and it's a good place to live."

Migrant respondents, such as Dao, subscribe to the American Dream discourse despite working many long hours in low-paid menial jobs with very little prospect for long-range mobility.[3] As what Jennifer Hochschild calls the "soul of the American nation," the American Dream ideology has for centuries served as a promise to the American public.[4] Those who hold on to this ideology, Michele Lamont asserts, "believe that the current distribution of rewards is fair, that opportunity is available to all, and that people can make it if they work at it."[5] Yet, without question, the promise of the American Dream goes unfulfilled for many in the country.[6] When we juxtapose immigrants' lives across transnational social fields, however, we see the complexities of the American Dream discourse across multiple social and economic positions. The ability to provide for their non-migrant relatives as well as to spend money when they make homeland visits reinforces their confidence in the rewards of their persistent hard work in the United States. Despite their precariousness in the U.S. labor market and their extremely frugal lives, migrant members of transnational families narrate stories of privilege and of gratitude for living in the United States.[7] In this sense, they believe they have achieved a version of the American Dream.

THEY WORK HARD FOR THE MONEY

When Dao returns to Vietnam, she stays in a crowded, narrow two-floor townhouse that belongs to her seventy-five-year-old mother in a run-down neighborhood of the Go Vap district of Saigon. Because Dao returns to Vietnam on a regular basis and has her own room in this house, a fact that, given the limited space in the house, highlights her importance as an overseas family member, she no longer packs personal clothes on return visits. She occasionally brings some over-the-counter medicines and whatever her family may have asked for as a "special request." "Nothing over $100," she laughs. "You can get whatever you want and need in Saigon these days. It's not like ten or fifteen years ago when you can't buy soap or Tylenol. It's all here now. There is nothing you need that they don't have in Saigon."[8] On one Sunday afternoon when I am visiting, the house is filled with more than a dozen people socializing with one another. The cacophony of conversations and the festive atmosphere make it seem that most of these people are guests at a family gathering. However, as it turns out, none of them are guests; all fourteen are occupants of the 800-square-foot typical Saigonese townhouse, with shared walls on the two main sides of the house. Dao reveals that three separate families live in this multi-generational household: Dao's elderly mother; plus Dao's two sisters and their husbands, and their two sets of teenage children, including four nephews and two nieces; plus an adult nephew, his wife, and a baby. Although she cavalierly discloses that she supports all fourteen of these relatives, I suspect it must be too stressful to make ends meet between her household in Charlotte, which she and her daughter, Kristy, both work to support, and the multi-generational household in Saigon. Yet, Dao explains:

It is not too expensive to support all of them here because my mother already owns the house. That would be the most expensive thing if we did not have the house that my mother has owned for many years. And for food, they cook every meal. They eat together, so it is much easier for them to buy things in bulk and share food. I give the whole family $250 a month for food. They have to pay for all the other expenses, such as electricity and gas for the stove. One of the nephews pays for the basic Internet service they have.

"What about emergencies?" I ask. "What about incidentals? When things come up, how do they take care of those things?" Dao explains further:

That's when it becomes a big problem; if something comes up and they need a large amount of money, then it becomes a crisis. About three years ago, when my nephew was twenty-two, he got into a motorbike accident, so I had to send back $1,800 for the hospital care. My mother also sometimes needs urgent care because she is not very healthy, and so that costs money occasionally. But I try to tell them to be careful with whatever they do because it is hard for me to help them if emergencies come up.

When asked how she has to economize in Charlotte to sustain monetary support for the Saigonese relatives, Dao shifts gears and discusses how lucky she is to live in the United States: "In America, it's not the same. Life is easy there. When you think about it, there are five adults working in this house—my two sisters, my two brothers-in-law, and one adult nephew—but their combined income is less than $500 a month. So all five make less than what I can make in about a week in Charlotte." She turns to her own situation in the United States as a comparison:

When you think about it, I am living in luxury. I have nothing to worry about. All I have to do is work hard and I can always make money. If I don't take six weeks off every year, I can earn as much money as all five of them make in a year. I think I am lucky that I can earn so much as long as I work hard in America. When the kids' father left us, I could still work and support myself. It's not like that in Vietnam. You have to be lucky to support yourself in Vietnam. In America, all you have to do is work hard; no matter what, you can always make money as long as you are willing to use your labor.

The research on Honduran transmigrants by Leah Schmalzbauer poignantly illustrates how low-wage immigrant workers return to the homeland to valorize their social status and self-worth. They are able to do so by the very fact that their incomes stretch further in the homeland than in the United States,[9] thereby helping them realize that their hard work in the United States pays off.[10] Despite structural limitations and a generally bleak economic opportunity structure for low-wage immigrants in the United States,[11] poor Honduran immigrants continue to embrace the American Dream discourse by way of their ability to purchase status-bearing goods in the United States and Honduras and to support non-migrant relatives in the homeland.[12] Schmalzbauer contends that through their exposure to the message that hard work can make anyone rich, immigrants "reproduce this ideology and that of American consumerism transnationally by sending messages, some true and some false, of success and opportunity to kinship networks back home."[13] Most important, Schmalzbauer asserts that sustaining and forging lives across transnational space makes the ideology of the American Dream more viable for poor immigrants than for other poor Americans.[14] She calls these Honduran transmigrants "transamerican dreamers" because they believe that no matter how tough it is in the United States, hard work will enable them to realize their dreams through consumptive behavior in the homeland.

My research on Vietnamese transnational families echoes Schmalzbauer's findings. Migrant respondents consistently talk about hardships and sacrifices that they endure in the everyday regimens of their low-wage work. Accordingly, when most migrant respondents describe their jobs in the United States, they relate stories of dirty work, long hours, and treacherous working conditions. Forty-three-year-old Khang Tran, a sarcastic, in-your-face kind of man who works as a machine operator at a warehouse distribution center near Falls Church, Virginia, describes such a line of work: "My work is very difficult in America. It's always heavy lifting and a lot of moving around with equipment and supplies and merchandise. It's like being a robot or a machine working all day without enough breaks." Elaborating on the challenges of his work situation, he says:

Sometimes the job can also be dangerous if I have to climb high up in the warehouse to retrieve heavy materials. The hours are very long because the warehouse is open very early and closes at midnight every night. Sometimes when I get home, I can't move my body and don't have the energy to eat. I just want to lie down and go to sleep right away when I get home, and start all over the next day. I don't have a choice in my schedule because the supervisor gives us what he needs on a weekly basis. Sometimes I have to work until midnight, and then I have to come back the following day at 5 a.m. to work. Some weeks, I can go for days without seeing my family.

Many migrants who arrived in the United States during the process of deindustrialization that intensified in the early 1980s experienced firsthand the erosion of well-paying jobs that once provided stability for the working class.[15] Over the past three decades, the shift from a manufacturing-based economy to a service-based economy has resulted in job termination for some low-wage workers, while many others have had to find multiple part-time jobs to make ends meet.[16] Thao, a female respondent in her mid-thirties, describes her multiple jobs as a nursing assistant and as a cashier at Walmart.[17] "I used to only work for minimum wage as a cashier at Walmart, but they changed their hours and hired many more part-time people so they could not give me enough hours," she explains. "They refuse to hire any more full-time cashiers. So a friend of mine recommended I take a short course to be a nursing assistant. I originally wanted to be a nurse, but I can't afford to quit work and go to school, so the short course is better than nothing." About her reasons for continuing to juggle two jobs, Thao says:

After I finished the course, I got a job working in the hospital, but they can't give me full-time work either. Because of that, I work at the hospital during the day three to five days a week, and at night I have the cashier job at Walmart. Even though the job at the hospital pays me $4 more per hour, I don't really like it. I have to clean after people and clean the hospital rooms. Sometimes I vomit several times a day when things get really bad there. If they could give me a full-time position with health benefits at Walmart, I would choose to work there full-time even though I would be making less money. I would just work more hours so I don't have to deal with the nasty hospital.

Other respondents also opt to work at lower-paying jobs, but make up for their low wages by working longer hours. Like Thao, some say they would rather work in low-paying jobs that are tedious and mundane than in higher-paying jobs that are dangerous and dirty. This view was articulated by forty-six-year-old Hong, a Florida-based eyeglass factory worker, who because she works in an air-conditioned factory does not see her work as "working class," despite the fact that she earns only $7.50 per hour. She says, "This company lets us work as many hours as we want. We get to work full-time and if we want to, we can work overtime for $10.25 per hour. But they won't let us report the overtime pay because in reality they have to pay us more than $10.25 if we work past forty hours a week, so we get paid cash if we work overtime. For the past eleven years, I work as much as my body can handle." Hong compares herself with other American workers:

I try to put in seventy to seventy-five hours a week because the overtime pay is a great deal for all of us. Some of the Americans complain about the work because they say it's boring, that it's too routine for them, and they can't handle it for a very long time. I am fine with it. I can do it for a very long time because my job is to put eyeglasses in boxes neatly so we can ship them out to the retail stores. The only problem is that sometimes my hand hurts by the end of the week, so I have to take a day off to recover. But it's still better than a lot of the other jobs I see the Vietnamese people work at around there, like working at the supermarket or restaurants.

In addition to occasional unfair practices, such as not getting proper overtime pay as just described, respondents report incidents of racism. Those who discuss additional struggles with discrimination and unfair labor practices in their work note that despite such problems, they continue to endure these conditions because they believe their lives will be better in the long run if they continue to sacrifice, work hard, and make an honest living. Hiep, a fifty-two-year-old father of three who has been working for more than fifteen years at a mushroom farm in Atlanta, Georgia, takes this view:

My wife and I have been working at the mushroom farm for over fifteen years. We pick thousands of pounds of mushrooms every month for the farm to distribute to their retailers. In the winters, it is extremely hard to work because they can't heat the inside of the farm. We could pick mushrooms for twelve hours in the cold weather. My wife gets sick easily, so even though she is always sick in the winters, she still goes to work with me. It's fine to work hard, but sometimes the stupid supervisors have favorites, and that really angers me. Some of them [supervisors] at the farm have favorites and their favorite workers are always the white people. They get to choose when they take days off and they get paid higher wages than us. The other Vietnamese workers and I have complained, but they don't pay us any attention.

Writing twenty years ago about the comparative outcomes of immigrants and domestic minorities, sociologists Min Zhou and Alejandro Portes pointed out that for many newly arrived immigrants, "a tour of duty in low-paid menial work is part of the time-honored path towards family advancement and economic independence."[18] For the Vietnamese migrants in this study, their time of arrival in the United States generally had no relationship to their views about mobility and hard work. That is, migrants were generally uncritical of the system of oppression embedded in contemporary capitalism,[19] and regardless of when they arrived in the United States, as a social group, migrants were generally optimistic about their circumstances. They do not deny the existence of racism or other structural barriers; rather, they tend to focus on opportunities,[20] no matter how limited, that they actually experienced in their lives.[21] When they evaluate the economic opportunity structure in the United States, they occasionally refer to experiences of discrimination or unfair labor practices, as in the case of Hiep; however, they view these problems as interpersonal matters, rather than a structural condition of their lives. Even when they discuss discrimination and unfair labor practices, migrants maintain their fidelity to the ideology of the American Dream.

LONELY PARADISE, HAPPY HELL

Despite experiencing unfair labor practices, invidious working conditions, and a bleak life in general, migrant members of Vietnamese transnational families turn to a transnational optic to make sense of their precarious circumstances. "When you think about it and compare America and Vietnam, it is a lonely paradise and happy hell," says Khang, the warehouse worker. Khang's comparison of the United States as "lonely paradise" and Vietnam as "happy hell" lucidly captures the perspective of many migrant interviewees, some of whom used the same metaphor of paradise and hell when comparing the United States and Vietnam. On an economic basis, migrant interviewees tend to think of America as paradise and Vietnam as hell. Yet, on an emotive basis, they feel lonely in the United States and happy in Vietnam. There is a certain irony in the fact that if the United States were *only* a lonely paradise, they probably would not accept the American Dream ideology. But because the happy hell of Vietnam is part of their transnational experience, they are able to merge the two and focus on the paradise part of the United States and the happy part of Vietnam. These intersectional economic and emotional feelings help explain the logic of transnationality among migrant respondents. In other words, this comparison is an astute illustration of how migrants occupy multiple positions within the transnational social field of the Vietnamese–United States migration corridor, a condition that Peggy Levitt and Nina Glick Schiller refer to as "simultaneity, or living lives that incorporate daily activities, routines, and institutions located both in a destination country and transnationally."[22] The glaring polarity between the lives of many they see in Vietnam, including their own relatives, and their lives in the United States cannot be ignored when they make return visits. In such instances, they may choose to focus more on the relative paradise they enjoy at home and momentarily try to forget the precarious nature of their economic lives in the United States.[23] In fact, it is common for interviewees to discuss their difficult working conditions in the United States, and yet to be mostly positive and optimistic, if not gratified, about their circumstances within the same interview.

The significance of interviewing migrant respondents in the homeland is accentuated by data that show how they describe their work lives in transnational relative terms. Without question, when I interview migrants in Saigon, their sense of self and status is valorized because they are situated in developing Vietnam. Even the lowest wage earner among them, who makes $5 per hour with no tips—because the owners take all tips from the servers—working as a waitress at a Vietnamese restaurant for "under the table pay" in Houston, maintains a sense of optimism.[24] I met twenty-nine-year-old Nga in the middle of the day at a chain café in Saigon, where I learned that despite having lived in the United States for only nine years, she is already on her fifth return visit. She talks about life in Houston:

There is no better place than America. Everyone wants to go to America. You can just take a look around Saigon and see how poor people are, how hard it is to get a job and make a decent living here. If people could go to America easily without needing a visa, 99 percent of this city would be gone. If I wait tables at a restaurant here, I would be a nobody, I would make less than $50 per month, and they would treat me like a slave. But in America, the government protects us. If you come to America with nothing, like me—no education, no skills—you can still get a job the day after you land in America.

The importance of having a positive outlook on the economic opportunity structure in the United States, and therefore the American Dream ideology, compels migrants to say they believe their lives would be much worse if they had never gone to the United States. Again, no matter how precarious they view their jobs in the United States, their outlooks are nonetheless optimistic, as exemplified by the following statement by Dao, the nail salon worker:

You really don't know how miserable it is in Vietnam unless you live here and experience the pain of being poor. This country has no jobs. You know, after the war people were starving to death, and that's why so many of us tried to escape to America or any other country that would take us. We knew that no matter how hard it is over there [anywhere in the diaspora], life could not be worse than life in Vietnam. My family was fortunate that we got to go to America because you can work hard there and save money, and one day you will have a good life. Even with my job working twelve hours a day painting fingers, and kneeling down for hours cleaning and massaging people's feet, it's still much better than being poor and miserable in Vietnam.

Regardless of their age, respondents view economic opportunity in the United States as far better than life in Vietnam. However, as discussed by Dao, members of the older generation have an additional frame of reference from the postwar years that makes their belief in the American Dream qualitatively different from that of the younger generation. In contrast, those in the younger generation look strongly to their peers in Vietnam for a reference point to help them understand the international economic disparities. This is most salient for migrants who came of age in the United States. They were not young enough when they arrived to go through a formal pre-collegiate education, nor did they come late enough with families of their own to immediately take on responsibilities for supporting a household. Phung, a thirty-four-year-old female typist from Los Angeles who makes $11 per hour and who came to the United States as a young adult, echoes the perspective expressed by Nga:

Some of us just don't have the intelligence to go to college and get degrees to get the best jobs in America. But even if you don't have a degree, you can still make a decent living over there [United States]. When I compare myself to my cousins here [Vietnam], I feel very lucky that I am not here. I mean, I am happy every time I come back to visit. I feel lucky that I can bring American dollars here to spend, but without my job in America, I could never afford to save and come back here and spend. People say we can be happier in Vietnam, but this is happy hell if you don't have a job, like many people my age here. I know many our age who can't afford to move out of their family's house, and most of them make only about $100 a month.

Similarly, this view is expressed by Kiet, a thirty-eight-year-old man who migrated ten years earlier to Southern California, and who now makes $32,000 a year driving semitrailers throughout the state:

You can't compare yourself to the people who came to America very young. They got to go to grade school there and got a chance to work their way up, make American friends, and do well in school. They got lucky. But people like me and other people I know, we came to America too late. We were already adults. We did not have good English skills, so we did not have too many options. We had to support ourselves and help support our families. Anyway, I am still doing better than my friends here in Saigon. I have friends here who can work all their lives and can never save as much money as I can save in one year. That's why America is the best country to live in, and everyone knows that. You can go there, like me, with no education and get a good job. Even though I need to work a lot of hours at my company, I don't have to worry about money like my friends in Saigon.

CHILDREN AND THE AMERICAN DREAM

Migrant respondents especially embrace the American Dream ideology through the potential achievement of children, whether or not they have children. This finding supports empirical studies that focus on Asian, Latino, and African migrants in the United States who embrace the American Dream ideology even in the face of abject poverty, discrimination, and severe deprivation.[25] When speaking of the mobility of the future generation, respondents in this study exemplify the "immigrant bargain," a term coined by Robert Courtney Smith to explain how migrants justify their hard work with the expectation that their children will do well and succeed.[26] Parental status is not a factor that influenced their optimistic view because the vast majority of them have children or intend to have children.[27] Respondents with children notably say they work hard so their children can succeed in the United States. Virtually all of those without children predict that their children will do much better economically than they themselves have done because of the opportunities they will give their children.[28] Virtually all respondents say that obtaining college credentials is the first move into the steps of mobility in the United States, and acquiring "office jobs" is frequently cited as an aspiration.[29] "I came to America too late to go to school, but if you are young in America, you can work hard, get a college degree, and get a good office job," says a female warehouse-packing worker in her early forties who lives in Arizona. "I want my children to get an office job; it's easier and you get paid more. You don't have to work like a slave, like us laborers."

Migrant interviewees no doubt set high hopes for their children to succeed, despite a general lack of mobility in their own lives. Although Dao allows her daughter to work at a fast-food restaurant almost every day of the week, because they need the money, she expresses high hopes that her daughter and son will move up the U.S. economic ladder:

Kristy and Kevin [her daughter and son] have more chances to succeed than I did because they came to America very young. If they work hard, they can get into a good school and get a college degree. I work many hours and work very hard so they don't have to work as hard as me in the future. I even told Kristy she does not have to work as a cashier, to only focus on her studies. But she said she watches her studies carefully. I try to get them whatever they need so they can do well in school, because if they do well, I can relax later in life. [*What do you mean by that?*] I don't want to depend on them, but I won't have to worry if they succeed and can get a good job in an office. Then maybe one day they will help support me so I don't have to work so much, like I do now.

Even migrants who have lived in the United States for several decades continue to view hard work in low-paid menial jobs as part of their "tour of duty" for economic mobility, especially when they think about the economic possibilities for their children.[30] This is reflected in migrants' discussions about their children's future in relation to the stark situation in which they themselves currently work. Repeatedly, respondents talk about their jobs as the next step toward a better future. "I do it for my children. I can give my all for my children because I know they will succeed in America," explains Khang, the warehouse worker. "I came to the United States when I was a young man, so I didn't have the time to go to school. I had to get a job right away to support myself, because my family was poor then." He elaborates on the importance of working hard and focusing on the opportunity available to his children:

Everyone was poor when we first came to America. So we had to start from the bottom and work our way up. Even if you look at my job now at the warehouse over there, it is still better than other people. We know people who work at the hospitals cleaning toilets and the hallways. [*How do you think your children will do better than you?*] They will work hard because they know how hard I work and they know that we don't have a lot of money. We tell them all the time that if they focus, if they work hard and not play too much, they can be a boss or a supervisor one day, not like my wife and me, who are just workers.

Another respondent, Hong, the eyeglass factory worker, describes her viewpoint in similar terms, crying midway through her thoughts:

When I work at the factory day and night, I think about every hour I put into the factory, every eyeglass I pack, I think about what that means for my children. I think about how they have the world out there and all the opportunities over in America to take advantage of it. [She cries as she continues.] I remind them how we escaped Vietnam so they can have a better life, and they have to work hard because America is good to you if you work hard. If you don't work hard, you will not succeed and you will have to labor away for the rest of your life. I tell them that I work hard and their father works hard, that we put in all our energy to the point when our body can no longer take it every week, when I can feel my body aching and waiting for the next day off. I tell my children all of this because I want them to work hard and succeed.

Writing about immigrants in a poor section of east New Orleans, Min Zhou and Carl Bankston found that despite a bad local economy, high unemployment, and sometimes broken families, Vietnamese refugee immigrants are optimistic about their children's future.[31] This is especially true among parents and community members who feel that ethnic solidarity and control help children succeed in the face of crushing poverty and disadvantage.[32] Consistent with this empirical finding, respondents in this study said that no matter how many hours they work, they keep a close watch on their children and rely on their friends and family in the community to watch over their children when they are not available. More generally, when respondents talk about community ties and dependency, they invariably speak about working hard because, although hard work may entail competition, it signals clearly that academic achievement leads to upward mobility, if not to true "American" success.[33] In this sense, affiliation with co-ethnics serves as a form of social control for their children, particularly when the children witness community members achieving what they see as the American Dream. As Hiep, the Atlanta-based mushroom picker and packer, sees it:

There is a man who works with my wife and me. He brought four children to America by himself, and his wife did not join him until fifteen years later. He has been working at the mushroom factory for longer than I have. He encouraged all his children to go to school and he did everything he could to make them succeed. On some days in the past years, you can see him bring the younger children to work with him, and he would check on them during his breaks to see if they study. Three of those kids are now very successful. One is a doctor and the other two are going to be pharmacists. I tell my three children every day about that man's children because I tell them if they work hard, they don't have to be like me, but if they don't work hard, they will have to pick mushrooms for the rest of their lives.

Among all the migrant respondents with children ($n = 28$), 17 percent ($n = 5$) report their children "made it" in the system of mobility in the United States. For these migrants, the experience of their children doing well in school, going to college, and obtaining professional jobs is the ultimate reward and measure of their tremendous hard work. These respondents have children working as an accountant, a software engineer, a pharmacist, a retail store manager (hired through an executive MBA training program), a bank manager, and a dentist. It is of empirical value to note that although almost all respondents hold on to the American Dream ideology, few actually see it manifest through their children or within their personal networks. Notwithstanding arguments made about ethnic capital as a key factor in determining pathways for Vietnamese children,[34] migrant interviewees whose children obtained professional jobs were, in the migrants' views, the ultimate evidence that the American Dream is within reach. Duc, a fifty-three-year-old Vietnamese restaurant worker from Northern California, describes the pride she feels in her twenty-six-year-old daughter's accomplishment as a software engineer:

My children are why my husband and I have worked so hard all these years. We always tell our children to just work hard, study, and do well in school. We told them to not worry about money, that if they just work hard in school, they can succeed. We have a son who is now in eleventh grade, and we hope he will listen to his sister and follow her the way she worked in school and got successful in her job. When she was younger, I didn't let our daughter out of our eyesight. We watched her carefully and made sure she worked hard so she can get into a good school and get a good job so she does not have to work as hard as her parents.

She invokes the promise of the American Dream in response to my gentle observation that many other respondents, despite extremely hard work and watching out for their children, do not report similar success by their children:

You can visit my daughter at her company and see that she has a great job now, and her office is so beautiful and the company gives her so much. [*Many Vietnamese Americans say they work hard, but many people I meet do not have children who succeeded. How do you think your daughter made it so successfully?*] I don't know why the other children don't succeed like you said. I think they must have gotten in trouble or have the wrong friends. I see that in some of the friends I have over there. They don't watch their children or they let their children have bad friends. When you have bad friends, you cannot focus. It's America. If you focus and stick with your plans, you can do it.

SPENDING HARD-EARNED MONEY

These findings might lead us to infer that the migrants' belief in the promise of the American Dream ideology is only or primarily held with respect to the future of children. However, when juxtaposed with the prevalence of monetary circulation in the homeland, the significance of the homeland for members of this immigrant group as it relates to their belief in the American Dream ideology is evident. Even for the vast majority, who have not yet seen the successful outcomes for their children or the children of those in their social networks, the ability to provide for non-migrant relatives as well as to spend money when they return to the homeland permits them to elucidate why they work so hard. Many say their hard work is what enables them to spend as generously, and sometimes lavishly, as they do. Moreover, the ability to provide for their non-migrant relatives reinforces their confidence in the rewards of their persistent hard work in the United States. This is poignantly illustrated by Dao, who talks vividly about her role as the provider for her fourteen relatives in Saigon:

If I stop giving them money here, they would not have enough food to eat. You can see there are many mouths to feed in this family! Before I was able to come back, my mother told me that they rarely eat meat for their meals. They cannot buy meat on the money they make, but my help—even though it is only $250 a month—gives everyone the chance to regularly eat meat. In addition to that, if someone gets sick or there is an emergency, they can call me. They can depend on me. I know that it brings them peace of mind that they can depend on me. I never forget to send them money monthly because I know they need it.

When asked how she handles emergencies for her non-migrant relatives, Dao explains that her savings—money she can only accumulate in the United States— permit her to be like an insurance policy for her family in Vietnam. This shows that frugality and hard work are entangled in her belief in the American Dream ideology, as well as enabling her to ensure her family's well-being in Vietnam:

You know, many people say that if you have an overseas relative, it can be like having very good insurance. [She giggles as she describes this.] That's what many locals here think and they show it. They don't worry about anything because they know if they quit their jobs or if they get into an emergency, they can just make a call or even send a message to their relatives abroad. Many will get the money right away. For me, I told my sisters that they and their husbands must work. They cannot be lazy and not work. But if they have an emergency, if something comes beyond their control, I will take care of it. They know I will take care of it, and they are responsible enough to not abuse it. So I do have a separate savings pot that I put away for emergencies for them. I guess it is kind of like insurance. But it is emergency insurance only!

Luu, the thirty-four-year-old Houston food preparer who makes $9 per hour and is a total provider, explains that in contrast to the attitude of her high-spending peers in the United States, her self-denial of worldly goods in America helps feed her non-migrant relatives. Like Dao, she provides an ex- ample of how belief in the specific element of frugality is invoked in the Ameri- can Dream discourse:

So many Americans, especially the Vietnamese people there, are so wasteful. They get a job and they go out and buy a nice car right away. I know some girls who work with

me, even ones who have kids, want to buy fancy cars to show off. The Vietnamese girls
I know who work in the same mall with me over there, the first thing they do when
they get their paychecks is go out and buy a fancy outfit or something wasteful for
themselves. They like to go eat at nice restaurants even though they don't make that
much money. I mean if you work hard, you should enjoy sometimes, but you should
not be wasteful. All that money they waste on stuff, I save mine and I can bring it to
Vietnam to feed my family here. Every time I see a girl buy an expensive shirt or some
makeup, I instantly think about how many days that money could feed my family here.

On the other end of the spectrum, non-providing spenders talk extensively
about the satisfaction derived from their ability to use their American dollars in
the homeland. Respondents who spend, rather than give, money speak about
how they reap the benefits of their hard work in America on return trips to
Vietnam, where they receive intrinsic satisfaction by spending money.[35] Chanh,
a thirty-seven-year-old construction worker from Los Angeles, explains how his
hard work pays off when he indulges and pampers himself in Saigon:

You know, life is so short. We work so hard in America. We make good money; if we
think about the money that our relatives in Saigon make, we make great money. All the
hard work I do in America, I have to enjoy it [*huong thu*].[36] I try to be frugal in America, to save money, but when I am in Saigon, I indulge and pamper myself. I don't think
about it. I mean, when I am in Saigon, I think less about the money because things are
not as expensive as the U.S. [*How do you pamper yourself here?*] I definitely eat out more,
even if I am staying for a long time with my family. I go out to eat whatever I want,
whenever I want. I take my relatives out for nice dinners and we go to nightclubs and
cafés. I get massages, things like that. Also, every time I come back here, I take my family on a trip to the Dalat Mountains. Everyone likes it there very much. There are many
things you can enjoy in Vietnam that you can't in America because it is cheaper here.

Similarly, another respondent, Hue, a twenty-nine-year-old female hair
salon worker from Northern California, with several family members living in
Saigon, including one younger brother and many first cousins for whom she
has much affection, explains that spending money on her family is her central
reason for making regular return visits:

The best times for me are when I am here [in Saigon]. I indulge in whatever I want,
especially taking care of my family. [*What do you mean by taking care of your family?*] I

know that my brother and cousins are always eager to have me back so I can buy them things and take them out around the city. Saigon is a very fun city, but if you don't have the money, you never really truly know the city well. If you go into the fancy new buildings and the fancy new cafés and nice restaurants, you can look at the price and see that most of the locals here who just have a regular job cannot afford to spend money in those places. My brother loves going to nice cafés and spends hours there, and loves going to nice restaurants and the movies. So when I am back here for a month every year, we spend time together, sometimes at the café all day just talking, eating, and hanging out.

Such an atmosphere presents contradictions in terms of patterns of savings and frugality practiced on the one hand, and cavalier and indifferent spending on the other. When probed about this contradiction, respondents invariably call to mind that the reason they work so hard in the United States is either for their children or to obtain money they can spend in Vietnam on themselves or on their non-migrant relatives. Giving and spending money provides immediate validation that their persistent hard work has paid off. The homeland offers tangible ways—through spending and giving money—that may not exist for low-wage Americans who do not have multiple spaces to occupy across transnational social fields. Chanh, who always brings his wife and four-year-old son on return trips to Vietnam, explains how he mediates this contradiction. Asked if he ever feels like he is spending too much or too frivolously, Chanh says:

I work like a dog for my family here [Vietnam]. Whenever I spend twelve to fifteen hours a day outside on a construction site, putting every tile into a house, or cleaning every pile of mess in the projects we do in America—every time my back aches—I think about it. I think about why I put in extra hours of work instead of just working eight hours a day. I think all the time about if the overtime is worth it to me or not. And my wife sometimes reminds me that I have to also consider my own health and our family when we are over there [in the United States]. But when we are here, we see how much we love it here, how much we enjoy life here. We can't forget that we work so hard over there because we have to be back there in a month! But we need to spend money here, too. We need to play and pamper ourselves sometimes. We have to if we work so hard.

Hue, the hair salon worker, echoes this perspective in a self-assured way. She takes it a step further by describing her sense of belonging in Saigon: "If I had a choice, I would live in Saigon forever. But I just don't have the chance to get

a good job here that will pay as much as I make in America. I make in one day
what many of my relatives make in one month here." When I ask if comparing
incomes in Vietnam and the United States is valid, Hue explains:

If you just work hard and save money in America, you can come back here and live
like an emperor [*de vuong*]. In America, I work over ten hours each day, and I just
take one day off a month. Because any day I take off is someone's monthly income
here in Saigon. When I come here to spend money, I feel the long hours of work I do
in America are worth it. I don't feel bad about spending money here because I work
many hours in America. I think about my relatives here who don't have the same opportunity that I do because if they did, you know none of them would be here.

. . .

Migrant members of Vietnamese low-wage transnational families uniformly believe that persistent hard work will pay off for them. In the face of bleak working
environments that provide little or no mobility in their lives, migrants believe
they are doing well in the very systems of contemporary U.S. and global capitalism that exploit them in low-paid menial jobs. In this context, the findings
reflect a number of studies over the past three decades that show that Americans,
including and perhaps most vividly the immigrant population, generally buy
in to the American Dream discourse despite structural obstacles.[37] The asymmetry between their views of the American Dream and the concrete reality of
their lives shows vividly that migrants working in low-wage jobs believe in the
concept of the tour of duty built into the pervasive discourse about immigrant
incorporation. Migrant workers' aspirations for their children's mobility is one
major factor that explains their continually positive outlook, especially for the
very few who have witnessed success by their offspring. Consequently, for most
migrants, regardless of parental status, the potential mobility of children helps
them cope with multiple disadvantages they face as members of the low-wage
workforce, including low pay, long working hours, dangerous working conditions, occasional discrimination, and unfair labor practices. When their lives
are juxtaposed across transnational social fields, moreover and importantly, we
see how migrants who occupy multiple social spaces are able to rationalize the
value of the American Dream despite any evidence to the contrary.

Migrants who make regular return visits to Vietnam give and spend money
on relatives, enabling the migrants to realize in the present the payoff of their

hard work. This chapter helps us better comprehend the successful marriage of the American Dream ideology and the system of global capitalism that exploits low-wage migrants. We saw that migrants, ranging from total providers to non-providing spenders, pinpoint their ability to give and spend money in Vietnam as concrete evidence of their hard work in the United States. In addition to benefiting from the intrinsic satisfaction of being able to provide for their families in Vietnam, migrants take pleasure in indulging in activities they might be unable to afford in the United States. This explains perspicuously why migrants continue to engage in self-sacrifice and self-denial through economizing many aspects of their lives and working longer hours at low-paid menial jobs. They empower themselves by using the money they earn and save to support relatives in the developing world, a social practice made possible by the economic disparity that prevails in the Vietnam–United States migration corridor. However, this social practice has limitations, as we will see in the next two chapters, which examine how and why migrants and their non-migrant relatives alter their reference points with respect to consumer behavior in the new Saigon.

CHAPTER 6

COMPENSATORY
CONSUMPTION

W RITING more than a century ago, Thorstein Veblen coined the term *conspicuous consumption* to explain the class of nineteenth-century nouveaux riches who ostentatiously spent money to tout their new wealth.[1] He pointed out that one's reputation during the period of new wealth formation depended on one's pecuniary strength, which had to be expressed through lavish spending.[2] Monetary lavishness was a "means of reputability."[3] For Veblen, conspicuous consumption was about wasteful spending that must lack utilitarian value to bring credibility to the spender.[4] Following Veblen's seminal work on status-driven consumption, numerous scholars have written about different ways people consume to express their status.[5] In this chapter, I spotlight how migrant men and women are segmented along gender and class lines in the ways they engage in *compensatory consumption*,[6] a term David Caplovitz uses to describe a form of status-driven consumption in which poor, working-class minorities in the United States spend money on expensive durable goods to compensate for their low occupational status.[7]

When low-wage workers have few prospects for improving their social standing, Caplovitz notes, "they are apt to turn to consumption as at least one sphere in which they can make some progress toward the American Dream of success."[8] As Eli Chinoy notes in his classic study of low-wage automobile workers, when confronted with the impossibility of occupational advancement, they "measure their success by what they are able to buy."[9] Compensatory consumption is thus used to shift the measurement of success from the sphere of production (i.e., the lack of prestige in their work) to the sphere of consumption. Compensatory consumption resembles conspicuous consumption in some ways,[10] but the two are distinguished in other ways. In short, if as Veblen notes, the theory of conspicuous consumption is a theory about the leisure class,[11] then compensatory consumption is a theory about the working class. Here, I expand upon the idea transnationally and along lines of gender relations.

Over time and during their return visits, low-wage migrants extravagantly spend money on goods and leisure in Vietnam to communicate status, but this lavish spending also serves as a response to their relatively deprived structural positions in the U.S. labor market.[12] Spending behavior by Vietnamese low-wage migrants in the homeland perhaps signals most strongly the gendered dimension of monetary circulation, especially through the proclivity to purchase commodities and leisure for others. Women are more likely than men to buy durable goods for non-migrant relatives, whereas men are more likely to pay for food and drinks at restaurants and bars, as well in various leisure activities throughout the city. I call this process *segmented compensatory consumption* because it marks how social groups engage in consumption practices differentiated along categorical lines of differences, such as gender and class.[13]

One effect of the fact that spending money on non-migrant relatives is highly segmented between men and women is that the visibility of women's expenditures on their non-migrant relatives is often understated in everyday public discourse.[14] Underlying the gendered segmentation of consumption is a common pattern whereby both men and women respond to blocked social and economic mobility in the United States by occasionally engaging in extravagant compensatory consumption.[15] The phrase *segmented compensatory consumption* accordingly illustrates the complex and powerful dynamics of this classed and gendered modality of action for migrant members of transnational families.[16] In a paradox of spending habits, precisely because they are unable to acquire status in the United States through the conventional avenues of obtaining college credentials and stable or prestigious employment, Vietnamese migrant men and women from the United States sometimes overspend on goods and leisure in Vietnam to repudiate their low status in the United States.[17]

LIVING LARGE IN THE CITY OF MEMORY

It is nearly 2:00 in the morning. As the server brings the bill to convey that the restaurant is finally closing, Quoc Bui, a forty-three-year-old Bostonian who is on a return visit with his wife and three-year-old daughter, asks to see the menu for the sixth time since we arrived for dinner, which started eight hours ago. Within ninety minutes of our arrival, the female relatives who joined us for dinner left, and the gathering turned into a drinking festivity for the men. I stuck around, as Quoc insisted each time I announced I was going home. "We never play like this in America, Hung!" Quoc explains. Each time I take a sip of the dreadful local whiskey he pours me, Quoc and his friends exclaim, usually in unison, as the others clap, "You can't just lick it! You have to drink the whole thing. You can't be like a foreigner. Drink it like a local!"

Although the conviviality persists between us and the other customers in three separate parties, the staff has cleaned the rest of the enormous restaurant. Some of the servers are waiting at the door near their bicycles for permission to leave their shift, which ended about three hours earlier. But each time a server comes to settle the bill, Quoc waves a 100,000 VND bill (equivalent to $5) to tip the server, and smiles, signaling that, in fact, the bill is not being paid yet. By 2:00 a.m., Quoc has tipped five servers a combined total of one million VND so they will stay and tend to his drinking festivity. Although each 100,000 VND bill is more than their daily income, there is a limit to how late these young servers will put up with even the most generous customers. When the owner finally intervenes, with as much politeness as one can muster at 2:00 a.m., one of Quoc's cousins whispers to him, "We really have to pay now and leave." Quoc takes a wad of cash from his trousers, conspicuously displayed to convey his "converted wealth" (i.e., the seeming conversion of low wages from the United States into high wages in Vietnam).[18] He then pays the 8 million VND tab, the equivalent of about $400, for dinner and unlimited local whiskey for nearly fifteen people.

However, the night out has not yet ended. As I climb behind one of Quoc's cousins, who is seated on one of the many motorbikes waiting outside for us, confusion arises about where we are to go next. "That place is closed," one person says. "That place is closed, too," another chimes in. After several rounds of brainstorming, one of the men yells, as he zooms off with Quoc on the back of his motorbike, "Follow me to Yesteryears!" About ten minutes later, after the streets of Saigon have cleared out for the late-night economy, we land at Karaoke Yesteryears, one of about a dozen unlicensed establishments that defy the city's curfew. Yesteryears caters to those who do not quite want to face tomorrow. People like Quoc come to a place like this because it offers them the chance to extend their consumption power in front of friends and family well into the wee hours. Here, men gather to continue drinking and to compete not so much to see how well they can sing the best melodies, but to see who can spend the most on liquor, food, and occasionally the intimate labor of hostesses.[19] Singing a peculiar amalgamation of Vietnamese revolutionary music and American pop, I struggle to stay up until nearly 5:00 a.m., when Quoc pays the bill of $180 for the eight remaining survivors of the night.

The night economy of the new Saigon is contoured not only by its gendered and classed idiosyncrasies, but also, and more important, by the status display practices of men from various corners of the globe. As one thinks about this social order in the temporal and spatial locus of the new Saigon, the racialized and classed bodies of men, including the migrant subjects, can be assigned to different hubs of the city. Foreign men concentrate at places such as the famous Apocalypse Now or the Queen Bar in the central business district, while the wealthy regional expats from South Korea and Taiwan find themselves in the high-end bars of District 5, the famous Chinatown of Saigon. Consumption practices in cities, as Ken Young argues, "are repetitive and concrete manifestations of people's vision of modernity and their own place in the social order."[20]

The following day at around 3 p.m., I text Quoc and invite him for coffee, as I normally do after a night out with respondents. It is much easier to interview people in the afternoon than at night because hanging out at cafés is a favorite afternoon recreational activity among migrants and many locals. They do so not to people-watch themselves, but to be watched by others. Afternoon interviews following a night out are also strategic moments for getting respondents to reflect on the spending behaviors of the previous night.

As I ride my motorbike to meet Quoc at the MTV café on the famous Pham Ngoc Thach Street in Saigon's café district, I remember that he lives with his

wife, daughter, and mother in a two-bedroom rented apartment in Boston.
Quoc commutes to work about forty minutes away at the Marriott Hotel in
the Back Bay district, where he is one of a dozen or so maintenance workers.
Before he started this job eight years ago, he had his own business, but he decided to work for the hotel because, as he says, "it gives me fewer headaches.
I don't have to worry about getting enough business. And we get health insurance." I also make a mental note that Quoc spent nearly $600 the previous
night, and more important, not only did no one help pay, but it was blatantly
clear that no one offered to do so. On both occasions when Quoc paid the bill,
the crowd in our party as well as in the establishment stopped whatever they
were doing to watch him pay, as if it were a silent theatrical sketch between
Quoc and the person collecting the money.

After ordering coffee, we engage in some small talk before reaching the
topic of leisure in Saigon, a subject that migrant men love to discuss. When I
ask Quoc about his favorite activities in Saigon, he explains:

Play and eat with no limits, play and eat with no limits [*an choi xa lang*].[21] That's what
Saigon is for. It's a great city. People really love to go out here. It's not like America,
where people are always inside their house. In Saigon, you can go out anytime and
there is always something to do. People will make time to be with friends and to just
hang out. Look at this café, full of people. People sit around, hanging out. You would
never see this in America at this time. People are obsessed with their work over there.
In America, I have to make appointments with people just to have coffee, but here
you can simply text everyone on your phone and someone will meet you right away.

A key to understanding the behaviors Quoc so vividly describes is to underscore what Angela Chao and Juliet Schor call "social visibility" in consumption practices:

Social visibility is important because of the moral hazard problem associated with
non-visible goods. Moral hazard arises because individuals have an incentive to exaggerate their consumption in order to gain social position. If consumption is not externally verifiable, self-reported levels of consumption are not credible. A second issue is
that self-reporting about consumption patterns (i.e., boasting) reveals the individual's
concern with status, which in some contexts undermines status. (Appearing not to
care too much about status is often necessary to attaining it.) For these reasons, social
visibility is a key dimension of status consumption.[22]

In the new Saigon, status claims through social relations are heavily predicated on externally "verifiable" attributes, especially the ability to visibly pay for goods and services. Giving money in private is not always adequate for displaying overseas status, unless recipients make public announcements out of respect for their overseas relatives. Thus, for many migrants, spending money publicly is sometimes the best, if not only, way to acquire status. Migrants who resist materialism and choose not to participate in the social visibility of consumption, whether or not they want to compensate for their low status in the United States, are disadvantaged in that they receive little or no social recognition or even affection and deference from non-migrant family members. They may also endure social stigma for being cheap and selfish. The worst social punishment, however, is to be labeled a "fake overseas Vietnamese."[23] This label communicates that the individual is a fake in the sense that he or she does not follow tacit codes of money and kinship within transnational families, and therefore is not worthy of being classified as part of the successful overseas population, most of whom feel tremendous pressure and desire to generously give and spend.

Dinh, the thirty-six-year-old carpenter from San Jose we met in Chapter 1, describes his favorite activities:

I love Saigon because everywhere you go, it's just play and eat [*an choi*]. There is no corner in this city where you can't go and have fun. The café culture, karaoke, and food are everywhere. At night, the clubs and bars are unbelievable. People here really play hard. When I come back, I rarely stay at home with my family. I always go out, and sometimes I ask them to go with me, but if they don't go, I just go by myself. There is no reason to sit inside if you come to Saigon. It is not a city for sitting inside the house.

To eat and play—in other words, to interface with the sphere of consumption—manifests as visible public displays of status claims. Because the sphere of consumption in the new Saigon consists of myriad ways in which one can buy services and commodities, it is important for men to consume in verifiable ways, by literally demonstrating the exchange of cash in public spaces in front of relatives, as exemplified by the long dinner and karaoke with Quoc.[24] On some occasions, men give money spontaneously, especially in public, to gain the recognition of many family members.[25] In their research on South Asian male migrants, Filippo and Caroline Osella report that "male sociality demands generous spending, even excess . . . . Cash is then a signifier of masculine status, notes reckoning the worth of a man."[26]

Dinh rarely stays home with his family when he visits, preferring to take them out and spend money on them in spaces that non-migrant relatives generally do not patronize until migrant relatives arrive in the city. The fundamental principle here is that some migrant men communicate to others their converted wealth by spending verifiably in public spaces. Spending money is a lingua franca of the new Saigon, articulating consumptive power. Yet hidden underneath, paradoxically, is the blocked mobility of their American selves. As in the case of Quoc, Dinh elaborates on why he likes to take his family on outings:

The locals here can't really afford many things in this city. You can ride around the city and see that many of the nice cafés and bars and restaurants really cater to foreign money, especially for Viet Kieu, in some districts. So when I come back here, I want to show my uncles and my cousins what a "modern" bar or café looks like. They always look impressed and surprised that there are these great places in Saigon that they have never been to. They love trying these new places because they normally would never come here. They see that if you have money, you can enjoy this city in a different way than they are used to enjoying.

The practice of spending money in public spaces, such as modern cafés and bars, offers clear examples of how migrants and their non-migrant relatives come to understand the interface of local frameworks of space and global processes in the new Saigon. In fact, many of these spaces of consumption are modeled after, and sometimes exceed, the design and materiality of cosmopolitanism found in major global cities such as New York, Tokyo, and London.[27] The emulation of such spaces as the Lush Bar and Monaco Dance Club can be mapped onto the contours of big cities in the developing world, such as the new Saigon, precisely because of the disparity in labor costs. This disparity makes such places affordable for low-wage migrants to consume upon their return, while prohibiting the local working class from taking part in this sphere of high-end consumption. Low-wage migrants find themselves interfacing throughout the city with other global aspirants, such as expatriate workers from multinational firms and their high-wage counterparts (i.e., returning migrants who earned high wages overseas and have accumulated capital). Nonetheless, this disparity allows low-wage migrants, such as Quoc and Dinh, to differentiate and clarify the asymmetry of their social standing with that of the locals. In this context, the local working class becomes the frame of reference for the low-wage migrant population. This is because other global aspirants (e.g., expatriates and high-wage migrants) are not in competition with low-wage migrant men in the public sphere of consumption.

To achieve the requisite social visibility and what Chao and Schor call the "external verifiability" of these consumption practices,[28] migrant men must satisfy two criteria: public consumption of leisure must be frequent, and it should involve large groups of people. It was rare to go on an outing with migrant men and their relatives in which fewer than ten people were present. For example, one could come home at 5:00 a.m. from karaoke with a party of ten, and then a few hours later host a lavish lunch for the same ten people at a restaurant, followed by later afternoon drinking. Migrant men often repeat this process several times a week throughout their visit.

The visible scene of such (masculine) consumption in the public sphere is so prevalent in Saigon that it is featured in *14 Days*, a Vietnamese film released in 2009. In the film, Vietnamese Australian actor Trinh Hoi depicts the return of a Vietnamese American migrant man who takes on conviviality full force. Seen from the standpoint of the local Vietnamese population, the film is a mockery of the extravagant and blatant ways migrants spend money on a fourteen-day return trip to Vietnam. The title, of course, suggests the temporality imposed on the overseas population, whose classed bodies, struggles at home in the West, and low purchasing power within the global labor market contrast with the internal locus of control that local Vietnamese workers have with respect to their flexible time and leisure. Hence, Vietnamese American men return each year for serious conviviality, but for only fourteen days—presumably the standard vacation time that American companies grant their workers.

In this sense, social visibility establishes what Luis E. Guarnizo and Michael Peter Smith call "translocal relations," which are relationships that associate migrants with specific historical and geographical points of origin and migration, and that form a "triadic connection that links transmigrants, the localities to which they migrate, and their locality of origin."[29] Thus, if cities, as Teresa Caldeira notes,[30] are urban configurations of power relations marked by social and physical boundaries, then it is not difficult to encounter the social divisions within the new Saigon, which reflect how class and gender are encoded in different axes of the city.

Caldeira points out that the proliferation of fortified enclaves, "the privatized, enclosed, and monitored spaces for residence, consumption, leisure, and work,"[31] has created a new model of spatial segregation that alters the character of public spaces in many cities across the globe. Such fortified spaces, she argues, abandon the public sphere of the working class, creating visible inequalities without disguise or subtlety. Within the new Saigon, for the migrant population, spatial divisions reflect the internal heterogeneity of this group. The signs and traces of working-class life are retained in the new Saigon, albeit in peripheral spaces, while fortified enclaves of the city are configured for the wealthier class in suburban spaces. The socially divisive grids of the city can be seen, for example, in District 2, where foreign expats reside and play, and in District 7, which is occupied by wealthy migrants and regional capitalists from Taiwan and South Korea. Far away, the local mass working class occupies localized spaces, such as in Districts 4 and 10.[32] However, as a distinct group, the low-wage migrant population occupy multiple, contradictory spaces when they return to the new Saigon. Although they may not be able to purchase private properties in fortified enclaves, such as in Districts 2 and 7, they can be seen in consumptive transactions, if only temporarily, at high-end cafés, bars, and restaurants, where they sometimes intersect with other global aspirants, including foreign expats, regional capitalists, high-wage overseas Vietnamese, and the local new rich.

Thus, low-wage migrants are simultaneously visible in different hubs of the city: they can be seen in the high-end cafés and restaurants of the business district, and they are also embedded in the poorer hubs of the new Saigon, where their relatives continue to live, eat, and play. Indeed, most low-wage migrants return to visit for months at a time, and when they do, they most often stay in the poorer hubs with their relatives. The convergence of the Vietnamese low-wage workers and the local working class in the latter spaces has created a juxtaposition of seemingly incongruent systems of stratification. However, the visible maintenance of translocal relations—the historical and geographical links between migrants and their non-migrant relatives—in these hubs makes them the likeliest spheres of transnational logic for the low-wage migrant class.

Merchants in these localized working-class spaces capitalize on the migrant networks in their neighborhoods by opening up restaurants and bars that resemble the spaces of local working-class life, with the familiarity of the pre-migration years and the visibility of working-class relatives, neighbors, and friends, but that are distinctly priced for migrants with foreign capital. These spaces have become instruments of social separation between the local working class and the global class of low-wage Vietnamese migrants, especially those from the United States.[33] For instance, Nguyen Tri Phuong, a popular street that cuts through District 10 and District 5 of the city and is famous for its late-night eating and drinking, maintains the "old" Saigon of many working-class residents, while it distinctly caters to the Vietnamese low-wage migrant population.

Before the late 1990s, it was a quiet street with very little commerce, but since then, this street has become a major gathering thoroughfare for low-wage migrant returnees. Nowadays, on any given night, groups of overseas men and their families socialize, eat, and drink at more than a dozen restaurants on the fifteen-hundred-foot block between Nguyen Chi Thanh and Ba Thang Hai Streets. Not only do the social interactions that these restaurants generate with local consumers relate to experiences of class and gender that are specific to these exemplary hubs within the city, but streets such as Nguyen Tri Phuong take on a masculine global representation—analyzed as economically differentiated—of consumption that few locals can compete with on the ground.

One weekday evening when I went out with Khang, the warehouse machine operator from Virginia introduced in Chapter 5, I observed a level of excessive eating and buying that became a normalized pattern for Khang on return visits over three separate summers. I experienced the same pattern with other migrant men I interviewed and with whom I participated in everyday activities of leisure. Khang invited me to join him and his family at Quy Thanh, a sidewalk restaurant typical of the evening scene on many streets in the city. When darkness falls, chairs and tables occupy virtually all the available pedestrian walking space in many parts of the city.

Quy Thanh is a working-class establishment that serves a mixture of cheap, typical Vietnamese dishes. It specializes in a range of seafood, from snails to live lobster. Merchants on this street direct servers to spot the big spenders— migrant men—who come with large groups. These guests often compete with each other for the most expensive and limited live seafood for the night, including lobster, jumbo shrimp, and the local delicacy garoupa fish, all swimming in tanks on display against the walls of the restaurant. The restaurant is thus a visibly segregated space, which one might call a *convergence hub* due to the way it incorporates the low-wage migrant class and the local working class. This restaurant and others along the street serve as convergence hubs that represent the sort of masculine segmented compensatory consumption afforded to the low-wage migrant population.

Other global aspirants—the local new rich, foreigners, and regional capitalists—are virtually absent, unless they come with one of the two groups these hubs primarily serve. These restaurants allow low-wage migrant men to establish for themselves and the social milieu a perception and an experience of social difference in the city. This difference is principally marked on any given evening by the ability of migrant men to control and dominate the expensive inventory of seafood, while simultaneously serving as an exclusionary mechanism that prevents working-class customers in the neighborhood from being able to buy from the inventory. Thus, although each restaurant on this street supposedly caters to the working-class niche by offering affordable entrées starting at about 60,000 VND, or $3, per person, or possibly less, the typical bill for most groups who accompany a migrant man totals hundreds of dollars.

Khang invited me for what he termed a "no-special-occasion dinner" with his family—a mixture that includes uncles and cousins, as well as his mother, who is also visiting from abroad. When I arrive by myself in a taxi, a server waiting on the sidewalk to greet customers immediately recognizes that I am not a local. He gestures toward the row of tanks housing the live fish, lobster, and shrimp so I will not be tempted by one of the other fifteen restaurants in sight. I signal that my party has already arrived. When I walk over to Khang's table, everyone has already started on the first course, grilled jumbo shrimp, which the menu on the wall indicates costs about $96 a pound. As I look around at the clientele, the scene is typical: an unmistakably stratified crowd of those who have money to spend and those who do not. At one point, I stand up and walk toward a group of servers, who are conversing while waiting for customers to call them. The team leader, Hanh, an articulate nineteen-year-old woman, describes the customers:

Some of the customers here just come and order simple noodles or the cheap seafood, like snails, but it's really the overseas Vietnamese men who we are told to wait on the most. You can walk around and see it. Any table that ordered live lobster or live fish is a Viet Kieu table. They spend the most money and they stay for a very long time. That's why the owners tell us we have to make sure they are happy.

When I return to the table with Khang's family, they have proceeded to the next course, live lobsters grilled with sizzling scallions. Khang asks me to take the first serving. As everyone makes his or her way through this course, several servers come to ask what the table wants for the next course. Khang turns to me and asks me to take the lead and order. I ask the table for their opinion about the stir-fried noodles, considering we have already tried live jumbo shrimp and live lobster. As I ask this naïve question, several people giggle, as if I have no idea what I am doing. Khang immediately takes the menu from me and proceeds to order live steamed garoupa fish, the most expensive item on the menu, around $130 a pound. After the server leaves, Khang jokingly tells me I failed at ordering. "Man, you can't order noodles at a place like this," he says. "People will laugh at you. They'll think you are from here."

"As in, think I'm a local Vietnamese?" I ask.

"Yes! You can eat noodles tomorrow by yourself if you want!" Khang exclaims.

WOMEN AND THE MATERIAL WORLD
OF PRIVATE CONSUMPTION

Migrant women are invariably passive participants in scenes such as the one I just described. They may participate in the consumptive public sphere of eating and drinking, but they rarely take part in the transactions of negotiating, ordering, and paying at restaurants, cafés, and bars. Moreover, they generally do not extend their leisure hours late into the night, as men do in public spaces of consumption. If they join relatives for dinner or coffee, they generally go home earlier than men, usually in the company of others. In contrast with migrant men, migrant women favor staying at home with their relatives, rather than going out to dine; they prefer to take part in more mundane daily activities, such as cooking, watching soap operas, and visiting distant relatives around town. Nga, the twenty-nine-year-old restaurant server from Houston, expresses her preference for spending time with her family in this way:

I don't really think of myself as a visitor or a tourist anymore when I come back. I mean, Saigon is home for me. It's home here just like it's home in America. Sometimes it's more home to me here than in Houston. Things are familiar; there are more family connections here. When I come back, I like to stay at home with my relatives. I like to do everyday stuff, you know, not to make a big deal out of being here, not to make myself stand out, like I know other Viet Kieu like to show off that they are from overseas. Many Viet Kieu like to go around town and spend their money to show off that they make money in America. They like to be seen. That's not me. I like to stay at home and just do everyday stuff.

Similarly, Trinh, a forty-two-year-old nail salon worker from Southern California, says:

I prefer to spend time with my relatives at home, to talk and catch up on things. Even though, you know, it's easy to talk on the phone, Skype, Yahoo, and stuff like that now, when I am back I like to be at home with my siblings. I like to stay inside and cook, and talk to people, to see them and watch them go about their daily routines. That makes me happy. I don't care what's going on in Saigon. I am not interested in going to cafés or being in the public. I just make it comfortable for me in the house and I stay inside.

How, then, do women engage in compensatory consumption if they primarily occupy the spatiality of private homes during their return visits? To say women prefer to stay home with their family does not imply they are entirely absent from public spaces of consumption or that they do not engage in externally verifiable spending. Indeed, during a quick stroll into any of the new shopping malls and ubiquitous old informal markets, one sees that these spaces are largely feminized in the new Saigon. This is especially evident in the spectacle of low-wage migrant women buying large durable goods for their families at electronics and appliance stores.[34]

Migrant women say they shop with their non-migrant relatives—both men and women—for the purpose of buying personal items such as clothes, perfume, makeup, and electronics, but most at some point purchase durable goods for their relatives' homes. Migrant men, on the other hand, rarely signal their affection and care by buying durable goods for their relatives. Of the twenty-two migrant men and twenty-four migrant women I interviewed, only about a quarter of the men ($n = 5$) said they had bought at least one durable good for their relatives, whereas more than 70 percent of the women ($n = 17$) had done so. These durable goods included bedroom furniture, air conditioners, refrigerators, stoves, mobile phones, and motorbikes. The only exception was that men and women had an equal prevalence of buying motorbikes for their relatives, with almost everyone buying at least one motorbike for someone.[35] Other studies have shown that immigrant women are more likely than men to favor purchases of durable goods over other types of spending.[36] Mariano Sana argues that "the acquisition of durable goods such as home appliances, furniture, and a vehicle offer safe means for status reaffirmation."[37]

Because shopping malls are new consumption sites in the city, spending money there is distinct from how migrant men spend money in restaurants, bars, and cafés. Shopping malls also are gendered because shopping revolves around family activities. One scholar aptly refers to new shopping malls as the "public parks" of Southeast Asian cities.[38] Therefore, and notably, migrant women tend to shop for large durable goods for families, and they do this as a recreational activity with different members of the family. Because the products migrant women buy are not consumed immediately, the consequent sensorial effects of the expenditures are long term, and because durable goods belong in private homes, status is generally conferred to migrant women within the private domain among friends and relatives. Scholars argue that people's closest associates matter most in interpersonal social comparisons when it comes to conferring status via material capital.[39] Thus, non-migrant relatives commonly visit private homes to touch, observe, and listen to the range of commodities purchased by migrant women, and in some ways, this kind of attention is in and of itself a form of status conferral. Those who do not come to view a new purchase may be seen as articulators of envy.

The sensory gratification produced by material goods is often accentuated because such materiality did not exist before market reform. On many occasions, when I visit the homes of interviewees, migrants and their non-migrant relatives (mostly women) make a point of showing me new purchases. Such expositions reveal material objects as "envelopes of meanings,"[40] signifying monetary circulation within the transnational family. Indeed, scholars have long noted the inseparable relationships between the material and the social,[41] but few analyses of material culture have focused on the sensorial effects of consumption.[42] In a city where commodity culture is relatively new and where the very act of shopping is a sensorial experience, reflecting the social and spatial consequences of global forces in the city, the objects people buy routinely convey the sensorial gratification of the purchase and the status-seeking nature of its buyers.[43] In contrast with migrant men, who prefer to spend money on experiences, migrant women typically spend money on objects to assert their status as migrants. However, these migrant women do not seek to convey their level of status within the low-wage migrant class; rather, they aspire for others to perceive that they are members of the overseas moneyed class, by virtue of the appropriation of material capital.

Material capital provides low-wage migrant women with the social instruments with which to emulate an imagined cosmopolitan, Westernized moneyed lifestyle in a culture and context where other forms of capital (i.e., cultural and social) are seen as relatively insignificant, a point I expand upon in the next chapter. As Max Weber points out, to join a status group—in this case, the imagined overseas moneyed class—people have to emulate the lifestyle of that group not only in behavior but also in terms of possessions.[44] At the least, migrant women must use material capital to differentiate their lifestyle from that of the local working class. To do this, they almost always buy a "standard set" of goods that has emerged in the context of the new Saigon—and in the eyes of their relatives in particular—as signifying their identity with and knowledge of the modern West.[45] Moreover, such goods help to convey the mobility of non-migrant members of transnational families to the local community.

The standard set of goods migrants purchase for non-migrant relatives normally includes at least a sofa for the living room, if the house or apartment has one, and a stove and refrigerator for the kitchen. To achieve full recognition, low-wage migrant women occasionally emulate their own kitchens in the West by purchasing microwaves, blenders, and the other smaller appliances. Many also buy air conditioners, although this last item often is viewed as a luxury because of the expensive utility bill it generates. These purchases must always be out of the ordinary and must not resemble what neighbors buy; instead, they mark the distinct purchasing power of the overseas population. Such purchases are by no means only for utilitarian purposes; in fact, these are hedonic purchases on many levels, reflecting the global convergence of capital and skills with cheap local labor, thus providing for the sensorial gratification of mobility within the framework of global and local capital accumulation in the city.

We see this in the case of Siu, a thirty-nine-year-old office worker from New Mexico, who bought her brother an opulent Italian-style sofa for his modest apartment in Saigon's working-class District 4. During one visit, Siu immediately invites me to sit on the sofa, rather than on a number of other seating choices. Within five minutes, as she sees me touching the fabric, she explains:

I bought that sofa you are sitting on about twenty months ago, but it still looks new. Feel the fabric. They say it was upholstered in a factory not too far from here, but with an Italian supervisor. Everything about it is Italian. It was made here, but it's from an Italian company with Italian designers. You see the sofa makes the apartment look Western. I wanted something different for my brother and his family, not the kind of sofas they make in Vietnam—the old traditional-looking ones that look backward and old style. Most of the homes here have terrible furniture, still very Vietnamese.

Similarly, on one occasion when I visit Dao, the nail salon worker, she has bought her sister a brand-new refrigerator. Without failing to disclose its cost, as we explore every inch of the appliance, she says:

It's the best one on the market now. The salesperson told me that they rarely sell this item because it's the most expensive refrigerator you can buy in Saigon at the moment. I paid about $2,000 for it. The Koreans make it; they have very high-end products these days. You see that it's stainless steel. If you look the next time you go into someone's house, you probably won't see stainless steel. It's rare in Saigon.

Objects, such as household durable goods, and their sensorial gratification, especially of sight and touch, are costly instruments of social difference. Yet virtually all low-wage migrant women purchase these goods to rebuff their low-income status in the United States. The decision to purchase a durable good is therefore meticulously made, and more often than not, migrant women buy the best and most expensive models of commodities. Dao puts it bluntly: "I prefer to not buy them anything because I just want to give them money so they can buy whatever they want, but if I do, I will only buy the best [*neu khong mua thi thoi, mua thi phai mua do tot nhat*]." Likewise, when I ask Nga, the restaurant worker from Houston, to comment on my finding that many migrant women prefer to buy their relatives high-end goods, she replies, "I think you don't get many opportunities to buy your family things here, and it's important to buy them the best stuff if you can." Nga elaborates on the value of commodities purchased by migrants:

I think it's also being a Viet Kieu, if you buy anything for your relatives, it's better that you buy them high-end stuff, because if you buy them average stuff, they will think you can't afford the real thing. So I think it's important to present yourself properly to your family here as a Viet Kieu. You can't be cheap, and you have to be careful about what you get them because they don't get these things very often and you don't come home very often. So you want to make sure that whatever you buy for them, they will remember that you bought it. If you buy something that is normal and everyone has in Vietnam, they will not remember you. They can't say to other people, "Look, that was bought for me by my Viet Kieu sister."

How low-wage migrant women go out of their way to buy the best durable goods is illustrated by a shopping excursion I made with Hue, the twenty-nine-year-old hair salon worker from Northern California. Hue invited me to go on a Sunday, a favorite day for shoppers, with her and her younger brother, Phuoc, a twenty-five-year-old factory worker who makes about $150 per month. We agreed to meet at Nguyen Kim, a well-known electronics store in the center of the city. When Hue suggested we go there, I remembered that a few weeks earlier when I had dinner at her house, Phuoc was somewhat surprised when he saw my old-model cell phone, which I had owned for several years. In Saigon, a cell phone is the best portable status signal one can project, besides the less portable motorbike. These two purchases can earn tremendous status for most locals, no matter their age or gender. Phuoc asked several times why I didn't have the latest Nokia cell phone, which at the time cost about $600. In that conversation, Phuoc hinted to me that he had been asking Hue to give him money so he could buy a new phone, but he wanted a "decent" one, not necessarily the new Nokia, which he said was too expensive. Recalling this conversation with Phuoc, I am not surprised that we are on a mission to buy a cell phone. Both Hue and Phuoc arrive at Nguyen Kim dressed up, as many Saigonese do on a Sunday, especially when they are about to make a big purchase. As Phuoc makes his way to the cell phone section, Hue and I chat near the display of printers. I have been looking to replace the one in my home office, and within three minutes, I decide to buy a low-end black-and-white laser printer. Immediately Hue asks me, "Why don't you buy that Hewlett-Packard one? It looks like it's the best one there." Attempting to be polite because I know that when Hue says it is the "best" one, she really means it is the most expensive, I explain that I just need something my assistant can use to print basic notes for me to read. This satisfies Hue's objection.

After I make my printer purchase, we go over to help Phuoc with his cell phone selection. On display are no fewer than 200 models and brands of cell phones, ranging from a basic one that costs about $30 to the latest Nokia that Phuoc mentioned several weeks earlier, which is actually $699. As Phuoc looks at several models in the $200 range, I watch Hue scan the high-end section of the cell phone display. As she looks at four choices, including a Samsung and three Nokia models, Phuoc becomes less interested in the lower models. I stand back to observe, but also to restrain myself from looking critical, if not disgusted, because I cannot imagine buying a phone worth approximately six months of Phuoc's salary. Then it dawns on me that the cost of any of the four phones Hue has chosen probably represents about two weeks of her pay at the hair salon in Northern California.

After about ten minutes during which Hue questions the salesclerk about each of the phones, she turns to Phuoc and asks, "Which do you like best of these four?" Clearly so as not to appear as if he yearns for a higher-end phone, Phuoc says, "I am happy to get whichever one you want to buy for me, sister [*chi*]." As I observe this interaction, two of the salesclerk's assistants come out to watch over us. Within minutes, one takes out the most expensive model, the very one Phuoc asked me about when I had dinner at their house. It doesn't take long for Hue to ask Phuoc, "How about this one? Do you like this one? Would you know how to use it?" Somewhat embarrassed and shy, but clearly craving the phone, Phuoc deferentially says, "I can learn it easily, but it's too fancy for me. Maybe we should stick with this lower end. It's nice enough for me." However, Hue has clearly made up her mind; with a quick and desultory gesture, she tells the salesclerk, "Ring up the $699 one."

.   .   .

Low-wage migrant men and women spend money in segmented consumptive spheres. To achieve status in the homeland through spending power, men tend to spend money on leisure in the public sphere, whereas women tend to spend money on durable goods for their families, usually to furnish the home. These transnational families develop unique allocative systems of personal relations of distribution that are specific to gendered economic meanings.[46] A sturdy theoretical and empirical basis exists for understanding the relationship between gender and money in society.[47] Social psychologists, such as Melvin Prince and Floyd Webster Rudmin, report that cross-culturally, both men and women see a man's financial portfolio as a central aspect of the overall male image, whereas money is not generally linked to women's overall image.[48] Other economic psychologists demonstrate that men's sense of identity, self-esteem, and power are directly linked to money matters.[49] However, women are more likely to view money in terms of caring and expressive pursuits.[50] This is perhaps the most striking aspect of gender and money addressed in the transnationalism literature. When money is linked to masculinity and migration, it is usually spoken of in terms of power, status, prestige, and self.[51] Yet when women are associated with money, the vocabulary shifts to discourses on care and intimacy.[52] Thus, the crucial implication of what I have described about segmented compensatory consumption is the potential for these discrepant structural positions to reflect how Vietnamese society understands in general terms the dynamics of migration, gender, and status.

Spending money to tout success and prestige is no doubt a common phenomenon across cultures, social groups, and historical periods. Recent literature shows that capitalist modes of production fashion consumptive behavior while constructing individuals' identities through the purchase of commodities. It is important to note, however, that status consumption ranges widely, according to variations in contexts of gender. Furthermore, Veblen discusses conspicuous consumption as wasteful spending that must not have utilitarian value if it is to bring credibility to the spender.[53] In contrast, compensatory consumption among low-wage Vietnamese migrants is more complex, at times involving lavishness, but at other times falling within the realm of utilitarian use. We see this, for example, in the purchase of durable goods for relatives. A close reading of low-wage workers' consumption in the homeland suggests it is a strategy for repudiating the structural blocked mobility they confront elsewhere, more specifically their inability to acquire status and prestige through the conventional routes of educational and occupational mobility in the United States. In Chapter 7, I examine how non-migrant members of these transnational families talk about the nexus of status and materiality in the new Saigon, highlighting how and why imbalanced expectations, competitive spending, and social comparisons intensify the Vietnamese transnational expenditure cascade.

CHAPTER 7

EMULATIVE
CONSUMPTION

TUNG PHAN is a twenty-nine-year-old electrician who
was born in a rural village of the Mekong Delta. He left his
village as a young adult to pursue a college education in the city. His older sister,
thirty-eight-year-old Bich, is a clerical worker at a large high-tech company near
Seattle, Washington. Bich, who supports several relatives in her village, agreed to
pay all her brother's educational expenses, but Tung failed at the university almost
immediately, so he commenced vocational training to become an electrician, a job
he has held for the past ten years, during which time Bich continued to provide
financial assistance. As a newly married couple, Tung and his wife rent a small
four-hundred-square-foot apartment in Tan Binh District, in the northern part
of the city, near the airport. His wife makes about 2 million VND per month as
a cashier at a large department store. Their combined monthly income is nearly
7 million VND, the equivalent of about $350. Approximately one-quarter of
their earnings goes toward rent and utilities. Despite their relatively low wages,
their ordinary apartment in a dilapidated building has some top-of-the-line
kitchen appliances, including a matching stainless-steel refrigerator and stove,
a microwave, a forty-two-inch flat-screen TV, and a window air conditioner—
five items they purchased with the $3,000 Bich gave them for their wedding.

Commodities, especially electronics and motorbikes, captivate Tung. In conversations, he routinely mentions the prices of commodities or the costs of his recent purchases. He also routinely inquires about goods from the United States and other parts of the world. Tung's sense of everyday life, in short, revolves around his curiosity and occasional obsession with the valuation of material goods. Thus, his observations of people in the new Saigon focus primarily upon their possessions. On one occasion, he says:

Many people now have things that my wife and I work very hard to save for, so we can also buy them. People, the successful ones, can buy the best motorbikes and the best phones. It's hard to live in the city and not compete with people because there is so much here that you can buy. The city is becoming more materialistic and competitive each day [dua doi, canh tranh]. It takes time to save money so you can afford nice things, and that's why my wife and I are trying to save a lot of money. [*What do you want to buy next?*] We have so many things we want . . . . The first goal we have is to upgrade our motorbike to a nicer one because my sister bought the one we have now for us three years ago, and it's not as fast as the new ones.

When asked to elaborate on his feelings about competition in the city and materialistic people, Tung explains:

It's natural that people want things, nice things. Everyone desires nice-looking things [mong muon]. In Vietnam today, compared with my childhood, we have so much now. You can live very well if you have money. You can have whatever you want. If you go to my village, you will see it clearly, too. But everyone wants to live in the city. Why? Because you can buy nice things in the city. You have access to things that people in the village do not have. You just need the money. I think if you have the money, you should spend it on what you want, on what brings you happiness. People who don't have things need to work hard; they have to make more money.

This chapter highlights the process of *emulative consumption*[1] among nonmigrant relatives in transnational families. This kind of consumption occurs when lower-income groups try to keep up with higher-income groups through the acquisition of goods as status symbols.[2] Emulative consumption is a foundational idea from both Thorstein Veblen and Georg Simmel.[3] More concisely, Simmel expands on the notion of *conspicuous consumption*, as conceptualized by Veblen, who mostly paid attention to emulation as an aspect of competitive spending within the class of the nouveau riche.[4]

For Simmel, the desire for status vis-à-vis the purchase of commodities travels down the class hierarchy through what he terms *trickle-down theory*,[5] and is not necessarily tied to waste and luxury, as formulated by Veblen.[6] This trickle-down theory is about emulative consumption by lower-income groups, which drives higher-income groups to constantly change trends in material goods to distance themselves from the lower-income groups who emulate them.[7] In macroeconomic terms, emulative consumption is what James Duesenberry calls the "demonstration effect"[8] and what Robert Nurkse specifically refers to as an "international demonstration effect"[9] in his examination of developing countries and their citizens' aspirations for material consumption. Nurkse argues that as developing nations "come into contact with superior goods or superior patterns of consumption, with new articles or new ways of meeting old wants, they are apt to feel after a while a certain restlessness and dissatisfaction. Their knowledge is extended, their imagination stimulated; new desires are aroused."[10]

Emulative consumption (among non-migrants) resembles compensatory consumption (among migrants) in some ways, but is distinguished from it primarily because non-migrant relatives in Vietnam do not face the same kind of blocked mobility and the same economic opportunity structure as do their overseas relatives from the United States. In short, non-migrants do not consume in order to compensate for perceived or actual blocked mobility. Yet the visibility of overseas money, spending, and recently developed expenditures has shifted the frames of reference for consumption on a global scale among non-migrants in transnational families.[11]

Emulative consumption in the homeland is reinforced by the fact that material capital is already the most significant status signal among a group of people living in a culture that is undergoing rapid economic reform, as well as by the fact that money within a primarily cash economy has become an important, if not the most significant, measure of one's worth.[12] Central to the experience of status in the new Saigon is the role of material status symbols, which are different from the non-material status symbols (e.g., gestures, mannerisms, and vocabulary) that Erving Goffman analyzed,[13] and that Pierre Bourdieu later elaborated upon as cultural capital.[14]

The experiences of poor non-migrant relatives living within transnational social fields provide a key challenge to Bourdieu's contention that the poor participate in status social fields with respect to consumption only because they have a "taste for necessity."[15] As well, and significantly, emulative consumption in the new Saigon is as much about valuing material capital in and of itself as it is about the experience of relative deprivation that motivates some people to emulate others.[16] Non-migrant members of transnational families frequently talk about the significance of money and material capital as they see it from their point of social standing in the world. For many, such material capital is drawn from the resources of overseas relatives in order to reconstitute class identities, boundaries, and parameters of self-worth.

Applying an emic perspective to respondents' viewpoints pertaining to material capital and social standing in contemporary Vietnam,[17] I do not attempt to establish or describe the nature of social class stratification or the objective description of class structure within the country, which is beyond the scope of the data for this project.[18] I also do not address the macro social inequality transpiring from monetary circulation, which has been an ongoing debate within the literature on money and migration.[19] Indeed, numerous studies have shown that monetary circulation often is the only mechanism toward upward mobility for some individuals in the developing world,[20] resulting in a collision with the systems and growth of social stratification in any society characterized by large outflows of migrants.[21]

THE IMPORTANCE OF MONEY AND MATERIAL CAPITAL IN LESS AFFLUENT SOCIETIES

The publication of *Distinctions*, by Pierre Bourdieu, nearly thirty years ago provided the foundational idea for our analysis of categorical differences along class lines.[22] According to Bourdieu,[23] distinctive tastes and lifestyles are the stuff that makes up status. His analysis centers on refinement, sophistication, and cultural knowledge—the sum of cultural capital—as key resources for signaling status.[24] In other words, for Bourdieu, cultural capital centers on expressions of "aesthetics, abstraction, improvisations, eclecticism, cosmopolitanism, and authenticity."[25] These dimensions result in variations in taste that help people produce standards of differentiation, mechanisms of exclusion, and ultimately class boundaries.

Bourdieu makes the case that people with economic capital can convert it to cultural capital, although doing so is not easy for everyone regardless of economic standing.[26] They cannot convert intentionally because it is part of the *habitus*, a kind of psychobodily mechanism that makes consumption "a matter of course rather than deliberate calculation."[27] In other words, the habitus is a "habituated dispositional aspect of status consumption: tastes and practices accumulate, they are not learned, and they are not expressed without thought, never strategically."[28]

Two central weaknesses in Bourdieu's model for class analysis are the elision of the poor in social fields of status claims,[29] and the fact that it does not examine how class identities are converted across international borders (e.g., how low-wage immigrants take on different class identities in their home countries).[30] As Nina Glick Schiller notes, Bourdieu's theory of power "does not directly discuss the implications of social fields that are not coterminous with state boundaries."[31] Within the social field of *only* a nation-state, then, Bourdieu argues that "taste classifies, and it classifies the classifier."[32] To achieve distinctive tastes with respect to consumption, individuals must distance themselves from the taste for necessity, "which shifts the emphasis to the manner (of presenting, serving, eating, etc.) and tends to use stylized forms to *deny function* [my emphasis]."[33]

In her intricate critique of Bourdieu, Michele Lamont's empirical evidence points out that,[34] contrary to Bourdieu's formulation, social actors within the same class can vary in how they appropriate various kinds of social boundaries, which are "conceptual distinctions that we make to categorize objects, people, practices, and even time and space."[35] In short, she argues that Bourdieu relies too much, if not exclusively, on cultural capital to signal status,[36] which is gained from economic power and dispositions of the habitus.[37] For example, Lamont reports that working-class men can use measures of moral standards, such as categories of the "caring self,"[38] to evaluate others.[39] Lamont's analysis of social class, therefore and importantly, focuses primarily on the ways individuals from different social classes use three kinds of social boundaries (socioeconomic, moral, and cultural) as mechanisms for what she calls "exclusive" and "distancing" behaviors.[40]

The theoretical assertions by Bourdieu, and the critiques of Bourdieu by Lamont, provide important insights into the accelerated shifts in conceptions of status since market reform in contemporary Vietnam. More concisely, morality as a measuring stick for status and worth has been gradually replaced by materiality as the most salient measuring stick to assess people's social worth, a point supported by Allison Truitt's recent work on the judgment of worth in the new Saigon,[41] and by studies examining key criteria for evaluating social worth and prestige in the context of market reform.[42] This is specific to non-migrant members of low-wage transnational families.

With few exceptions, most non-migrant interviewees use socioeconomic status (i.e., pecuniary strength) as the most salient feature in their evaluations of people and as the primary measuring stick for judging people's success.[43] Moreover, the small sample of local respondents in this study confirms this perspective. Both non-migrant and local respondents consistently talk about the importance of migrants not only having but also displaying pecuniary strength if they are to project the image of success. To do otherwise would imply failure at living abroad. In the eyes of non-migrant and local respondents, the economic opportunity structure of the United States should afford great monetary success to migrants, no matter what routes they take to obtain monetary power. In some sense, those who have never traveled abroad subscribe equally, if not more, to the American Dream ideology than do migrants.

When non-migrant respondents describe their judgments of people's success in general, they rarely discuss anything other than the acquisition of capital and material goods as a measure of success, as illustrated by Tin, a forty-year-old bartender at a nightclub:

Money gives you power and nice things. That's how we know you are successful. Successful people should have nice things. They should wear beautiful clothes and drive the latest motorbike. You know, in Vietnam now, it's a very materialistic culture. People judge you if you don't dress nicely when you are in public or if you spend money on cheap stuff when there are better-quality things that you can buy. To be successful, you should make a lot of money so that you can have a high standard of living, because now in the city, you can live like they live in modern countries. Nowadays, you don't have to go anywhere to have a good life. You can stay in Saigon and have a comfortable, modern life if you have money.

Similarly, Thanh, a thirty-one-year-old bookkeeper at a clothing store in central Saigon, distinguishes between the salience of money and higher education in signaling success and status:

We live in a very materialist culture of Vietnam, very competitive [*canh tranh*]. You can call it a show-off [*khoe khoang*] culture. People want to know how much money you make and how successful you are in your business or in your job. You can have the highest degree or go to study in the richest country, but if you don't make a lot of money, it does not matter for most people. It's all about the money you have and how you spend it.

Respondents over the age of fifty (i.e., who were in their late twenties and early thirties when economic reform started) identify moral character more frequently as an important dimension in their judgments about people than do younger respondents.[44] However, when I broached the topic of money, the older generation pointed to money as slightly more important than other dimensions of status, such as morality. Lien, a sixty-two-year-old merchant with a brother living abroad, provides an interesting illustration of this phenomenon. She describes her preferences with respect to a son-in-law, a husband for her unmarried daughter in Saigon, as follows:

I want her to choose a successful husband, someone who makes good money and can support the family without any worries. Many people here in Saigon these days go over there [overseas] and study, but they come back and cannot get a good job. They think they are successful just because they went to study overseas, but you are not successful unless you have money. I prefer that my daughter marry someone who has never been anywhere, as long as he is successful and financially stable. Because, in Vietnam, you cannot do anything if you don't have money. You can be educated, but it does not help anyone if you have education and can't make good money.

Manh, a fifty-five-year-old unemployed man, provides another good example of how the older generation judge one another through material status symbols:

When people walk into the streets, they only need to glance at you to see if they want to associate with you. The first thing they look at is your motorbike and the phone you use. In Saigon, looking good in your clothes and what you carry are important if you want people to acknowledge you. If you look like someone who does not spend money on these things, people will not want to get to know you unless you can show that you have money to spend. It's all about respect and status. To get status in this city you need to have money. It's a very competitive city [rat canh tranh].

Tuba Ustuner and Douglas Holt report on the importance of money and material capital in relation to other forms of capital in less affluent societies. In their research in Turkey, they argue that the country "has a consumption field in which classes compete to mobilize their economic and cultural resources via their consumption in order to claim higher social standing."[45] A central feature of their empirical findings is that different social classes use different consumption strategies to signal and confer status, ranging from pecuniary displays to cultural sophistication. In comparing those with low and high cultural capital, based on measures of education and income, Ustuner and Holt report that among those with high cultural capital, the "expression of cultural capital operates, not through Bourdieu's habitus, but rather through a strategic 'by-the-book' pursuit of tastes that have been explicitly defined and circulated through the discourse."[46]

In contrast, those with low cultural capital seek to emulate Turkish high society by consistently consuming goods and services that "serve as conspicuous signals of their pecuniary distance from Turks with fewer economic resources."[47] Of significance to our analysis here is that in Ustuner and Holt's study, respondents with low cultural capital (i.e., those with low incomes and low levels of education) tend to draw upon their pecuniary power by applying a particular set of formulaic activities, such as going to specific destinations and buying specific household items, to signal status.[48] Challenging Bourdieu's assertion that the poor employ consumption strategies only in their taste for necessities,[49] Ustuner and Holt demonstrate that individuals with low cultural capital in less affluent societies actively participate in consumption fields by using pecuniary displays and material capital to claim status and social standing.[50]

The measuring stick for evaluating status and social standing in Vietnam has changed dramatically since market reform. Until recently, morality and talent (e.g., academic achievement) constituted the typical and perhaps only measuring stick used in Vietnam for evaluating status and social worth.[51] However, according to some preliminary survey data from Nguyen Thi Tuyet Mai and Siok Kuan Tambyah, status differentiation has become more complex since market reform, with pecuniary strength emerging as an important, if not the most important, indicator of perceived prestige. In the past, touting one's pecuniary strength did not convey status, and wealth was insufficient to demarcate one's position in life. In fact, social standing was once predicated on high moral values and a life of thrift.[52] In the last quarter of the twentieth century, market reform and accelerated economic growth led many Vietnamese to believe that money and material objects showcase one's success and achievement.

Material capital in the new Saigon is a powerful resource for claiming status and is increasingly a key mechanism for social differentiation in the context of transnational families. Among the fifty-two non-migrant members of transnational families and the twenty-three local respondents, few attribute social status to such dimensions as highbrow culture, sophistication, and aesthetics. They also rarely draw upon "moral" standing as a signal for status. As Bao, a thirty-two-year-old retail clerk, exclaims: "It's all about money, money, and money. Money is above everything else [*tien la tren het*]!" A local respondent in his late thirties expands on this idea, noting that physical attributes and other social markers that once marginalized people, regardless of economic standing, are now overlooked in favor of pecuniary strengths: "You can be ugly, you can be gay, you can have no arms or limbs. But if you have money, you are okay!"

One of the sharpest examples of the importance of material capital for self-esteem and worth for non-migrants is the motorbike, which has become the principal purchase to signal status for individuals and families in Vietnam. Freire aptly refers to motorbikes as the "consumption icon" of the new Saigon.[53] Thus, the motorbike enables not only physical but also social mobility, and the kind of motorbike one buys can signal where one falls (or has fallen) in the new systems of social ranking.[54] Truitt notes that motorbikes in Saigon serve as "exemplary symbols of purchasing power, machines, and embody the promise of autonomy and freedom of movement associated with trade liberalization."[55] Outnumbering all other forms of transport, motorbikes are viewed as a liberating agent, not to the nation or its people, but to the individual consumer. In short, motorbikes signify "the consumer desire stimulated by the opening of Vietnamese markets to the global economy."[56] In a new economy where motorbikes literally and metaphorically articulate human mobility and progress, they are one of the first gifts non-migrants request from their migrant family members. How such a commodity can redefine or reconstitute social standing and worth in the new Saigon can be understood through the story of Thong, a forty-six-year-old manual laborer in Saigon, and his nephew, Phong, a thirty-two-year-old furniture deliveryman from Los Angeles.

I met Thong, the youngest of Phong's father's siblings, after several encounters with Phong. On one occasion, Thong reveals that Phong has offered to buy him an SH motorbike. This brand and model has just gone on sale in Saigon and at about $7,000, costs almost twice as much as the previously most expensive motorbike in the city. Because I had not heard of the SH, I ask if we can view a model at the showroom on Le Duan Street. Thong and I arrange to meet there later in the day with Thong's wife and two young children, whom I meet for the first time at the showroom.

Seeing the diffidence of Thong and his family at the showroom, I cannot help but wonder how their lives might improve if they were to spend the $7,000 on something other than an extravagant motorbike. They could, for example, start a decent small business or even buy a small plot of land on the outskirts of Saigon. When asked if it was his idea to buy the SH, Thong says, "I wouldn't dare think of it [*khong dam suy nghi den*]. It was Phong's idea to take me here, and so we came to make him happy." However, when asked how he would feel about owning the SH, he says,

Who doesn't want to live like an emperor [*de vuong*]? It's a beautiful motorbike, and living here, if you have this bike, everyone will look at you. In Vietnam, if you have money, you have to spend it [*co tien thi phai xai*]. If you don't have money, no one will look at you. But if you can show you have money and are willing to spend your money, people will take notice of you [*de y*]; they will look at you and say you are the modern type [*dan hien dai*].

Thus, it is clear that while Thong could use the $7,000 for other purposes, such as buying necessities, or putting it away as a buffer for future emergencies, he is receptive to Phong's offer of the bike as a gift.

About ten days later, Phong sends me a text message to let me know he has already purchased the motorbike. Later in the week, while Thong is out of town, I ask Phong to meet me so I can ask him about the motorbike purchase. We meet at the Windows Café, a popular gathering place among Saigonese hipsters. Phong arrives on the SH motorbike, which he has borrowed for a week while Thong and his family visit relatives in the village. Anyone who visits a café in Saigon will see that motorbikes are parked outside of these establishments according to unmistakable standards of hierarchy. This display highlights the material power of their owners, who bask in the glory of seeing others admire their objects as they sit outside, as near as possible to the line of motorbikes, so people can associate these private properties with their owners.

On this occasion, Thong has gone to visit his children's grandparents in the village where Phong's parents were born. Four of Phong's aunts and uncles and various other relatives live in the village. Some of these villagers are poor farmers, but many are unemployed and depend on the financial support of Phong's parents from overseas. Thong himself occasionally sends some of his meager income to the villagers. That $7,000 would have bought this entire network of kin in the village at least a year's supply of food. Thong is the only one of these villagers who moved to the city. Because Thong was the youngest sibling and was unmarried at the time, he had the financial support of Phong's parents, and later Phong himself sent regular stipends. For more than a decade, Thong struggled to get a good job or start a business in the city. Phong describes his uncle's living conditions:

This man really struggles. He tries to support his wife and two children with about $200 a month, working as one of those guys who put water pipes in new houses. He works for himself, so he doesn't have a regular income. That's why he and his wife, they all live in a bedroom that costs them one million dongs a month [$50]. It's sad when you go there. The room is about 250 square feet, and they have a tiny cooking stove in that room, two mattresses on the floor for him and his wife and the children to sleep.

At this point, I ask Phong candidly how and why his uncle's living situation warrants the purchase of a $7,000 motorbike. If anything, I note that the bike seems inconsistent with his needs. Phong explains:

I think about me and him, and when I compare us, I think I would be so depressed if I were him, if I had to live in that disgusting small room, even by myself. Imagine living in that place with a wife and two children. How can you have the energy to do anything else if you live in a place that is depressing like that? I would be so lazy that I would never want to leave that room. I think in some ways, I might even save his life with this motorbike. He is going to go from hell to heaven. I think it's going to make life better for him. It might take me about nine months to save $7,000, but with the SH, my uncle is a different person. So I am changing his life with just nine months of my savings.

Guliz Ger and Russell Belk observe that countries undergoing accelerated economic change, particularly in transitional economies, can expect a dramatic rise in levels of materialism, which is defined as "the importance a consumer attaches to worldly possessions. At the highest levels of materialism, such possessions assume a central place in a person's life and are believed to provide the greatest sources of satisfaction and dissatisfaction."[57] Other scholars also argue that, with respect to the relationship between happiness and materialism among the poor, self-esteem and sense of pride stem from owning possessions based on the cost, rather than from the satisfaction that such possessions yield.[58]

In his research on consumption in transitioning economies, Belk argues that luxuries are particularly appealing to consumers in these economies because of "feelings of deservingness due to prior deprivations."[59] We might not expect to find the appeal of luxury commodities, such as the SH motorbike, in places around the world, such as Vietnam, where the majority of people struggle to fulfill basic needs. Yet the desire for luxury in transitional economies is sociologically coherent because years of material deprivation have made the appearance of luxury highly seductive. In transitional and less affluent economies, some people sacrifice necessities for luxuries, a pattern Belk terms "leaping luxuries" to imply that consumers have leapt over to luxury, forgoing basic comforts, necessities, and fundamental hierarchical needs in order to satisfy higher-order needs.[60] My fieldwork contains extreme examples of leaping into *unaffordable* luxuries, including people who buy fancy motorbikes but cannot afford the fuel for them, or who own expensive smartphones but cannot afford to connect to the multimedia services. Or people, such as Thong, who agree to the purchase of a fancy motorbike while supporting a family of four in a rented room.

The trade-off is that non-migrants acquire prestige through the status conferred by material goods, rather than satisfying basic needs, such as adequate nutrition or comfort. Thus, the concept of luxury is socially constructed;[61] as Belk points out, "the definition of what specific goods constitute luxury is therefore specific to a particular time and place and is always socially constructed."[62] Over time, many products shift from luxuries to necessities, and the shift often takes place in the context of relative deprivation.[63] Thus, for example, it might be fine if everyone in a neighborhood washes their clothes by hand, but the situation is viewed differently when the majority of the neighbors begin to acquire washing machines.

What were once luxuries in economically developed countries (e.g., televisions, automobiles, washers, and microwaves) can quickly turn into necessities under macroeconomic acceleration, such as in a transitioning marketized economy. Leaping into luxury, of course, can be both pleasurable and useful, as when it buys membership into a group that brings psychological well-being or when the object provides comfort, such as a refrigerator that keeps food fresh.[64] The story of Thong's extravagant SH illustrates how leaping luxuries communicates status, permitting one to feel like an "emperor" even if one must sacrifice necessities to obtain these luxuries. In Thong's case, status was chosen over necessities, such as starting a business or saving to buffer against future financial needs. The fact that material capital confers status as well as serving as a measure of worth has led to an increase in leaping luxuries, even when this seems in every respect inconsistent with the general lifestyle of the possessor of the object. To be clear, the possibility of leaping luxuries in the new Saigon is made possible for some families only because of their links to transnational kinship.

THE REVOLUTION OF RISING EXPECTATIONS

Commodities can provide immense pleasure when they offer a level of comfort that has not been experienced before. Non-migrant members of transnational families often relate to specific commodities in a manner that Eric Kit-wai Ma refers to as their "sensory contact to modernity."[65] New and useful commodities also help possessors psychologically and socially display evidence that they no longer have to avoid the pain and deprivation of being without what many other upwardly mobile urbanites have come to see as a norm in their standard of living. Objects provide the sensory gratification that owners associate with the superiority of Western capitalistic material culture.

Such goods serve to bestow a sense of social superiority and to provide an almost instant reconstitution of social position within their communities. A poignant example of this concept is found in the story of An-Phi, an unemployed thirty-four-year-old woman. She describes the value of an air conditioner that her older brother, a forty-two-year-old taxi driver from Hawaii, recently purchased for her: "The heat in this city, as you can feel every day, is unbearable. Sometimes it is impossible to do anything—to sleep or eat—when you have to be in this heat. And our apartment was always so humid because of the bad insulation we have in these large buildings." Moreover, her fantasies about air-conditioning reflect her desire to emulate the consumption she has witnessed in her neighborhood:

I have a neighbor two doors down from my apartment whose sister bought her an air conditioner almost five years ago. I used to go and sit in there sometimes and pretend

I wanted to visit. But honestly, I have to say, all I wanted was to go and sit there for as long as I could just to enjoy the cool air. I wanted to take naps there sometimes. If I could find an excuse to be there and gossip and help a little with her household chores, I would try to take a nap in that wonderful cool air, just as they do in modern countries. When Cong bought me this air conditioner, he gave me oxygen to live on [laughs]. I started to go outside less, and my husband and I stopped going to cafés and malls so we can be in an air-conditioned room.

Similarly, Tan, a twenty-four-year-old economics student who lives at home with his parents, tells the story of when his uncle gave the family an air conditioner:

I used to hate studying at home because it was very hot. I got used to air-conditioning because one of my friends' houses has had air-conditioning for many years, after his overseas family gave them several air conditioners. I prefer to go there and study, and sometimes I studied there all day. I never came home—except to go to sleep, because my friend didn't have space in their house for me to sleep. I would not come home to my parents until it was time for everyone to go to sleep.

Perhaps more important than simply providing comfort and alleviating that which was once seen as an extreme deprivation, objects help non-migrant members of transnational families socially differentiate themselves and reconstitute their social positions within their milieu. Like their overseas relatives, whose visible consumption and external attributes help display power and status, non-migrants take on the display of objects to communicate pecuniary strength, even if that strength is credited to their overseas family. Many non-migrants with overseas relatives see themselves as socially superior along socioeconomic boundaries because of the status symbols that commodities display and the ways in which specific ones, such as motorbikes and air conditioners, serve as iconic signifiers of modernity and affluence in the new Saigon.

Moreover, and importantly, commodities often articulate belonging in a transnational family, which in itself can confer status to non-migrants. Air conditioners, motorbikes, flat-screen TVs, and other modern objects signal that one has arrived at modernity. Regarding the display of material objects at home, Duong, a thirty-year-old hotel receptionist, says, "In this society now, it's important that your family has some essential stuff to show that you have money to buy things. You have to be presentable to be respected. If you have overseas relatives, you sometimes have to invite people to come over when your relatives come back home, so you have to have some nice things in your house, to not have just an empty house."

Linh, the teacher we met in Chapter 3, reveals that her cousin, Gloria, bought Linh's family a forty-two-inch flat-screen TV during one return visit. At the time, this was a rare item on the Saigon commodity frontier. Linh explains the importance of having that TV:

We were the first family in the neighborhood to have that kind of TV model. Everyone knew it because when Gloria bought it for us, many of the neighbors came to observe it. We try not to brag [*khoe khoang*] about it, but I am very proud and happy that Gloria bought it for us. The neighbors see that Gloria takes good care of us. We also sometimes after that invited people over to watch films with us because it's a friendly neighborhood. Everyone knows that we have the biggest TV, so they come over sometimes even when we don't invite them.

In the context of transnational families, a recently developed *consumption-scape* has fashioned new models of gaining prestige and status on the level of neighborhoods and private social relations.[66] As non-migrants in transnational families emulate each other by primarily using the pecuniary strength of their overseas relatives, commodities and leisure that were once seen as luxuries gradually enter the discourse and social practice of the general population.[67] Thus, a "revolution of rising expectations" has emerged in the context of transnational families in the new Saigon.[68] As different social groups acquire commodities to communicate status and to stake claims to their place in the social order of the new Saigon, non-migrant members of transnational families raise their expectations for an elevated standard of living, due largely to new reference groups with which they can compare themselves.[69]

These reference groups comparatively exclude the local working class, to which most non-migrant members of transnational families belong and among which they generally live. Instead, non-migrant members of transnational families have gone global in their social comparisons when it comes to aspiring to possess and purchase, especially in durable goods and leisure. Rising expectations about standards of living serve contemporaneously with the distinct pattern of compensatory consumption among their migrant relatives, thus shaping the transnational expenditure cascade among transnational families in the Vietnam–United States migration corridor. The spending of money by migrants to buy commodities for their non-migrant relatives is socioeconomically consequential for the latter on a number of levels.[70] At the most basic level, we see a "mass keeping-up process" with respect to consumption among transnational families, and by extension in Vietnamese society in general.[71]

For example, after receiving an air conditioner for her apartment, An-Phi plans other purchases, as she reveals:

I want to buy an LG refrigerator because that brand is the best in the city right now. The Koreans can make very good electronic products, and most people here now prefer the Korean kind over the Japanese ones because it's cheaper and it's just as good. The last time my brother was here last year, he promised me that when he comes back next time, he will buy us a refrigerator. That's why right now we are using a tiny one, but only temporarily.

Similarly, many non-migrant respondents develop acquisitive fantasies centered on the latest durable goods, particularly household items. Yen, a twenty-two-year-old recently married, unemployed housewife, notes why she eagerly awaits a return visit from her sister, Nga, a restaurant worker from Houston:

I am eager for Nga to visit us soon. I've been married for over a year, and we have not seen Nga since the wedding. She is the only relative I have abroad, and she helps me with many things in Vietnam. [*Like what?*] When she came for the wedding, she gave us $1,000, which we put away. She also bought us some kitchen appliances for our rented apartment. But she also promised us that the next time she comes back, she will buy us a flat-screen TV for the apartment, which we need because I spend a lot of time at home and I don't want to get bored staying at home doing nothing.

We see the revolution of rising expectations most explicitly in the gradual proliferation of the household "standard package." A number of researchers point out that in less affluent societies, the proliferation of consumption practices drives people to aspire to a standard package of goods and commodities to signal their entrance into particular social classes.[72] In the 1970s, Richard Coleman and Lee Rainwater described a similar pattern within the process of middle-class formation in the United States.[73] They referred to a "standard set" of goods that individuals bought when they entered middle-class life in the American stratification system. Indeed, to earn respect, the middle class needed to make certain purchases, including a well-furnished home, a car, and yearly family vacations. The list of household goods began with items such as a daily newspaper and a washing machine, but over time expanded to include a dishwasher, TV, and computer as necessities.[74]

Like the new economy of needs that formed in mid-twentieth-century American culture, a standard set of goods is frequently part of the consumptive repertoires of transnational families in the Saigon of the early twenty-first century. This standard package includes a nicer-than-average motorbike; a respectable cell phone; and other household durable goods, namely three important items: a refrigerator, a stove, and an air conditioner. "You *need* these things if you want to live like a modern person in the city," Tung explains.

Vien, an owner of a small shop who is in his late sixties, makes a similar observation: "Only poor people, the really poor ones, sleep without air-conditioning in Saigon these days. Most of the people I know with overseas relatives have air-conditioning in their houses." I ask Tung what he thinks are the minimal things people in the city should have. He answers:

If you live in the city nowadays, you need at least a nice motorbike, not the kind that a village person drives in the city or the kind that the really poor drive, but a nice one—maybe a Spacy or if you are really successful at your job, you should buy an SH. And then you should have a nice phone. Those are the two things people see when they meet you. In the house, you need now a nice refrigerator and a nice modern stove, but that's for the women to take care of, so I am not sure about all the details. For me, I also think you need a nice TV, a DVD player, and air-conditioning in your house—but that's more of a luxury, which my wife and I decided we *need* because we both really like it [emphasis added].

THE FANTASY OF EMULATION

Teeming with shopping malls and luxury boutique shops, the central business district of the new Saigon encapsulates the preoccupation with acquisitive fantasies.[75] In this atmosphere, it is not surprising that the aspiration effect is widespread, as evinced by the many window-shoppers and people on motorbikes slowly going down the main boulevards with their acquisitive gazes on new commodities, such as expensive plasma TVs, SH motorbikes, and air conditioners. However, not all of these aspiring shoppers make purchases. As one non-migrant respondent explains, marking social differentiation: "Only

poor people go to the department stores because they want to be there all day
in the air conditioner buildings. If you have money and you want a product,
you call the shop and they bring the brochures to your house. You don't have
to go anywhere." Thus, the vast majority of window-shoppers only fantasize
about global goods, which are the only products normally on display, because
Vietnamese products are seen as inferior to Western goods.

The following anecdote about a local respondent illuminates how pecuniary
displays by the overseas population generate acquisitive fantasies among members of the general population, who may have no association with migrants.
I met Huu when I serendipitously stopped in a shop to get a pair of trousers
fixed. A thirty-nine-year-old local tailor, Huu had migrated to the city nearly a
decade before from a village in the Mekong Delta and has worked in the same
shop for nearly five years at the same rate of 4 million VND per month. His
family remained in the village, where his parents now live with his older married brother. Among his family of five other adult siblings, the highest earner
in the village makes about $50 per month, which makes Huu's income seem
extraordinarily high in comparison.

About a year after meeting Huu, I ask to visit his residence to capture
some comparative insights into the living standards of non-migrants, most of
whom have the financial support of their overseas family, and of locals, who
have no association with transnational actors. So I arrange to visit Huu at the
boardinghouse where he rents a room, on the outskirts of the city in the Binh
Thanh District. He tells me he pays $30 a month to the friendly family, who
rent rooms to other Mekong Delta migrants[76] who, like Huu, have come to the
city from villages where they could not find jobs. Huu has a thin mattress on
the floor in one corner of the room. Next to the mattress is a cup in which he
puts his toothbrush and toothpaste. I remember the scene vividly because of its
sharp contrast with the other homes I have visited in Saigon. Because the house
has six other boarders, no one is allowed to leave his or her belongings in the
bathrooms. Huu takes that cup upstairs whenever he needs to brush his teeth.

Not only is Huu's room the most modest residence I had visited to that
point in my fieldwork, but also it is distinguishable from any of the homes
of non-migrants with overseas relatives because of its lack of objects and durable goods. Huu's room does not have air-conditioning or even a fan. There
is no TV in the house and no refrigerator in the kitchen. As a result, Huu

never eats in the house; instead he eats the *com bin dan*, or "food for common people," sold by street hawkers, as does everyone else who lives here. If the owner of the house ever cooks, she has to buy groceries for each meal, which has been the practice for most Vietnamese since before the standardization of refrigerators in the late 1990s.[77]

After visiting his boardinghouse, I invite Huu for coffee to inquire about how he came to the city and about his life in general within it. "I come from a poor family in the village, so none of us got a chance to better ourselves with school and we didn't have any connections that could get us good jobs," he says. "If you are from a village, you try to leave it as soon as you can to go to the city because it's the only place you can find a decent living. If you don't do that, your only option is to stay in the village and be a farmer." He indicates that his move to the city was the next best thing to migrating abroad:

I decided to take the risk when I was in my early thirties because I saw my life going nowhere in the Mekong Delta . . . . There were some people in my village who have Viet Kieu family, and that was the best thing that could happen to them. Their Viet Kieu family usually helps them by paying for them to settle in the city so they don't have to be farmers. None of my family was lucky to go abroad. My father tried to escape by boat years ago, but after failing three times, he gave up.

Then I ask Huu to tell me about his life in the city, specifically about how he has adjusted in the past five years of living here and about the value of having an overseas relative. He responds:

It's hard with city life. You know it's not easy. I tell people in the village all the time that if they come to live in the city, they have to be prepared to have a difficult life, a life of hard labor. I've been working at the tailor shop for more than five years and my life is still the same. I have not seen any improvement, except that I was trained to be a tailor. I haven't been able to save any money living here because it's too expensive. I am lucky I don't have to borrow money to live day by day, but it's still very hard. You saw my room—I have nothing in it. And my motorbike is an old one I bought from a pawnshop [*tiem cam do*]. I think if I had just one relative abroad, if one of us had been able to leave the country when everyone tried to escape, it would be so much easier for me and my family. I would at least have a good motorbike to drive in this city. But life is just plain and ordinary for me because I just try to live day by day.

Huu's story shows how within the everyday discourse of the new Saigon, the fantasy of fulfilling mobility dreams often is anchored in transnational family ties when other possibilities seem limited. Compared with other macrostructural variables, such as international tourism and the presence of multinational firms in the developing world, the presence of the Vietnamese migrant population makes a significant contribution to these mobility dreams and acquisitive fantasies because of the tangible reality of social networks and the modality of social comparisons that pervade lives in the new Saigon. Ger and Belk point out that "immigrant workers returning for home visits act as walking displays for the glittering consumer goods they bring back from their adopted cultures. Immigrant and guest workers are now a major flow of people influencing global center-periphery relations."[78] In the context of the new Saigon, it has become a mundane exercise for locals to spot Vietnamese returnees on the streets of the city, and especially in specific hubs and axes of the consumptionscape. One does not have to spend much time with returnees to figure out that they come from abroad because their identities are articulated through distinctive fashion items, such as tight jeans, sunglasses, or shoes that signify their overseas status. Most of all, as I have shown, the visible spending habits of migrants make them stand out in the consumptionscape of the city, which ultimately trickles down to ordinary citizens, who, as Huu noted, simply try to live day by day.

· · ·

The discussion of emulative consumption raises several important issues. For many non-migrant members of transnational families, material capital as a status signal in Vietnam generally trumps other forms of capital, such as cultural capital, with respect to social differentiation in the social order of the new Saigon. There is no doubt that other factors, such as global and local mass media, international tourism, the spread of popular cultures at home and abroad, and the proliferation of marketing by multinational firms in the country, have influenced spending behavior among non-migrant members of transnational families, as they have affected Vietnamese society in general.

However, the economic behavior of migrants, especially in triggering the transnational expenditure cascade, exacerbates the matter exponentially. Money and consumer goods provided by overseas relatives, as well as the visibility of their cash in episodic spending, reveal forcefully to non-migrants possibilities of consumption that they never before imagined. Simply put, access to money from overseas relatives makes it possible for individuals in the homeland to think about new acquisitions that mark status and social hierarchy. Moreover, consumption of commodities is the sensory contact that many non-migrant relatives associate with mobility and modernity. This consumption practice often involves new commodities that are inconsistent with the lifestyles of the individuals. For example, the leap of luxury is clearly experienced when Thong receives an extravagant motorbike from his nephew. In this gift exchange, Thong opts to forgo necessities in favor of the boost in status that accompanies a fancy new motorbike.

In the new Saigon, the commodity frontier can fulfill comfort while also bringing possessors a sense of distinction and social boundaries in their cultural milieu. This consumptionscape challenges Bourdieu's assertion that the poor engage only in a taste for necessity, and furthermore calls into question Bourdieu's foundational idea that only cultural capital produced by the psychobodily manifestation of the habitus can trigger status signals. The reliance on overseas money for consumption is at once pragmatic in alleviating that which was once seen as deprivation and that which is interpreted as pecuniary strength within personal social ties. The consequent revolution of rising expectations means that we see some evidence of the making of envy, as was the case with An-Phi, who wishes to have an air conditioner in her house because, and perhaps only because, her neighbor has had one for so long. Such envy is what compels many Vietnamese in the new economy to strive to keep up with their neighbors and friends. But even more consequential is the way in which new classifications and classifiers in the new Saigon raise the transnational expenditure cascade, which then trickles down to ordinary citizens, for whom acquisition is only a fantasy.

CHAPTER 8

THE CYCLICAL
ENTRENCHMENT
OF MONETARY HABITS

DIEP NGUYEN is a twenty-six-year-old married secre-
tary living in Saigon; her thirty-eight-year-old brother,
Kiet,[1] is a semi-truck driver in Southern California. Their parents reside in the
United States with Kiet; in addition to supplementing their parents' meager
Social Security checks, Kiet has taken responsibility for financially supporting Diep. He paid for Diep's tuition at a two-year vocational program so she
could obtain a secretarial job. After paying for her wedding, Kiet gave his sister
a number of relatively expensive gifts, including a $500 watch he brought back
from California and an $1,800 motorbike.

When Diep had a baby, Kiet gave her $1,000 for expenses associated with the
birth. When she went back to work after giving birth, Diep asked her brother
for money to pay for a three-year program of English classes that would make
her more marketable to foreign companies in Saigon. By agreeing to send her
the money, Kiet counted on the acquisition of English skills to enable his sister
to earn more and then gradually become financially independent.[2] During the
time she took English classes, Diep started to work full-time for a local firm
that paid her 4 million VND a month; now, combined with her husband's
monthly salary of approximately 6 million VND, this amount puts them above

the average-income bracket in Saigon. Yet Diep continues to rely on Kiet for money, a situation that he identifies as a strain on their transnational relationship. As Kiet explains:

It's been ten years,[3] and I've saved nothing in America because I have to also support my parents since they get less than $1,200 with their [combined] Social Security money. But Diep keeps asking us for money. She always asks my parents first, and they always want to help, but I know my parents don't have money, so I try to send it to her whenever I can. When I go back, I see her life is fine, but something always comes up, and I end up having to give her whatever I save.

This chapter examines the perspectives of migrant members in transnational families, focusing on their descriptions of how their non-migrant family members misuse money, inflate needs, and manufacture crises in order to receive money. The majority of migrant respondents gain tremendous personal worth and satisfaction by sacrificing for their families, even when they know money may be spent frivolously. Yet, despite the satisfaction these respondents experience, many also describe feelings of stress and anxiety in their role as transnational providers. Problems related to the misuse of money, inflated needs, and manufactured crises arise frequently enough and cause sufficient worry to migrant respondents that they warrant a lengthy treatment here. Migrant respondents invariably cite the nature of habits and routines as central features of monetary circulation. By this, they mean both their own habits of spending and giving money, and their non-migrant relatives' habits of expecting and receiving money.

How have the processes of giving, spending, and receiving money become routinized, normalized, and part of the conventional economic behavior in transnational families? From the standpoint of migrants, although the original purpose of giving and spending money was to pay for non-migrant family members' necessities, that purpose has shifted so that they now have a habit of giving and spending money to raise living standards and support new lifestyles. On the one hand, migrant respondents recognize that they habitually send, give, and spend money; on the other hand, they are aware that their family members have made a habit of relying on them, even when the reliance is unwarranted. This habitual behavior is thus routine and ordinary: "a *straightforward* operation of routine and tradition, where action taken for *whatever reason* in the past continues to be taken over time as a matter of habit. The original *'purpose'* of the action may persist, but it continues as a matter of course rather than strategy" (emphasis added).[4]

Because sending, spending, and giving money have become routinized, these habits are sometimes difficult for migrants to extinguish. They know that altering their giving and spending habits would jeopardize the social relationships they have built precisely through their relative pecuniary strength. Thus, a circular and cyclical incongruity exists between migrants' complaints of excessive spending habits by their non-migrant relatives and the continual flow of money that migrants send to and spend in the homeland. Moving away from the view of monetary circulation and consumption practices as purposeful or decisional social actions that lead to raised expectations in the transnational expenditure cascade,[5] the analytics of habits reveal another kind of social action that is "relatively unmotivated."[6] Similarly, nineteenth-century psychologist William James described the notion of habit as "sequences of behaviors . . . that have become virtually automatic,"[7] and Charles Camic later called it a "modality of action."[8]

THE DARK SIDE OF GIVING AND SPENDING MONEY

The literature on money and migration frequently uses the language of "remittance habits" and "spending habits" to describe the ordinary routines within what Luis E. Guarnizo calls the "economics of transnational living."[9] Habits associated with monetary circulation are ways in which "migrants pay to remain members of the transnational community. Remittances buy membership, and larger amounts confer higher status in the transnational community."[10] Migrants also derive great personal satisfaction from knowing the money they send to the homeland as well as give and spend there helps improve their impoverished family members' standard of living. As Daniel Miller points out, buying commodities for family members is in some ways an act of sacrifice that signals devotion and affection.[11]

Monetary circulation sometimes allows migrants to hide their low status, thereby sustaining the illusion that they are successful in the United States, even if in reality they are struggling for economic self-sustenance. How do migrants come to understand these social realities, given the inconsistency between their habits of giving and spending and their true economic abilities? In other words, why do they continue to send, give, and spend in circumstances in which they have no need to do so?

When faced with these questions, migrant respondents reply in ways that reveal the complexity of and entanglements within tacit codes of obligation, altruism, and status in transnational families, which have produced routine social practices of monetary circulation. Social theorists have identified such tacit codes, or unspoken rules, as central features in the organization of civil encounters and intimacies.[12] In short, tacit codes of familial conduct within transnational families have produced monetization that is routine and conventional. Cong, a forty-two-year-old taxi driver from Hawaii, who once purchased an air conditioner for his sister on a visit to the homeland, explains how these tacit codes work:

I think when it's your family, you just care for them and you know they live in a poor country, so you tend to overlook your doubts about them. I mean, in the beginning when you first go back, you want to buy them a few things or give them a good amount of money. And then when you leave, you feel guilty that you are leaving them behind for America—I mean, the place where everyone wants to go. You feel like you are so lucky. After a while, when they ask for money or when you go back, you give it without thinking about what they will do with the money. You can't not give them money because it would not look right.

Similarly, Trinh, a forty-two-year-old nail salon worker, talks about monetary circulation as part of the tacit codes of her family. She explains that it is difficult for her to talk about the problem of money directly with her non-migrant brothers:

You know that our culture is very much about not talking problems. It's sad, but sometimes we don't talk about things until it becomes a huge conflict, and then people just get angry. With my brothers, I almost feel uncomfortable when I don't give them money when I am here in Saigon, but I also feel uncomfortable when they ask me for money. It's just part of our culture that we are expected to give our families money if we have more money than them. It's normal to me.

Perhaps because of the tacit codes about money in transnational families, some migrant respondents say that at some point they face stress and anxiety about their inability or unwillingness to give and spend money on their families. The ways migrants describe their stress and even anger about habits of overspending on their non-migrant families reveal the tremendous level of contradictions and tensions in their transnational, but paradoxical, worlds. Even in cases where migrants express anxiety over the burden of supporting non-migrant relatives, they continue to send money home or spend it on relatives during return trips.

Some continue to circulate money when they know their non-migrant relatives misuse the money they send, and others do so even when they know the recipients have more lavish lives than they do. A number of studies have shown that migrants tend to hide the harsh realities of their lives to avoid "shameful social categorization,"[13] to prevent their non-migrant relatives from worrying, or to simply project that they have achieved the American Dream.[14] Other studies have documented that migrants do not share stories of their harsh lives abroad because they fear their non-migrant relatives would conclude they were in fact lying to avoid sharing "their wealth."[15] Succumbing to the social pressure to project the illusion of success—the ability to economically sustain while also providing for families back home—can be tremendously costly.[16]

These dimensions of monetary circulation, specifically the hardships and complaints that migrant respondents shared, shed light on monetary circulation as a particular kind of social action that has become a matter of routine and convention over time. Phung, the thirty-four-year-old typist from Southern California, explains the discomfort embedded in situations in which her relatives ask for money without disguise, even though she sends money automatically every month:

I don't think about it most of the time because I set the amount of money I give each month to certain people, so the only time I think about it is when someone writes me a letter or they call me and ask for money. I also think about it when I am in Vietnam because that's when people give me problems about money, when it's in my face. They don't have any issues about asking you up-front, and sometimes I just feel uncomfortable with that.

Trai, the thirty-six-year-old department store worker from Southern California, says his two sisters talk only about money when they communicate with him, which puts a strain on their relationship: "The way my two sisters spend money is like they treat money like water. They think it's free and flowing.

Every time they contact me, especially the older sister, it's all about money. If it's not about asking for cash outright, she asks me to buy her something from America. Sometimes she skips the whole part about 'how are you?' or 'how is life?' like that's irrelevant to our lives."

Some migrant respondents report epiphanic moments in which they came to see money in their transnational families as a personal and familial problem. Vu, a thirty-nine-year-old butcher from Orange County, California, explains:

When I used to do my budget in the past, I did not put the "Vietnam money" into my budget. But a while ago, it became part of my budget. I started to make it more automatic, to send money without thinking about it because it's so easy to send money. But things have happened that make me wonder why I started doing it so automatically. I think that, for me, it has become more stressful as I see that my sister and her family always seem to never have enough money. It sometimes irritates me that they ask for more money than what I can give.

Similarly, thirty-four-year-old Doan, a retail worker from Missouri, talks about how she automated her habit of giving money:

I have these two cousins in Saigon who I feel close to, and actually I feel closer to them than to my own brothers and sisters in America. When I first met them about ten years ago on my first visit to Vietnam, they were angels to me, and I felt like I had to help them because they were so poor. I began to make it an automatic part of my budget to send them money. Whenever I would go back every other year, I made sure I had money to give them. But I think now looking back, I should not have made it so *routine* to send them money because they expect it. They don't really think of it as a gift anymore. It's like a welfare check they receive every month from me. Sometimes that makes me feel kind of used, you know.

Some migrant respondents who acknowledge that monetary circulation has become stressful in their lives say they regret expending money on family members. Some say they should not have given or spent so much money in the first place because it led to habitual expectations from their non-migrant relatives. Doan explains:

You know after a while, you just feel like you are a money machine, like you are an ATM machine. After a while, you realize that when they talk to you, in the end, a lot of it is about money, a lot of it is about what they need and how poor they are. I think, for me, in the beginning, I made the huge mistake of buying them nice things. Like I bought my male cousin a motorbike. I did it only because I thought it was a one-time thing. You know how, in America, our cars are our feet—that's how it is for the motorbike here. So I thought I was helping him one time only. Somehow, they always ask for more, and I give more, to the point now that I feel broke from helping them out. It's sad because when I think about it, most things I buy them are things they don't really need. It makes me wonder what would have happened if I hadn't spent so much money in the first place. Would I have become close to them?

Similarly, Han, a forty-five-year-old amusement park worker from Florida, describes her observations of the material landscape of the new Saigon: "From the beginning, I didn't want to spend so much. I have too many expenses in America, so I can't afford spending so much money on my family in Vietnam. I only give money to my seventy-three-year-old father, but he doesn't need that much. It's the younger people I have to worry about. They want many things! Saigon is exploding with things, and everyone is materialistic." She continues by describing the mistake her sister made by overspending on their non-migrant family members:

I think my sister, Tuyet, has too much of a generous heart. She doesn't try to understand how everyone is so much about materialistic things. She can't control herself. She wants everyone to be happy, and I think she made the mistake in the beginning of going too much with her heart. She gave too much money. I think it's a problem now . . . they always ask her for money. I can see that she is stressed out about it and shocked about it sometimes. But it is hard for her to stop because that's what their relationship is about.[17]

Other migrant respondents feel unequivocally that their relationships with their families in Vietnam have evolved into relationships based on nothing but money. Cong has a more positive outlook than do some others, but he still has reservations about the routine of monetary circulation:

It is *normal* for families to depend on each other for money because—I mean, especially because—people in Vietnam are so poor. They can never have what you have in America. All the comforts we have in America, they can only dream about it in Vietnam. But if they have family abroad, sometimes their dreams can come true [laughs]. I think, for me, I try not to give too much, even though it is normal for me to send money regularly. Each time I go back, I try to buy one or two nice items for my sister, but I try not to make it a big thing because I think she will think it can happen all the time. I know that if you have family in Vietnam, giving money has to be a part of your relationship with them. You just have to be careful about it.

Unlike Cong, Giang, a forty-one-year-old warehouse-packaging worker from Phoenix, Arizona, had a falling-out with her brother precisely because of tensions in their relationship caused by money. "They [family members in Vietnam] can be greedy over there," she says angrily. "You know, my brother may sound very polite to you, but to me, it was all about the money. He thought I could print money in America and he would ask for impossible things." She continues, describing the sorts of things her brother wanted:

He asked me if my husband and I could help him buy a car because he wanted to start a transport business. In Vietnam, you have to pay up front all the cash to buy a car. Before that, it was about something else, and before that it was another thing. It's always about money—if not for him, for his kids. Even when we come to visit, he tells us how he has to spend so much more money to pay for the electricity bill or to buy food to cook when we stay with him. It's all about money, and it's hard to explain [*kho noi*], but sometimes you have to liberate [*giai phong*] yourself from them.

THE RISE OF A HOMELAND BOURGEOISIE

Monetary inflows from migrant members of transnational families in various parts of the world have produced what Robert Courtney Smith calls a "remittance bourgeoisie."[18] This is one powerful way to think about the reality that an entire class of people in the developing world has emerged over the past few decades in the context of transnational families. In his research on Mexican transnational families, Smith points out that members of this new social class enjoy more-comfortable lifestyles than do many others in the developing world because of the inflows of dollars they receive from migrants who live in nations that are more prosperous.[19] Leah Schmalzbauer explains how money inflows from migrants have created new ideologies about "class formations" and the "diverging social and economic realities" between migrant and nonmigrant family members.[20] Others, such as Joanne Dreby, underscore that these new class formations exist in the developing world precisely because of sacrifices that low-wage migrants must make in order to produce and sustain the relatively new class of the remittance bourgeoisie.[21] Therefore, and significantly, as Sarah Mahler points out, migrants face the task of "stretching their meager salaries past self-sustenance" in order to achieve a surplus for monetary circulation in the homeland.[22] These analyses by Smith, Schmalzbauer, Dreby, and Mahler gather particular strength because they raise the importance of the formation and permanent development of a social class in the homeland among non-migrant members of transnational families, through routines and conventions of giving and spending money among the migrant members. Thus, the growth of a remittance bourgeoisie in the developing world must be considered in the context of the perniciousness that characterizes the lives of migrants, who themselves are emerging as what Gayatri Spivak calls a "diasporic underclass."[23]

Some migrant respondents describe how their non-migrant relatives view monetary flows as a matter of habit, to the point that the non-migrants have better lives than the migrants themselves. Thirty-eight-year-old Bich, a clerical worker from Seattle, talks bluntly about her brother, Tung, whom we met in the last chapter:

At first, yes, I thought "oh poor guy." Vietnam is so poor and they have few opportunities, so I started to give my brother regular [consistent] money. I began to slowly realize that, you know, everyone has to work in order to live, and yeah, it might be different in Vietnam for them, but as long as you have the necessities to live, you can be here or there. It's the basics that matter most. Then he started to ask for new things. Every time we got on Skype or Yahoo messaging, he asked for something new and fancy. When he asked for money to buy a matching stainless-steel refrigerator and stove in his tiny apartment, I said, "You know, my husband and I don't even have those things."

Similarly, Vu, the butcher, reveals with a sense of anger how his relationship with his sister became monetized. He came to realize his sister has a better standard of living than his in Orange County, California:

When I found out they had a maid in their house, I was angry. Even though I know they only pay the maid $100 per month, it still bothers me because I work so hard and I still do everything for myself. I cook and clean, and shop for my own food. My sister and her family in Vietnam, it's like they want to be fancy. They want to be aristocratic [*quy phai*]. I mean, they can take care of their own house. Why do they have to pay for a maid when I send them $300 a month for food?

At least a dozen of the migrant respondents noted that when they bought their non-migrant family members a nice (and usually relatively expensive) commodity, such as a TV, air conditioner, motorbike, or mobile phone, or when they spent money on a lavish leisure activity, such as eating at expensive restaurants, they did so believing it was an extravagant luxury or gift. However, they soon discovered their non-migrant relatives wanted more items that were equally extravagant to match the original purchase, or their relatives took on the habit of wanting to go only to fancy places. A good example of this problem is found in Dao's description of buying a TV for her large multi-generational household in Saigon. Dao, the fifty-one-year-old nail salon worker from North Carolina, explains how her non-migrant family members abuse her generosity:

If I didn't come back as much as I do, I think they [her family] would spend the money I regularly send them on unnecessary things. I remember about three years ago, I bought the family a nice large TV. When I got ready to return to North Carolina, I gave each of my two sisters $200 before I got on the plane. I gave them money so they would save that money for food for the family. But the next year when I returned to Saigon, I found out they combined the money to buy a big stereo system with a karaoke to connect to the TV, so the sound would be loud and clear for them to sing karaoke. I got angry at them about it. I even told them they couldn't use the money like that without asking me.

Similarly, Vu talks angrily about how his sister spent $300 on luxury sheets for the bed he bought for her family:

She complained about having a bad back and that she really wanted to get this special mattress from the bed store. On one of my visits, I went with her to the shop at the mall. Even though I didn't plan to buy it, I somehow decided to buy it for her. It was an expensive bed. I think it was something like $500. Then on another visit, I found out from her son that she spent $300 on sheets for that bed. It was such a fucking waste of money . . . . I got so pissed off at her for it because I was thinking to myself, "If she can spend $300 on sheets, why did she ask me to buy her the bed?" It's so frustrating, you know, when they think you have so much money, and they have no idea.

In these cases, we see a pattern that resembles what Grant McCracken terms the "Diderot effect," whereby the acquisition of a new purchase leads almost automatically to the acquisition of more purchases.[24] This is not done so much to compete with or emulate other consumers, but rather to support a lifestyle that only surfaced with an initial purchase. Buying subsequent goods serves the purpose of making more consistent a lifestyle that matches that initial purchase. In his study of consumption among rural mainland Chinese migrants to Hong Kong, Eric Kit-wai Ma reports that when migrants give gifts to their left-behind rural relatives in China, those gifts can "destabilize an individual's habitat by introducing alien items that are inconsistent with the existing lifestyle pattern. They out-shine existing furniture and clothing. This destabilization can be resolved by upgrading the old or hiding the new."[25]

Furthermore, Ma suggests that consumption among migrant relatives through the buying of commodity gifts implants a Diderot effect in the recipient family.[26] The Diderot effect is based on the story of the eighteenth-century French philosopher Denis Diderot, who went into tremendous debt after he received the fancy gift of a dressing gown. He became displeased with the decor in his house after receiving the dressing gown, not because his old furniture and artwork were unappealing or useless, but because they were noticeably deficient when viewed in comparison with his new gift. His displeasure led him to go into debt to buy new artwork and furniture that matched the dressing gown. "I was absolute master of my old dressing gown," Diderot writes, "but I have become a slave to my new one . . . . Beware of the contamination of sudden wealth."[27]

The case of Kiet and his sister, Diep, illustrates the Diderot effect, one of the few instances in which social tensions within the transnational family developed when migrant respondents felt that the habitual consumption by non-migrants included the misuse of money or general deception designed to convince migrants to send money from a distance. Diep asked her parents for money to pay for her English classes, which she said would help her obtain a job with a foreign company that paid much more than the 4 million VND she earned at a local Vietnamese firm. Kiet knew that whenever Diep went through their parents for money, he would have to provide it, because, as he says, "she knows my parents do not have money to give her so easily. So when she asks them, she knows they would tell me about it and it's up to me if I want to give her money or not."

He agreed to send her the initial $1,800 she needed to pay for the first six months of English classes, although he realized he would have to send her $150 each month for thirty months so she could complete the module of English classes. Essentially, he agreed to pay for about three years of classes, which totaled $2,700. This was in addition to the $1,000 he had already sent Diep when she and her husband had a baby as well as another $1,800 he had given her to buy a motorbike. "That year was an expensive year for me," he says. "But, you know, I thought it was a good investment for her." About nine months after she apparently started her English classes, Kiet made one of his regular trips back to Vietnam. At that time, he did not notice much improvement in her speaking skills. "I try to be reasonable about it," Kiet explains, "because I didn't really know the quality of the classes she was taking or the school she enrolled in, so I thought we had to wait for the three years to be over."

Three years passed and Kiet made another return visit. On this occasion he learned through family gossip that Diep had used the money Kiet sent to buy her husband a fancy watch. When he confronted her about this, she did not deny it. Kiet learned that she bought her husband the watch because they wanted him to have a watch that matched the one Kiet had given her in terms of style and elegance. She also bought herself some jewelry to complement her watch. According to Kiet, she admitted to not liking the English classes and said she felt she was too old to learn another language. She felt sorry about it, he says, but could not explain why she did not tell him early on and return the money. Kiet thinks his sister lied to him about the money in the first place because she had, in fact, taken only one month of classes, which explained why her English did not improve.

The experience left Kiet suspicious of his sister each time the issue of money was raised in their family. It also led to a few dramatic arguments with his parents in America. Even though Kiet's parents recognized that Diep deceived them, they had more tolerance than Kiet had and they continued to give Diep small amounts of money. This became a strain on Kiet because he no longer trusted his sister to wisely use money, and because she was depleting the scarce resources of their parents, whom Kiet had to support financially. Kiet reflects on the experience:

It's hard because I wanted to help her have a better life, you know, to have her learn English so she could have more opportunities. And I even started the paperwork to sponsor her and her family to America. Even though it's going to take a long time, she will eventually get the visa to come, and the English classes would be useful for her if she ever comes to America. But, you know, she drained so much of my money. I should have known that she had gotten used to living a good life and that she has no idea we work so hard in America. It leaves a very bad picture in our family because we never can trust her when she asks for a large amount of money. It's easy to send $100 or $200, but she cannot ask for more from now on.

VARYING RESPONSES TO THE MONETIZATION OF TRANSNATIONAL FAMILIES

We have seen that while monetary circulation began as decisional and purposive, over time it has turned into a routinized and ordinary part of the social organization of transnational families. These activities provide a range of personal and social benefits for most of the migrant respondents. These positive outcomes include feelings of gratification from helping impoverished family members, the knowledge that they have gained membership in a sturdy transnational community, and elevated feelings of social and personal worth. For some of the respondents, however, habit persistence in transnational monetary circulation has negative consequences in the long run, among them tremendous feelings of stress, anxiety, and dissatisfaction, and general malaise from the relationships they have sustained with non-migrant relatives.

Some migrants say they feel their families have deceived them at times, which led to a culture of suspicion in which they became doubtful of claims about illnesses and emergencies. Some respondents have difficulty dealing with these dilemmas because they genuinely want to maintain social relations with their relatives in the homeland, but they recognize that to keep such relationships, they have to continue monetary distributions. As might be expected, a number of migrant respondents express sadness, anger, and emotional pain over the fact that monetary circulation has become so habitual that their transnational relationships are essentially monetized to the point that they face a moral, personal, and emotional dilemma over their desire to extinguish their familial connections in the homeland. Vu summarizes his dilemma with his sister and her husband as follows: "How can I continue like this? I mean, I know they make only about $100 a month each, but family should not be all about money." Doan from Missouri describes how her cousins want to eat only at fancy restaurants when she visits, noting that this exemplifies how money has become the sole focus of their relationship:

It bothers me a lot, you know, when my cousins only want to eat at fancy restaurants. I wonder if I couldn't afford it, or if I didn't pay for us, what would happen to our relationship? I mean, I took them to some nice restaurants the first few times I came back, but they got so used to it that when I ask them to go eat street food with me, they refuse. It's so weird because I know that without me they eat on the streets all the time! But if I ask them to go to a five-star hotel buffet, they rush there. It's weird because you want to treat them occasionally, and if you don't take them to nice places, they think you don't care for them. But, you know, we don't eat fancy food every day, either.

Some migrant respondents note that when they fail to send money from a distance or to give and spend money upon their return visits, their non-migrant relatives resort to faking sickness or manufacturing crises. Doan describes this quite animatedly:

They are always doing fine if you take them shopping. Or as long as you give them money, they are always doing well. They will always show up for anything you ask them to do with you, like they are your best friends, if it is about trying fancy restaurants or going to nice bars. But I did this test where I stopped paying for things, I stopped asking them to fancy restaurants, and guess what? I stopped hearing from them. Then the only time I would hear from one of the cousins is when she calls to say she is sick and she wants to borrow money, which you know, basically means she wants me to give her the money. I learned the hard way when one of them called me and asked for $500 and told me she was in the hospital. So guess what? I went to the hospital and her ass never checked into that hospital [laughs].

The case of Dai, a twenty-eight-year-old mechanic from Northern California, is another example:

It's like you expect them to always be sick or to always have an emergency just so they can get money from you. I got so tired of hearing about crises that I stopped taking it seriously. It's even funny to me because why should I give a few hundred dollars just because you are coughing? It doesn't make sense. I mean, they get a little cough, and they say they are in the hospital or need to go to the hospital. Why? Somehow they think that if they tell me they're in a crisis, I will give them money to take care of it. It can be annoying sometimes, you know?

Three types of responses are given by migrants who say the habit of sending, giving, and spending money has had negative consequences for them. Migrants who recognize the problem but fear that ending monetary circulation would threaten the depth of their relationship with their non-migrant relatives typify the first type of response. These respondents say they are resigned to living with the situation because their family ties mean more to them than the costs they incur by giving and spending money in the homeland. In short, these respondents emphasize the importance of responsibility and economic assistance to the family, which they want to maintain. Some of these respondents continue to rationalize about the disparate costs of living in the United States and Vietnam, which they say is a reason to continue their financial assistance. Noting that her brothers are her only ties to Vietnam, Trinh, the nail salon worker, explains:

I have only them as family in Vietnam, and they have me only in America. So if I don't help them, no one will. They need support from time to time, and there is no way for them to make the kind of money I send them regularly. When I send $300, that's how much one of my brothers makes in about two months as a truck driver in Saigon. I try to help them as much as possible, but there are times I can't send the amount of money they ask for.

Similarly, Cong from Hawaii says:

It's family, you know, you can't just abandon them. If I stopped giving them money, it would be a huge problem for us. I think they would feel very abandoned and that I don't care for them. That's the way it is. If you have family overseas, you expect them to help you. We are like a lifeline to them. Luckily—unlike many other Viet Kieu—I was careful and did not give too much from the beginning. But it is still my responsibility to help them because my sister and her husband can only make in a year what I make in less than a month here.

Some of these respondents acknowledge they would bring shame to their family if they did not continue to give money. Dao explains the importance of her family's reputation:

Saigon is a big city, but people here look closely at their neighbors and friends, and they gossip. They know everything because everyone talks to each other all the time. So I think my family would lose face [*mat mat* = lose reputation] if people knew I didn't send money to them regularly. When you have family overseas, you have to have something to show for it. You have to eat better food than others, you have to wear nicer clothes. It doesn't have to be fancy, but you have to show you have a little more than the others. I myself would feel ashamed for my family if people thought I didn't give them enough to have a better life than the others around them.

Similarly, speaking about his own feeling of worth, Mach, the thirty-eight-year-old hotel maintenance worker from Boston, says, "When I come back to visit my family, I want people to know I give them money. It's my reputation, too. I feel proud to see that my family can have more than others. Sometimes it is difficult when they ask for too much, but that's the way it is."

The second type of response by migrants is to minimize their spending when they return to visit and to avoid honoring excessive requests for money. Doan illustrates this in the following comment:

I decided on the last trip that I would not give my cousins any money if they ask for a ridiculous amount. But I still want to give them a little money whenever I come back. You know, we have a history of being so close, and I think for me, it was them in the beginning who made Vietnam so important to me, so much part of who I am. So I can't abandon them now. I am sad the way things have turned out, that they see me as only important to them because of the money.

Similarly, Kiet says the following of his sister:

Ever since we found out that she took the money I sent her for the English classes to buy her husband a watch, I decided that I am not going to give her large amounts of money anymore. I told my parents they can do whatever they want because I know they don't have much to give her. But for my part, I will just send her about $100 or $200 a month. I think that's good enough to support her. I won't let her think that she can take us for granted, that she can turn to us for money to spend on anything she wants without telling us what she does with the money.

The third type of response migrants have to the problem of monetization in their transnational families is more drastic than the first two types. These respondents completely end monetary circulation because they say it has gotten to the point that they are unable to handle the emotional stress of what they deem bad habits related to monetary circulation. A few of these respondents say their transnational ties in effect ended after they stopped giving to and spending money on their relatives. Loc, the retail clerk from Dallas whose parents, one brother, and one sister, live in Saigon, explains his situation:

My brother decided that he didn't want to have anything to do with me after I decided I had to cut him from my support. I gave him too much in the beginning, and he took advantage of it. He was buying things I would never buy for myself. I also got to the point where I had to cut back on my sister and parents, too, but I just gave them less. There was one incident in which my brother and I had a big fight over me not giving him money, and I decided I needed to cut him from my money. That's when he decided he no longer wanted to talk to me. That was three years ago.

Similarly, Phung explains she had to cut off ties with one uncle because he gave her the cold shoulder when she was unable to give him the large amount of money he requested:

I learned the hard way that money can change people instantly. I had one uncle I got close to when I visited on the first few trips. He was very kind to me, always making sure I was well taken care of when I visited with my friends or my mom. He would drive us everywhere and cooked us elaborate meals at his house. So I gave him some money regularly. It was automatic for me to give and give. But then two years ago, he asked for $10,000 so he could start a business, and I just didn't have that kind of money to give him. When I didn't give it, he thought I didn't want to help him, and eventually he was really cold to me when I visited. You can just tell how they are—their passive-aggressive behavior when you're there and don't give them money. So I decided, "You know what, I'm done with you if money is the only thing you think about."

Two respondents told me that by ending monetary circulation with their non-migrant relatives, they effectively ended their transnational journeys to Vietnam. After Chinh, the thirty-eight-year-old mechanic from Northern California, realized money had become the only aspect of his relationship with his uncle, he ended that relationship. He explains that because his uncle was his only tie to Vietnam, he is no longer interested in visiting the country:

When my wife and children first came to Vietnam twelve years ago, we felt like we discovered Vietnam for ourselves and for our children. Going there when you have family in the country is different from going there as a tourist. But my uncle began to ask for too much. We couldn't keep up with his requests for money, so my wife and

I had to decide the hard way that we weren't going to give him money anymore. We couldn't have him be dependent on us forever because we had already given lots of money over a decade. But once we saw that he treated us differently when the money ended, we didn't want to go there anymore. We didn't feel like he was a true family member to us. So we stopped going to Vietnam three years ago. It was hard on us because we love going there, but he was our only family there and it's not the same if we go and don't have family to hang out with.

Hien, the forty-eight-year-old nail salon worker from North Carolina, started to minimize the amount she gave her brother in Saigon because she was going through financial problems in the United States, including the foreclosure of her house. Before the foreclosure, she had promised to send $2,000 to her brother to pay his son's educational fees at a private school (which he considered only because he thought he was getting money from Hien). But with the foreclosure pending, she had no money to give him. Eventually, after she recovered from the financial loss of her house, she contacted her brother. He never replied. Hien and her husband made a return visit two years after their foreclosure and went to her brother's house, but her brother screamed at her and forbade her from coming to his house again. Crying, she describes what led up to the break in their relationship:

We helped so much over the years. It was not like we never helped him; we gave him money all the time. I could understand if he got angry because we lived luxurious lives in America, but we were not. We had a very tough time making payments on our house after my husband's job changed and we didn't have enough money to cover expenses. We told my brother this, but he kept asking us for money. My husband and I could never give him enough. It was never enough.

To make her brother less angry, Hien continued to send him $150 every month from a distance during her financial crisis, and continued to explain her mortgage problems. However, to her dismay, her brother refused to understand her situation, a problem she attributed to her habit of sending money every time he had asked in the past:

We were not lying to him that we didn't have the money. It was the truth [cries]. When we told him, he said we were selfish and "how could we not have $2,000 to spare?" [*Why do you think he refused to believe you?*] My husband and I think we were too easy and too generous with him from the beginning. He got used to the money we sent him whenever he asked. It was never as much as $2,000, like the last time he asked us. But since we were reunited in 1999, we sent him $300 to $500 every time he asked.

· · ·

The role of habit formation and habit persistence in monetary circulation underscores the routine and normative nature of these social actions. Habits are important to consider over time because, for many members of transnational families, giving and spending are related to what Elizabeth Shove calls the "social organization of normality"; that is, their raised consumption levels are associated with raised perceptions of comfort and convenience, and the general reconfigurations of "standards" in everyday life.[28] This new social organization of normality in transnational families frequently generates additional expenditures, which are introduced to coordinate and complement a lifestyle (rather than just a standard of living) that sometimes originates with a single purchase or an experience of leisure.

These habits are in part related to the revolution of raised expectations and emulative consumption, but they have a more specific significance in terms of the Weberian concept of social action,[29] because habits of consumption are not necessarily intentional or deliberate, and therefore not emulative in character. Economists point to the centrality of habit formation in both macroeconomic terms and micro interactions of monetary processes.[30] Some scholars note that levels of expenditures can increase not through absolute price changes of commodities, income fluctuations, or intentional emulation, but through mimetic processes.[31] In other words, whereas raised expectations in consumption patterns stem from decisional and aspirational effects, habits evolve through normative and routinized patterns. As Rachel E. Dwyer notes in her theoretical synthesis on the importance of habit within consumption studies, "shifts in the social context and level of inequality will result in changes in consumer behavior because of the positional nature of the standard of living even without intentional emulation."[32] This is what Shove refers to as the "social construction of routinized needs and wants" in her analysis of the rise of comfort and convenience as key expenditures in modern societies.[33] As reference groups shift, consumers begin to interpret specific commodities as a "conventional standard of decency."[34]

When expectations for flows of money become normal, migrant respondents report feeling they have to keep up with the new expenditures that their non-migrant relatives take on, some of which the migrants say are unnecessary to the lifestyles of their relatives. Migrant respondents endure a range of stress, anxiety, and even anger about providing money to their families; such feelings can themselves become routine for the migrants. Some face situations in which their non-migrant relatives misuse money, inflate their needs, or manufacture crises in order to receive money. These experiences reinforce the circular and cyclical pattern whereby even when migrant respondents' habits of giving and spending money produce negative consequences, they continue to distribute money for a range of reasons, including to avoid shame and to maintain ties with families in the homeland. Nevertheless, a few migrant respondents discontinue monetary circulation. In extreme cases, the discontinuance of monetary circulation involves the dissolution of transnational ties. For some migrants, the dissolution of their transnational ties also ends their transnational return visits to Vietnam, which for many, began only because of the family ties they had in the first place.

CHAPTER 9

THE HIGH PRICE OF
ESTEEM CONSUMPTION

H UE VO is the twenty-nine-year-old never-married hair salon worker from Northern California who, in Chapter 6, bought the fancy $699 Nokia mobile phone for her twenty-five-year-old brother, Phuoc. Hue adores her younger brother. In addition to giving him $300 on a monthly basis,[1] she expresses her love and affection for Phuoc when she makes return visits to Saigon by buying him material things, such as the phone, nice clothes, and other commodities. Although they are only four years apart in age, Hue treats her brother like he is still a teenager and thus feels responsible for him, much a like a parental figure.[2] The reason she feels this responsibility is partly because Phuoc is the only member of their immediate family who stayed in Saigon when the rest of the family migrated to America in the early 1990s. Due to complex circumstances, they left Phuoc in Vietnam with his grandparents.[3] For more than a decade, Hue has sent money to Phuoc each month. The other family members in the United States are strapped for money themselves, so they rarely send money to Phuoc.

During a previous visit, before Hue purchased the pricey phone for her brother, she bought him a motorbike—a fancy red Honda Dylan, just one notch below the SH.[4] Buying the Dylan cost Hue $5,000, an amount she did not have to spend, so she took out a cash advance on her credit card to pay for it.[5] The credit card loan has a 24 percent interest rate. She pays a monthly installment of $150 for the Dylan, only $50 of which goes toward the principal of the loan.[6] That monthly payment, plus another $400 in other monthly credit card payments, plus her $300 monthly support to Phuoc, add up to more than 40 percent of her net monthly income. Yet, despite these hefty credit card payments, Hue says,

He has to have things like other people [*phai co voi nguoi ta*]. I feel sorry that he was stuck in Vietnam, so I try to make him happy without us. You know, we left him when he was only nine because my grandparents begged my parents to leave him with them, and for some reasons they agreed to it. He took good care of the grandparents all these years. He is a great kid, very respectful and considerate of me. I try to help him as much as I can, and taking out a credit card loan occasionally is not a problem [*vai tien cho nay cho kia cung khong sao*].

This chapter brings into focus the experiences of migrant respondents who acquire and accrue credit card debt to finance their expenditures in Vietnam.[7] Turning to the U.S. side of the transnational expenditure cascade, I focus on my visits to the homes and workplaces of Hue Vo in Northern California and Vu Huynh in Orange County, Southern California, to illuminate examples of choices some migrants make when they use their credit cards excessively to finance their transnational lives. Although a robust literature exists on the financial indebtedness of migrants, particularly temporary and contractual labor migrants, who borrow money to leave their home countries as emigrants,[8] virtually no empirical research has been done on the nature of financial indebtedness, and especially credit card use, among those who have settled in developed countries and are leading transnational lives.[9]

A focus on consumption vis-à-vis credit cards captures a specific emotional side of the transnational expenditure cascade, echoing what Allison J. Pugh refers to as consumption within an "economy of dignity."[10] Stories of indebtedness reveal how migrant respondents, rather than spend money simply to display their status, are motivated to spend according to a confluence of status and what I term *esteem consumption*. Thus far, the focus in this study has been on status-driven consumption, which at times is about external attributes and the judgments of others, all involving some degree of competition in relation to localized status. Esteem consumption, in contrast, is about the desire to feel competent, respected, and dignified, rather than about the tendency to project bitterness, envy, jealousy, and competition with others. Even when speaking about the precipice of financial indebtedness, migrant respondents tell stories of esteem consumption and the development of sturdy bonds with the homeland stemming from the only source of money they have to give and spend in Vietnam.

Going into debt is not an easy problem for migrants to initially discuss. I serendipitously stumbled upon this topic when I learned from thirty-nine-year-old Vu, a butcher from Orange County, that he was broke and no longer able to make visits to Vietnam.[11] Such unmanageable debt is an exception to the rule, to be sure. However, it is important to elaborate upon exceptional cases in social science research because, as Clifford Geertz notes, social science data can be complex and disorganized, much like a kaleidoscope in which "one always see the chips distributed in some pattern, however ill-formed or irregular."[12] I initially anticipated that debt would be considered a shameful aspect of one's financial portfolio[13] and would be generally a taboo topic to broach. This was, in fact, rarely the case once I started to investigate the topic. In many instances, respondents who had reached the limit on all their credit cards asked if I could help them obtain more cards or higher credit limits.

Respondents had taken on non-collateralized credit card debts that were explicitly not linked to assets.[14] No one took out equity loans on a home to finance his or her transnational life.[15] One respondent borrowed small amounts of money from informal usurers,[16] payday centers,[17] pawnshops, and other institutions associated with what Gary Rivlin calls the "poverty industry."[18] Several other respondents took out personal loans from friends and relatives, but these loans were generally small and had no interest, which meant they were on the bottom with respect to repayment priorities.[19] Given these various parameters, loans associated with purchases and cash advances made with credit cards are the most socioeconomically consequential for migrant respondents, for at least three reasons.[20]

First, credit cards affect the users' future financial well-being because they are linked to credit scores,[21] which in turn potentially affect future financial borrowing privileges to buy things such as a car or a house, should the users ever qualify to buy one.[22] Defaulting on credit card loans can also lead to legal repercussions, which many fear.[23] Second, credit cards are the largest source of money to which migrant respondents can turn when they need capital.[24] A few respondents drew relatively large cash advances from their credit cards, amounts they were unable to obtain from any other source, with the largest debt being nearly $30,000. Finally, credit cards were the easiest means for migrant respondents to obtain money simply because they had them.[25]

Given the predatory nature of credit card lending in the United States, especially for low-income individuals and ethnic minorities,[26] it is relatively easy to get a credit card,[27] and even those with low-wage jobs, such as the workers in this study, often can get high credit limits.[28] In fact, despite the great recession of 2007–2009, Rivlin has documented how the credit card industry and other financial institutions have turned into a poverty industry that specifically preys on the working poor.[29] Rivlin writes that this industry remains prosperous "despite hard economic times and also because of them. People struggling to get by, after all, are often good news for those catering to the working poor and others at the bottom of the economic pyramid."[30] Interview data show that more than 60 percent of respondents had at least five credit cards,[31] and no one had a credit card limit under $8,000.[32] Despite their low wages, many carried relatively high credit limits on their cards.[33]

To understand why migrants make seemingly unreasonable decisions to take on credit card debt, we need to evaluate the context of their lives in the United States, and then to view their lives transnationally.[34] To many observers, some of these choices may seem irrational, misguided, and even irresponsible. For these low-wage migrants, however, credit cards opened up a world of opportunity to prove their sense of competence and social worth as well as to gain a sense of esteem in ways many other low-wage workers cannot in the absence of transnational homelands. Their day-to-day lives of low status, hard work, and bleak opportunities in the United States are unquestionably transformed through the satisfaction and pleasure of giving and spending money in the homeland. From a public policy perspective, this pattern bears tremendous significance in terms of the financial lives of low-wage immigrants in the United States who take on provider roles through debt acquisition for their non-migrant extended relatives in the homeland.

"MONEY IS NOT EVERYTHING"

When I first met Hue at the hip Terrace Café on Le Loi Boulevard in the center of Saigon, I had two immediate words to describe her: *personable* and *confident*. Few respondents ask questions during first meetings as personal as those Hue asked; most take weeks and sometimes months to gain trust and rapport before feeling comfortable enough to ask questions of a complete stranger. One of my full-time assistants recruited Hue to participate in the study after meeting her at a beauty parlor in Saigon, where she was having her makeup done and her hair fashioned for what was to be just an ordinary night out in the new Saigon. Hue loves to pamper herself at hair salons, but even though she works at a hair salon in the United States, she says both the clients and the workers at the salon are "low class," so one cannot really get pampered.[35] Because true "beauty work [*lam dep*]" is unavailable at the salon, she only gets her hair cut there, and not styled. "I don't really get my hair done in America," she says. "Nothing fancy to expect there."

Saigon, however, is another story. Hue goes to the beauty salon at least every three days when she makes return visits. She has a number of female cousins who take her out "round and round the town [*di vong vong*]"; she often spends the entire day at beauty salons, spas, and massage parlors, and going to her favorite restaurants. When I ask about her regular trips to the country during our first interview, Hue explains quite energetically: "I love, love this country. I would live here if I could find a decent job, but the pay is too low for the work I do. The girls here make only $100 or $200 a month at the hair salon. My dream is to come back and open up a small business, maybe a hair salon of my own. But for now I try to come back every year for at least a month. I don't know anyone who doesn't love being here."

Hue's sense of satisfaction during her time in Saigon is anchored not only in the close ties she has developed with her brother, as well as with her female cousins, who follow her everywhere she goes when she is in Vietnam, but also in pleasures that are virtually absent (and unaffordable) from her life in Northern California. The excitement and cosmopolitanism of the new Saigon is about being pampered, eating cheap and delicious food, and having fun at nearby sunny beaches. Hue explains, "I always feel nasty and crappy in San Jose, always tired and depressed. If I have a moment of being down in Saigon, I go to the spa or ask one of my cousins to go with me to a beauty salon and get our hair done or get a facial. Or we can easily decide to go to the beach and stay at a seaside hotel, without worrying too much about the price. In California, I can never do that."

Hue's exuberance about life in Saigon is reflected in her stylish choice of clothing and what always seems like a perfect ensemble of flawless makeup, nails, and hair. This version of Hue is one of style, sophistication, and beautification—an expensive version that does not easily travel back to the United States. About two years after our first set of interviews in Saigon, I was taken aback when we met in San Jose and I encountered another version of Hue.

I visited her at the hair salon where she works, in a run-down shopping plaza in San Jose, the city with the second-largest Vietnamese population in the United States. As Hue greets me, she exudes the same friendliness as when she was in Saigon, but she no longer has the elaborate makeup, stylish hair, or confidence. Instead, she looks at me timidly, like someone who has just done something wrong and has a secret to hide. "This place is gross, isn't it? I hate it," she says about her workplace. "It's so depressing here."

In truth, I am surprised by the conditions at the tiny salon, which is no more than about 400 square feet, with equipment that seems decades old. Jokingly I say, "No, I think it's retro, very American, I love it: quiet, your typical shopping plaza in the middle of suburban hell."

Hue laughs, and tells me she normally does not dress up when she goes to work. "I wear something comfortable because I am here all day," she says apologetically. "So, sorry I look terrible today." Again I have the sense that she has a secret, and she is revealing it to me. As she takes me through the world of her suburban life in San Jose, I learn a darker side of Hue, and eventually the secret that she is, in fact, not the version of Hue I met in Saigon. This darker side reveals that the formation of a transnational life has offered her, as it does so many low-wage migrants, the opportunity to experience a phenomenon among immigrants that Ketu Katrak describes as "the possibility of living here in body and elsewhere in mind and imagination."[36]

Hue was almost thirteen years old when she came to the United States with her parents and an older sister. They were initially given Section 8 government housing assistance to rent a two-bedroom apartment in the working-class section of San Jose.[37] She never liked school, so she turned to romance to bolster her sense of competence, esteem, and accomplishment. While many of her peers got attention by doing well in school and getting recognition from their teachers and parents, Hue sought social validation from her peers, especially boys who paid attention to her. By the time she reached ninth grade, she was ahead of her friends in terms of relationships. "I wasn't a nerd," she explains. "I preferred having a life." That meant getting involved in a serious relationship before any of her friends even entertained the thought of romance. By graduation, she was already planning to marry Tai, her high school boyfriend.

Then things shifted. Tai enrolled at San Jose State University, while Hue continued to work at the hair salon where she began working in high school. During his first year, Tai met another girl and had no problem breaking up with Hue. About two years later, heartbroken from the failed relationship with Tai, Hue met a man fifteen years her senior. She dated this man for nearly two years before she learned he was married and had two children. Although the man told her he had no plans to leave his wife, Hue stayed in that relationship, hoping he would change his mind. Eventually she realized that was not going to happen, so she tearfully broke up with him. This second breakup turned Hue into a bitter young adult, as she explains candidly:

I told myself that was it. I didn't want to deal with another asshole. I put all my emotions into two men and I thought I was going to marry them, but they were liars. They just wanted to get into bed, you know, like stupid assholes . . . . I didn't know I would end up like this, angry all the time. I got depressed. I stayed home and watched Korean dramas all the time. I got sick of hearing my parents talk about how lazy I had become, and how I was not useful to them.

Hue's parents had high expectations for her when they first came to the United States. The implicit immigrant bargain was that she would work hard in school,[38] achieve the American Dream, and in exchange they would provide the emotional and material support for her to make *their* dream come true. They had hoped Hue would go to college and lift all of them out of their low-income status as a family unit. After all, Hue was only thirteen when they left Vietnam, so they felt it was realistic for her to work hard in school, go to college, and get an education like so many other immigrant children in and around San Jose. But it did not take long for her parents to predict that Hue would not do well in life. Her decision to date at a young age created painful tensions with her parents. Her father forbade her from having a boyfriend, and her mother told her she would not amount to anything if she did not go to college. Because they disapproved of the relationship, Hue felt its eventual breakup was partly her parents' fault. She still harbors resentment toward them for it.

Hue's parents held her to a higher standard than they did her sister, who is eleven years older and who was not expected to get an American college education because she had already completed high school in Vietnam, and therefore her parents felt it was too late.[39] Shortly after arriving in the United States, Hue's sister met someone and married him. Within a short time, the sister had a baby and moved out of the family's home. By the time she was in her mid-twenties, Hue had caused her parents additional disappointment: she had not yet married. Speaking about her relationship with her parents, Hue says, "They were negative people to begin with, so I didn't pay them any attention. I thought about moving out on my own, but none of my girlfriends want to move out. They are afraid they can't afford it, and they are afraid of their parents. If I had my choice, I would go live on my own, but it's hard to leave home around here."

When Hue says it is hard to leave home, on one level she is referring to the cultural expectation that women in her community are not supposed to leave their family before marriage, no matter how old they are. On another level, it is a reference to the structural barrier of the cost of housing in the heart of the expensive Silicon Valley, which essentially prohibits low-wage workers from living alone.[40] Because housing is the most expensive item for low-wage workers, it is virtually impossible in most cities to survive as a single person on low-wage work. Many are forced to live in shared housing to make ends meet, as documented poignantly by the well-known journalist Barbara Ehrenreich.[41] These circumstances made it hard for Hue to advance socially or financially. Prior to rediscovering Vietnam when she was twenty-four, Hue was generally unhappy with her life. Looking back on her experience, she says:

I was lost, a bit depressed, you know, before I went to Vietnam. I didn't have many friends, and things with my parents were going downhill by the day. I think they were disappointed in me earlier than I knew because they were set on depending on me in the future. Now they know I'm not going anywhere with my job. I don't feel poor, but I will never be rich enough to support them. That makes it hard for us. They know I'm not going to be rich to help them or anyone in the family in the future.

Katherine S. Newman and Victor Tan Chen point out that middle-class families with stable finances "enjoy the luxury of autonomous nuclear families and loving, unconditional relationships free of the taint of monetization, but those of lesser means have to beg, cajole, and guilt-trip their family members into sharing some of the burden."[42] My study reveals that struggling low-income immigrant families live in multi-generational households out of necessity, with their hopes for escape pinned on the younger generation's ability to fulfill the immigrant bargain for success.[43] The decision to forgo college had real social, if not psychological,[44] consequences for Hue. For most of her twenties, she has had to deal with her parents' daily reminders of their disappointment. They once encapsulated their disappointment by informing Hue she is "not too useful to them." Hue thought she would eventually meet a stable, even wealthy, man in Silicon Valley, but her long work hours and her occupational niche made it difficult to meet, let alone date, such men.

Hue decided one winter to make her first return trip to Saigon with her sister and brother-in-law, who had recently visited his left-behind relatives for the first time since migrating to the United States. Before this trip, Hue was frugal and extremely good at the game of deferred gratification. Over five years, she diligently stashed $150 nearly every month from her pay at the hair salon, and saved a total of $8,000. With her savings, she bought a ticket to Saigon for about $1,000. She spent only half her remaining savings on that first trip, when she reunited with Phuoc for the first time in more than ten years. During that trip, she became better acquainted with some cousins she only vaguely remembered from childhood. Of that first visit, she says:

That was it for me when I went on that trip. I wanted to go back again and again. Since then, I go every year. There were two times when I waited one and half years to return, but I've been six times in the past five years. I think you know what I mean when I say that when I am there, I am a different person. Being here in San Jose makes me depressed. I wish I could live in Saigon forever, but at this point, it's not realistic. Maybe in ten years I will try to start a business there.

Making return visits allows Hue to be a "different person." There, her brother and her cousins do not judge her on the basis of her economic or professional achievements (or lack thereof). If they use money as a measuring stick to judge Hue, it is likely a positive appraisal because she treats them very well on her return visits. She brings clothes for the female cousins, and has treated Phuoc to the motorbike, a fancy phone, and a number of other material items. Of her brother, she says:

He's a great person, very respectful. I never felt close to my parents and sister in America. I think because they were always disappointed in me, it was hard to like them when they put so much pressure on me. I was not into school. So what? Phuoc is not like them; he does not care that I work in a hair salon. My cousins are the same. They don't think so lowly of me because I didn't go to college. So we have been able to talk more, be more open with each other about life. We are friends, you know.

It is not surprising that Phuoc and Hue's cousins treat her with respect, given how she showers them with gifts and cash, all of which are cast against the invisibility of her low-wage, low-status labor. In some sense, Hue compensates for not being a good immigrant daughter to her parents by being an extremely competent, if not exemplary, transnational total provider to her brother. She consistently sends Phuoc $300 a month from a distance, which is twice the amount of his income as a supervisor of a factory assembly line. Initially, like many respondents who needed to make ends meet when the expenditures in Vietnam required more money, Hue took on extra hours at work. Some weeks she worked fifteen to twenty hours more, rationalizing that the additional wages would be enough to send money monthly to Phuoc. Eventually, however, this pattern became tiring and Hue could not sustain it. She began charging small amounts on her credit cards. At first, it was just for her general living expenses, such as gas or groceries. Later she also began to take cash advances from her credit cards.

Most migrant respondents who go into debt say it began as a one-time event, undertaken with every intention of paying within a reasonable period for a pre-set expenditure,[45] such as a house renovation, tuition for someone to take English classes, or a trip to Vietnam.[46] Over time, however, debt became a routine part of transnational living; for some, it became unmanageable or even financially catastrophic.[47] In Hue's case, financing major events with credit cards resulted in long-term, nearly unmanageable debt. One winter, for example, she extemporaneously paid for an entire trip to Saigon with her credit card. A friend from San Jose begged her to come along, and even though she had no money, she badly wanted to go.

Hue decided she could work extra hours after the holidays to pay off the credit card. Once she was in Vietnam, however, she spent more money on her non-migrant relatives than she had anticipated. The Dylan motorbike she bought for Phuoc was the first big-ticket item for which she took out a cash advance from her credit card on that trip. Then one of Hue's cousins—her best friend in the country, she said—asked to borrow $3,000 for renovations on an apartment the cousin had just bought. Feeling generous and indebted to the cousin for several years of deep and loyal friendship, as well as feeling distant from the bills mounting up at home, Hue borrowed the sum with another credit card advance. All these big items eventually added up to a balance of $21,000 on six very high-interest credit cards.

A notable point here is that respondents generally report they did not have credit card debt prior to leading transnational lives.[48] Before they formed transnational relationships and established the habit of giving and spending money in the homeland, they were frugal individuals, like Hue, with few reasons to spend money in the United States beyond their everyday necessities.[49] In short, transnational journeys to Vietnam were in some ways journeys into the world of new expenditures, eventually leading to credit card debt.[50] Another surprising pattern was that respondents who went into debt were quite cavalier about the large amounts they owed credit card companies,[51] even when the interest rates were as high as 30 percent.[52]

Hue reflected on the connection between her return trips to Vietnam and her high credit card debt on another visit I made to San Jose. We sit in an ordinary coffee shop that once again reminds me of the contrast between her life in San Jose and the version of Hue I met a few years earlier at the hip Terrace Café in Saigon. It is as if she is two different people. On this visit, I ask how she went from being a fiscally disciplined person who saved $150 every month for five years to accumulating $21,000 in high-interest credit card debt. She says:

It sounds like a lot. I mean it is a lot, but I think I can pay it off in a few years. I don't regret because I got a chance to go to Vietnam when I wanted to go, only because of the credit card. I'll work hard to pay off the money. It's not a big deal. My brother is in love with his motorbike. You know Saigon, it's important for young men to have a nice motorbike. So I think it was worth it to go into debt for him.

When asked if Phuoc or her cousins understand that she has gone into tremendous debt for them, Hue explains it this way:

It's not important for them to know. I mean, I am honest with my brother about how much I make. It's not like I lie to him, like many Viet Kieu who exaggerate their incomes when they go back there. My brother knows I am not rich, but it's okay. He was reluctant for me to buy him the motorbike, but I told him not to worry about money. I have it, and if it's a problem, I would let him know. I told him that if it becomes a big problem, then he would definitely know. But it's not a big problem for me to pay the monthly bills for now. Sometimes you just have to live, you know, and not worry too much about money. Money is not everything.

Although Hue has not yet reached the limit on all her credit cards, her monthly payments now account for more than 40 percent of her net income. At about $600 a month for credit card bills alone, with interest rates averaging nearly 25 percent, it will take her more than ten years to pay off all her cards. Yet Hue remains positive, viewing her credit card debt as a trade-off that enables her brother to travel on a commodity frontier he would not be able to participate in without her assistance. This debt has also given Hue the opportunity to travel on an emotional frontier that has changed her outlook on life. For with the respect and deference Phuoc gives Hue in Saigon, he provides a haven that counteracts the heartless world of her family in San Jose, California.

INFORMATIONAL ASYMMETRY
IN MONETARY CIRCULATION

Going into debt for their non-migrant relatives is an economic sacrifice that many migrant members of transnational families are willing to make. Credit cards provide migrants a window of opportunity for gaining worth and esteem in circumstances of insufficient cash and savings, wherein they might not otherwise acquire it in the United States, even among their own families. Migrants, such as Hue, take on debt and rationalize to themselves that the monthly payments, while a large portion of their net incomes, are part of their ordinary living expenses. These low-wage migrants make do in creative ways, economizing and self-sacrificing at different moments to keep their debt and income in equilibrium. In most circumstances, they willingly and rationally take on the sacrifice. In many of these contexts, migrants such as Hue are able to stay afloat financially only because they save money by living in multi-generational households. Nonetheless, debt can become a tremendous problem if migrants exhaust all their resources. The issue is made worse if their non-migrant relatives misuse the money that migrants send. Vu Huynh's story illustrates this dark side of financial indebtedness.

Vu is a simple, soft-spoken, never-married man with a worn smile. He lives in a quiet working-class suburb of Westminster, Orange County, a city widely known as "Little Saigon" because it boasts the largest population of overseas Vietnamese in the United States.[53] He works as a butcher in an ethnic supermarket on popular Bolsa Avenue. When I called to arrange another in a series of interviews with him, Vu said, "Just come any day. Every day is the same for me."

However, when I arrive on that clear, perfect Southern California evening, and he greets me at the door, still in his butcher's uniform, he seems a bit irritated. I figure this might be because it is late in the evening and he has just returned, as he explains, from an excruciating seventeen-hour double shift in the meat department. It is a tough job, where he is immersed in animal blood and the putrid odor of seafood twelve to seventeen hours a day. On this day, he had only a twenty-minute lunch break, which he took in the back of the supermarket, with his cigarettes and a Tupperware container filled with salted-fish fried rice. He packs this same lunch for himself four times a week to save money.[54] As we step inside, I see he has been eating his dinner, a bowl of instant noodles, in front of the TV.

Vu begins our conversation by reading me a letter he received today from his thirty-two-year-old sister, Trieu. It ends with the following: "I am not feeling well these days. I need medications. Since I am not working, it is hard for us to afford the tuition for your nephew's schooling. I hope you can help us this month with $500, so we can take care of some problems the family is facing right now. Take good care of yourself. Your loving sister."

He used to be "super-excited," he explains, about receiving letters from his family in Vietnam, and opened them as soon as he saw the airmail stamp. In the early days, these letters contained long, thoughtful descriptions of daily life, including stories about nieces and nephews in school contests, cousins getting married or giving birth, family outings to modern shopping plazas in the new Saigon, and various rites of passage. Even though Vu rarely wrote back, he would pick up the phone and let his family know he appreciated their letters. But over the past five years, the tenor of these letters has changed. Now most end with a plea for money. Vu explains that he has been receiving different versions of the letter he just read to me, each telling the story of someone being sick and ending with a plea for money. Although Vu is no longer super-excited to receive mail from Vietnam, whenever he receives such a letter from Trieu, he nonetheless makes a quick call to tell her he received it, and then he runs to one of the ubiquitous remittance centers of Little Saigon, down the road from his apartment, and sends her money.

This evening, however, Vu says the latest letter made him extremely angry. At first I speculate this might be because he is particularly tired after working a double shift, or because he sent money recently and this new request seems excessive. In fact, it turns out Vu is angry because he learned earlier in the week that his sister used the money he sent her last month to buy a $300 set of luxury sheets.[55] Most of all, he is furious because at the same time he learned through gossip from other relatives that his sister is living large with the hard-earned money he sends her from a distance, including employing a live-in maid. Moreover, it turns out, this is not the first time there has been an issue. For example, during the previous year, Trieu told Vu she was sick when, he later learned, she had not been ill at all.

Trieu's letter today was the final straw. Acting on impulse, Vu picked up the phone and called his sister. He told her that was it—he was no longer going to send her money. "I called them, screamed, and cursed at them," Vu explains. "I was so goddamn furious about it." He elaborates:

I think it's the principle of it that got me angry. I had to wonder if they were starving themselves to buy the expensive sheets. Or did they get a maid so they can show off to their neighbors? It's just stupid. But really, I'm angry because I am so broke right now. And when I found out she was lying to me all this time, while I've been slaving away and borrowing money, it doesn't make sense to me.

Vu estimates the maid probably costs his sister $225 a month, when room and board are factored into her pay of $100 per month. He has been sending his sister between $200 and $300 every month for the past decade so she can buy food and necessities. It does not take too long, then, to understand Vu's equation: Trieu's splurge on the maid is about the same amount Vu has been sending for food on a monthly basis. At the bottom of the equation, however, is the fact that Vu feels duped because his sister hid from him that she has been employing a maid with his hard-earned money, including money he has taken out in cash advances from his credit cards. Thus, he calculates that his current debt acquisition has been used to finance his sister's new lifestyle in Saigon, which began with borrowed money to renovate her house and later grew into other expenses. As he explains:

With the money I make, I can support myself easily. I never have money problems. But when I started to go back to Vietnam, I wanted to help my sister and other family members with money because, you know, I guess because I am single and I can work easily. I am healthy and I can work long hours. I always take the extra shifts on the weekends if they ask me. I made a promise to my sister that I would help her renovate her house, and I thought it was fine because it was an investment for her and she would have a house to show for it. But it's just so stupid of her to want a fancy life by hiring the maid with the money I send them every month for food.

By the time Vu found out about Trieu's habits of living large in Saigon, he had already gone into significant debt to give her money and to finance his transnational journeys to Vietnam. Now he explains clearly and deliberately, like a witness on trial, that he does not believe his sister is or was sick or that she has been taking any medications, as she said in the letter. In fact, from Vu's perspective, his sister's life in Vietnam is better than his in the United States:

When I first went there, I had the responsibility to take care of her, to make sure her life was stable. But I slowly realized that it's not so bad in Saigon. Her life is fine. She has a family, and she and her husband work. They make enough money to support themselves. With the help I was sending them for the past ten years, they were living nicely, I have to say. They have better lives than many people I know in Saigon. And I think their lives are better than mine here in America.

Vu describes how he reached a turning point, after which he could no longer support his sister. During the first few years of return visits, he explains, "I used to be so worried because it was hard for people in Saigon early on, and I thought if I could afford it, I would send her money regularly." He continues, "Vietnam was just opening up to Viet Kieu to return; no one really knew what people had and how they were living. I wanted my sister to have a better life than others." As a result, he promised his sister and her husband that he would help them renovate their house. They already owned the land and lived in acceptable conditions, but they (and Vu) wanted their house to look more Western, with modern plumbing and full electricity.

When Vu brings out pictures of his sister's house, it is clear that the elaborate, three-story typical Saigonese townhome is different from the tiny, four-hundred-square-foot rented apartment in which Vu lives. The cost of the renovations to the Saigon house came to about $30,000, but Vu had no such amount. He was forced to take out loans from several sources, but never explained his financial situation to his sister. In addition to the savings he had been sending from a distance, four years ago he took out $8,000 in credit card advances to pay for the middle segment of construction on his sister's home. Two and half years later, in his last cash advance on his credit card, he took out another $2,500 for what his sister promised would be the last financial request for their renovations. Then, he made a final cash advance on his credit card for $3,000 to finance his last trip to Saigon.

During that last visit, now more than two years ago, Vu gave his sister $1,000 before he got on the plane to return to Orange County. The money was intended to supplement her wages and those of her husband so they could buy food for an extended period. Instead, as he found out shortly after returning to the United States, she chose to install a new air conditioner in her three-story house, built with money Vu had sent in many increments over the previous ten years, some from savings but most from credit cards.[56] She also used the remaining portion of the money to buy her seventeen-year-old son a cheap, but new, motorbike so he could go to school six miles away from home, a trip he had made by bicycle for the past four years. Vu says:

Of course, I thought they didn't need an air conditioner. But what could I do? I gave them that $1,000 to buy food and things they need. I always remind her and her husband, "You know you should spend this money wisely, on things you need. If it's not enough, I can send more. But don't be wasteful." When they decided to spend it on things they don't need, I didn't agree with it. But I won't send them more money if they ask for it. That was supposed to be extra money for a while.

After all was said and done, between the house renovations, his trips to Saigon, and his own living expenses in Orange County, Vu had reached the limit on all his credit cards and had no other sources to turn to for money. In short, he was broke, and could no longer afford to make return visits to Vietnam or send his family members money. In fact, he was barely able to pay his rent of $1,100 and his living expenses. His debt came to about $30,000 from credit card advances and purchases, not counting other miscellaneous expenses he had not yet paid off. In addition, he had borrowed $10,000 from a close friend in Orange County. During my previous visits, Vu had mentioned his financial problems and asked me to help him with debt consolidation for the $30,000 in credit card loans.[57] Repayment of the $10,000 loan was not urgent because his friend was not charging interest.

Vu's $30,000 debt was in the form of five high-interest credit cards, with a minimum interest rate of 18 percent. The highest interest rate was an astounding 29 percent. By this time, he was paying more than $700 in monthly installments on the credit cards, or a little more than one-third of his net income. Because of the exorbitant interest rates, only a little of that amount went toward the principal. It would take him nearly fifteen years to pay the $30,000 in credit card balances at $700 per month.[58]

Until recently, Vu says, he did not regret what he did to help his family, even though it was very difficult for him to sustain financially. "I would go, spend all my money there, and then come back and toil away in the butcher shop for another year before I did the same thing again," he explains. "I just lived by the day, and made plans as each month came along." This paycheck-to-paycheck lifestyle was worth it because those seven trips Vu took to Vietnam gave him the most joyous moments of his life. The farther he got away from the "nasty supermarket," as he calls it, the better he felt about himself. The closer he got to his family in Vietnam, the more meaning he felt he had in his life. As he explains, "At the beginning, I loved going back there. When I got off the plane, I felt that feeling of being home. It was my place, Saigon was my city. I never have that feeling in Westminster. It's the opposite. When I returned to America each time, I would get so depressed when the plane landed at LAX."

Now that he is no longer making return visits, Vu has to rely on his life in the United States for his sense of social worth and esteem. Despite living in a very populous Vietnamese community, however, he has few friends and no lover in sight. When he gets lonely, he spends a good portion of his paycheck at a strip club, or gambles a little at a casino in Los Angeles. He has been thinking about going to Vietnam to find a wife because in Orange County, he says, "I can't afford to be a good man to these women here. They are too materialistic." Therefore, in addition to providing Vu with family time, his trips to Vietnam have helped him feel validated in the homeland with his status as a migrant in ways that are not possible in Orange County.

The next time I saw Vu, I asked him how his relationship with his sister was evolving; in particular, even though I knew some of the reasons much earlier, I asked him more formally why he had not told his sister about his debts early on. He explains, "I guess I thought it was my own business to deal with. I also thought she was being responsible with money over there, so I was fine with sending them money. It wasn't something I thought much about. It was not like it was a secret. It was my money, my problem. It got me really angry when I learned she was misusing the money." After Vu eventually told Trieu about his debts, and explained why he was no longer sending her money, she continued to write letters asking for money. "My blood boils because I don't know why she doesn't understand that I am working my ass off, and they are fine and still are asking me for money," Vu explains helplessly. "They are fine by their standards, and my standards. It's not like I don't tell them that I am in debt and that it's making me lose sleep."

Vu's experience amplifies and reiterates the point that credit cards provide the opportunity for migrants to travel into an emotional frontier that they would be unlikely to encounter otherwise, since they would have insufficient funds. But Vu's story also illustrates the serious ramifications of informational asymmetries about monetary circulation in transnational families, the worst of which is that migrants often end up in financial tatters because of debt.[59] The complicated links between discrepant understandings about the use of money, especially when it is earmarked ambiguously, and subsequent decisions related to its use lead to serious misconstructions. Many kinds of informational asymmetries occur in transnational families, but financial informational asymmetries can have severe consequences because many non-migrant relatives truly have no conception of the cost of living in the United States or the magnitude of their overseas families' buying power (or lack thereof). Interview data reveal that none of the migrant respondents told their families in Vietnam they had gone into debt for monetary circulation, or to finance their transnational journeys home.[60] Thus, in these cases, informational asymmetries stem from financial secrecy and ambiguity. Yet migrants said that no matter where they got the money they gave, they objected to their relatives' misuse of it.

. . .

This chapter has unpacked the complicated connection between economic behaviors and an economy of dignity through the experiences of migrant respondents who take on credit card debt to finance their transnational lives. The data suggest an additional layer upon which monetary circulations occur; some of these data integrate the elements of status-driven consumption covered in previous chapters. However, a magnified portrait of migrants' day-to-day lives, their sense of self, and the juxtaposition of extreme financial fragility shows that some migrants turn to credit cards to finance their transnational lives because credit cards open up a huge window of opportunity for self-valorization.[61]

Although using credit cards is a limited and risky strategy financially, this practice offers migrants the possibility of gaining a sense of competence, worth, and dignity transnationally that might never be obtained otherwise. This analysis does not suggest that low-wage Vietnamese migrants who take on high levels of credit card debt believe it is the best way to navigate their financial precariousness. In fact, most respondents exercised tremendous fiscal discipline before they started to lead transnational lives. We saw this in the case of Hue, who managed to save a sizable amount of money before she went to Vietnam for the first time. Her difficult life with parents who gave her little respect compelled her to turn to spending and giving money in Vietnam to gain a sense of dignity in her life.

This issue of financial indebtedness is unquestionably a major problem that affects consumers at all strata of the new global economy. In late 2011, the total outstanding consumer credit owed by U.S households was $2.4 trillion, with revolving credit card debt accounting for approximately $800 billion of this amount.[62] Those who have credit card debt have an average debt of nearly $16,000.[63] The accumulation of debt among migrant respondents in some ways echoes the macroeconomic crisis in early-twenty-first-century capitalism,[64] but is distinguished from it[65] because non-asset indebtedness is a central feature of everyday life for low-income communities.[66]

The final picture that emerges from this chapter is that while credit cards offer a window of opportunity to gain worth, esteem, and dignity, they also have dark consequences within transnational families. We saw this with clarity in the example of Vu, who learned that his sister had been spending money frivolously without his approval. Vu sacrificed for his sister by taking substantial cash advances from his credit cards, which had exorbitant interest rates. Yet he happily took on this debt to pay for the renovation of his sister's house—before he discovered that, in his view, she was misusing the money. In the case of Hue, although 40 percent of her net income goes toward monthly credit installments, she remains optimistic and content with the satisfaction she has gained from the money she spends on her brother, cousins, and herself in Saigon. Who knows if her story will end as angrily and resentfully as Vu's? And how many more migrants have stories similar to those of Vu and Hue? What we do know is that regardless of the high interest rates and mountains of debt that migrants have accrued, the emotional gains that they have obtained through transnational relationships and through the transnational economy of dignity are, without doubt, priceless to them.

CHAPTER 10

TALL PROMISES

I N T H E C O N T E X T of Vietnamese low-wage transnational families, great divides exist with respect to how different members perceive and evaluate the adequacy of expenditures and flows of money.[1] In this chapter, I return to the stories of the six respondents from the vignettes in Chapter 1 to examine problems associated with unfulfilled promises made by migrants.[2] In the context of transnational families, migrant relatives routinely make promises for monetary circulation that create hope and aspirations about consumption. These promises have significant implications because they encourage acquisitive fantasies and mobility dreams in individuals who perhaps have no other avenues for material improvement in their lives. In some cases, non-migrant members of transnational families defer, modify, or simply abandon major life decisions (e.g., about marriage, job choices, and migration to the city) when it seems that promises made by their migrant relatives offer better alternatives.

The temptation for migrants to make promises, especially while visiting their relatives, is extremely strong for a number of reasons. The most prevalent reason has to do with the temporary presence of migrants in the homeland. After they make promises, they soon leave and perhaps assume that the left-

behind relatives will forget that any promises were made. Given the disparity in incomes and cost of living between life in the United States and life in
Vietnam, it initially might seem to migrants returning for visits that it will
be feasible to fulfill such promises, since everything in the homeland seems
affordable to them. In addition, the specter of social networks promotes expectations that migrants' promises will provide non-migrant family members
with nicer things and improve their lives. By the same token, promises that go
unfulfilled can easily foster anger, resentment, and feelings of abandonment.
Many non-migrant relatives revealed that it took years for their family members' promises to materialize, if they did so at all. Non-migrants report that
broken promises can cause tremendous personal embarrassment, especially
when such promises were delivered in public.

In an atmosphere of consumptive temptations and seductions within the
transnational expenditure cascade, migrant members of transnational families
might be expected to make some degree of unrealistic promises about monetary
circulation. We also can expect, as I have emphasized throughout, that some
non-migrants inevitably develop unreasonable expectations, given the new material landscape within which they are embedded. These broken promises and
unreasonable expectations are compounded by the dynamics of transnational
relationships in which members of transnational families do not know what
goes on "on the other side."[3] The concomitancy of broken promises and un-
realized dreams and fantasies can escalate into interpretations by non-migrant
family members of deception and even braggadocio and boasting.[4] Social frictions that arise from false promises for monetary circulation are generally minor,
but more major ones occur frequently enough to warrant a close analysis because social frictions can turn into blowups to the point that family members
minimize communications, cut off relationships, or even disown one another.

Rather than casting non-migrants as passive recipients of monetary circulation,[5] or migrants as duplicitous status seekers, a close look at unfilled promises
of money or other kinds of assistance by migrants shows that they often are con-
founded by seemingly unreasonable requests and expectations by non-migrant
relatives for gifts and monetary assistance. This can result in awkward tensions,
reflecting and refracting the glaring differences between lives across transnational
social fields.[6] The temptation to promise family that money will be spent and
given, even if it is known in advance that such promises are unrealistic and thus

could possibly threaten amicable and affectionate relationships, is so great that almost everyone makes promises on some scale.

Moreover, these problems are exacerbated by the fact that transnational family relations frequently are complicated by concealments related to money.[7] This is not to say that migrant family members fail to display money; on the contrary, many transnational familial social frictions originate in the very fact that overseas relatives spend money without disguise or subtlety.[8] Instead, "concealment" here means that it is common for migrant respondents to avoid discussing their real wages and the reality of their precarious lives in the United States.[9] A number of studies confirm this pattern among migrants who make occasional or regular return visits to the homeland.[10] To compound the matter, migrants spend excessively in ways that are not commensurate with their income levels, leading many non-migrants to believe their overseas relatives have more money than they actually do.[11]

Transnational familial social frictions arise out of the temptation for migrants to promise money and material goods to their non-migrant relatives. In general, stories about migrants making more promises than they can keep, or simply making unrealistic promises in passing, are common, if not universal. When such promises go unfulfilled, non-migrant family members find themselves in predicaments in which they must negotiate what seems like a breach of promise, a lie, or simply "boasting without the goods," as one non-migrant respondent said. Like the transnational families in the El Salvador–New York migration corridor in Sarah Mahler's study, when Vietnamese low-wage migrants cannot sustain monetary circulation, they feel too ashamed to return home, but rarely do non-migrants initiate a breakup of transnational relationships.[12] This pattern demonstrates the reality that migrant family members often,[13] though not always, hold the upper hand due to their economic power over non-migrant family members.[14]

These power differences are not always about economic asymmetry in transnational social fields. As Jorgen Carling observes, "Asymmetry does not imply that migrants are always in a powerful position vis-à-vis non-migrants or the other way around. On the contrary, transnational practices are shaped by the multi-faceted nature of the relationship, with migrants and non-migrants experiencing vulnerability and ascendancy at different times and in different contexts."[15] The following cases show how power shifts over time and in different contexts between different members of transnational families. These "dark sides" of transnational families can lead to blowups,[16] which range widely in intensity, with varying consequences for social relations. Some relationships might continue without any further monetary circulation, while in rare cases, migrants tragically sever social ties with their non-migrant family members, and in some instances also terminate their transnational journeys to Vietnam.[17]

THE MIRE OF BROKEN PROMISES

Lan Bui, twenty-seven, works with her husband at a small tailor shop in a working-class neighborhood on the outskirts of Saigon, making a total of $250 per month. They own a small plot of land where they built a house,[18] which is only partially completed due to insufficient funds. Lan never smiles fully, but she speaks strongly about herself, her family, and especially her sister Cam, who is nine years older and works as a supermarket cashier in Philadelphia. Lan's two children stay with her parents most of the week in Thu Duc, and she and her husband only visit on weekends because it takes seventy-five minutes to get home on their motorbike.[19] The family receives financial support from Cam and her brother, Luc, who also lives in Philadelphia.

In initial interviews, Cam spoke with adoration, sympathy, and much affection about Lan. Cam describes how much she herself has sacrificed and denied herself to save and give money to Lan. Despite her precarious job as a cashier, Cam economizes in almost every facet of her life in order to save. For instance, she canceled her phone service and instead uses prepaid calling cards that she buys at wholesale retailers, a practice that saves about $50 per month. She also canceled her cable service and forgoes most opportunities to socialize with friends unless she can do it at home. Cam's only extravagance is the lottery; she purchases lottery tickets on a regular basis, with the dream that winning would allow her to raise the standard of living for her family in Vietnam, especially for Lan. Yet no matter how much she economizes, even in a good month Cam is never able to send more than $200 to Lan. She also sends the other family members in Thu Duc collectively about $100 for food and necessities. On one visit home, Cam bought Lan a brand-new motorbike that cost almost $1,500, which made Lan one of the first in her circle of friends and fellow workers to own a motorbike. Although Cam has not been able to make other big purchases for Lan, she consistently sends money, as she promised. "Sometimes if it's a bad month and I can't save enough money, I take out a loan from my credit card and send Lan $50," Cam explains. "At least she will still have some food money."

Whenever Cam returns to visit, she makes sure she has saved enough before getting on the plane to give larger amounts than she usually sends, a typical strategy employed by many migrants before they go back to the homeland. "I can't go home empty-handed, with no money to give them," Cam says. "I felt awful when I did that once at the airport. Everyone just looked at me, waiting, I know, for me to give them money before I got on the plane." It is thus frequently a matter of shame and stigma if migrants come and go without revenues to spend and disburse.[20]

Hearing Cam's perspective and having visited Lan and her husband on five previous occasions, I am surprised when I next meet Lan to learn that she feels her sister does not provide for her well enough or love her enough. As Lan explains:

It's hard for me to say, but you can say that even though I have overseas family, a brother and a sister, it's like I don't have anybody over there [*co cung nhu khong*]. I waited too long for Cam to help me, but I stopped believing in her promises a long time ago because it's embarrassing for me. It's hard for me to say, but when I look at other people with relatives abroad, I feel very eager to be like them [*thay ham*]. Other people have overseas relatives who take good care of them. They have things to show for it, and they can go in public and show off to other people the things their families buy for them. They live in nice homes with air conditioners, and they drive new motorbikes. I am still driving the same motorbike Cam bought for me eight years ago. I feel like I am a local with no one abroad.

Before Cam was able to return home for the first time in 1999, she and Lan were constantly in touch through handwritten letters. Lan explains that they shared many stories of their everyday lives, and Cam encouraged Lan to hold off on a number of decisions. Specifically, she instructed Lan to defer plans to move to the city for work or to marry at an early age—plans many of Lan's peers were making at the time. To help convince Lan that she should not move to Saigon, Cam sent her pictures depicting the grandeur of life in an American city, Cam's car and apartment, as well as the "fancy supermarket" where Cam works. Although Cam makes barely $12 per hour as a cashier, her pictures cut a stark contrast with the life Lan leads. Then, before Cam made her first trip home, she sent Lan $200, which was the first time she had sent her sister money since migrating to the United States.

At the time, Lan was only seventeen, but she had already started working at a garment factory in Thu Duc. According to Lan, Cam made promises to arrange for Lan to marry someone from the United States, and promised to help Lan move from Thu Duc to Saigon if the arranged marriage did not pan out. This way, Lan could learn a trade so she would not have to work in the harsh conditions of the factory. "She said she would help me financially in the future and that I shouldn't worry about moving to the city to find work," Lan recalls. "She told me to not fall in love in Vietnam and that she would try to find someone from America to marry me so I could join her there." Lan naturally found these grand promises quite enticing, and did her best to ignore any inkling that they ultimately might not be fulfilled. She elaborates in calculated detail:

She gave me only $200, and she was gone for over ten years. What did she expect me to do with that $200? Buy a house? Support myself in Saigon? I couldn't even buy a nice bicycle with that amount. And each time I got a letter from her, she told me to not fall in love. She said to me that if I fall in love, I would be stuck in Vietnam forever, and that there was nothing she could do for me. I listened to her. I listened to her because I thought that if she didn't find someone from America for me to marry, then she would help me go into the city and learn a trade, because the factory was very difficult for me. She promised that she would help me go to the city and learn a trade at a beauty salon. Every day when I went to work at the factory, people who knew I had a sister living in America asked me why I had to toil in the factory. I told them I didn't want to stay at home and be bored, and that I was sure Cam would help me when she got the opportunity to return home. People just listened to what I said, until I quit the factory and they thought I moved to the city with Cam's help.

When Cam made her first return visit to Vietnam, she had not found anyone in the United States who would make a suitable husband for Lan, nor could she afford to help Lan move to the city at that time, as she originally thought she could. As Lan explains:

The first time she came back, she told me to be patient and that she would try the second time she comes back to help me move to the city and find me a place to become an apprentice in a beauty salon so I could go to America. She said she would introduce me to someone in America, and I could work in a beauty salon when I got sponsored there. She said many Vietnamese people in America work in beauty salons and nail salons. That first time when she came back, she gave me $300, and that was all she gave me. She said she would continue to look for someone to marry me and bring me to America. I listened to her. I was obedient. I didn't want to anger her. So I just listened. I never wanted to fall in love with anyone in Vietnam.

When non-migrants tell stories of broken promises and false hopes that their migrant families led them to hold on to, their narrations are more often than not punctuated with anger and resentment. These feelings are reflected in Lan's account as she describes how she moved on with her life after she figured out Cam was unable to deliver on her promises. "When she came back for the third time, she didn't talk about anyone coming back to marry me. It was as if she had never ever talked about it. I was too ashamed," Lan explains. "I had to have some dignity of my own by not appearing desperate. I didn't want to ask her again about her finding me a husband from America." Lan becomes emotional as she narrates the results of her crushed hopes:

I fell in love with someone I met from the factory. I said to myself that I could not depend on my brother and sister anymore, so I got married in order to depend on my husband. It was too long, and I didn't see much help. I had to plan my future, my life. My husband taught me—and he always tries to remind me—that we can be poor, but as long as we have our dignity, we can be proud. We don't have to depend on anyone. So I got married and had two children [*she cries as she continues the story*]. If I knew my sister could not find me someone from America, I would not have gotten my hopes up so much. I would have loved someone else who came along earlier. I feel ashamed for trying to depend on her for so long because I didn't know if she could help me or not. And because she is my older sister, I wanted to be obedient. I am ashamed because I told so many people here that my older sister would find me a husband from America or help me move to Saigon.

We can imagine the anticipation and fantasies that transpired as Lan anxiously waited from her late teens until her mid-twenties for Cam to fulfill her promise to help Lan with marriage and migration, both of which are major events for many women with aspiring mobilities in the new Saigon. The public humiliation that Lan experienced from many years of telling people she would eventually go to the United States is a common problem among non-migrant relatives who dream about migration.

Because Lan never had the opportunity to migrate, Cam has sent her financial support almost every month from the time that Cam made her first return home, in part as an effort to compensate for the broken promises. In her version of the story, Cam reveals, "Well, I did, you know, promise I would introduce her to a guy in America. But it's not that easy. I have been asking around, but you can't just go shopping at the mall for a husband. You have to be gentle and polite about it, and not just go up to anybody and ask, 'Hi, do you want to marry my poor sister in Vietnam?'" Cam elaborates on how Lan wanted to move quickly on a marriage arrangement:

When I told Lan that it takes time, she was upset, I know that. She wanted to come to America. She is too anxious. But I couldn't get just anyone for her. And about moving her to the city, I didn't realize how expensive it would be to live in Saigon. We went to look at some places in Saigon, and I asked around and met some beauty salon owners who could help her and let her work there. But in the end, I discovered it was too expensive to have her live in Saigon. So I told her it was better that she stay in Thu Duc with my parents, and I would send her $200 a month. I send that amount almost every month. Sometimes I send $100 or $50, but I try to make up for it during the holidays. It's not easy, and I keep telling her that.

Given her reasonable explanation, why did Cam keep telling Lan not to fall in love, according to Lan, or why did Cam not simply tell Lan early on that she was unable to help? In short, it seems from an outsider's point of view, that Cam's promises were not actionable. Why did Cam continue over a period of seven years to tell Lan she would help her move to the city when she had discovered on her first visit that she could not afford to do so? Cam explains:

I myself also had hopes that I could find someone to introduce to Lan so she could get married and go to America. I didn't know from the beginning that it would be so difficult. It's not easy to meet people and find a good person. But Lan was impatient. She's still so young emotionally. She wanted me to find someone right away, the first time I came back to Vietnam. And she wanted to move to Saigon as soon as I returned. I had to be sure we could get a good place for her to live and that I could help her. But I didn't have the money to help her move to the city. I told her to be patient with me, but she got married to that factory boy. That's why they live in that house with a dirt floor. It's sad to see her that way. She's still young, so I am not sure why she wanted to get married so early.

Unfulfilled promises can be emotionally consequential, as in Lan's case, because such promises lead to feelings of hope and anxiety related to the overseas relatives' ability to eventually fulfill those promises. Lan thought Cam could find her a husband in the United States, and if not, would help her move to the city. At the heart of the issue is that Lan felt either option—migration to the city or, preferably, marriage with someone abroad—would be a passage of upward mobility for her. Both of those promises seemed reasonable in Lan's view, so she waited for nearly a decade for Cam's help. In Lan's case, the overseas family member actively initiated the promises. As her story illustrates, promises sometimes are made under the guise of family control. In some ways, Cam wanted Lan to remain single so she could help her marry someone *Cam* found suitable. Moreover, marriage, migration, and mobility are inextricably linked in the world of transnational families.

Cam made promises to Lan because she wanted her sister's life and the lives of the rest of her family members to improve materially. "I wanted her to marry someone in America because she would have a better life, and she wouldn't be stuck in Vietnam," Cam explains. "Now her children will be poor forever." Lan's story is mostly a story of aspirations and the seductive temptations on the part of her sister to truly help out, even though the promise was unrealistic and went beyond the resources available. Promises to help individuals build homes, migrate, and bring their children to the United States often are made casually without much consideration of firm resources.

Given the broken promises and disappointment related to long-held fantasies about mobility, we can expect Lan to feel some degree of sadness, resentment, emotional turmoil, and stress. Yet despite these feelings, migrants and non-migrant families usually avoid confrontations. After non-migrants discover they can no longer rely on the promises made by their migrant family members, relationships generally continue with acquiescence, and issues of trust, loyalty, and affection are minimized. Lan, for instance, explains that her relationship with Cam is "normal, and I still respect her as my sister. But I have to be careful about what I hear she says she will do from now on."

THE TRANSNATIONAL SILENT TREATMENT

In at least half a dozen cases, non-migrant relatives related tearful accounts that ended with them never hearing from their migrant relatives after a particular trip home.[21] These non-migrant family members speculated that because their migrant relatives could not follow through with a promise, they chose to remain silent and stopped all forms of communication. In other families, migrants overspent their savings and could not continue monetary flows, so they cut off communication to avoid embarrassment and shame.[22]

The following anecdote illustrates how Quang Tran, the airplane cabin cleaner from Atlanta, Georgia, discontinued communication with his sister, fifty-four-year-old Truc, after failing to make good on promises he made to her. Truc is unemployed; her husband supports the family (including their twenty-one-year-old son and fourteen-year-old daughter) as a taxi driver with the 6 million VND he earns monthly, a third of which goes toward the rent of their five-hundred-square-foot apartment. Despite this low income, Truc plans to send her son to study in Australia, which will cost about $18,000 a year, an amount that would take her and her husband a lifetime to save. She hopes her son can stay in Australia after finishing school and sponsor the family to live there. This is the larger plan Truc has set in motion, at least conceptually, for the eventual migration of her entire family to Australia. She says that about four years ago, Quang promised to help send her son to Australia. She details his intentions:

I know that it is a lot of money. But Quang said he could make it possible. He said that in America there are many ways you can borrow money, not like in Vietnam, where it is impossible to borrow money unless you have a lot of properties. And if you borrow money in Vietnam, the interest is so high that it would take a very long time to pay back. We need to have the money until my son finishes his schooling in Australia, and because that would cost so much interest, I asked Quang for help. He told me he would help at least for one year, the first year my son goes to Australia, and then he would take out a loan for my son and me. He knows my son is a very hardworking student, and that we would pay him back in the future so he can repay the bank, so he is willing to take the risk and borrow money for us.

About three years after Quang made the promise, her son was at a point where he needed to decide whether to stay in Vietnam or transfer to Australia in order to complete his college education. At that time, Truc learned that Quang would be unable to help them out. She says the following about what transpired:

We haven't heard from him in over a year now. He told me he would come back to visit about nine months ago, but we didn't hear from him. We don't know what's wrong with him. We tried calling, e-mailing, and writing letters, but we never heard back. We asked several times if he could help us because my son needed to arrange the paperwork and we had to pay the fees in installments. I didn't want to pay any fees until I heard from Quang that he would send us the money. But we didn't hear from him, so I thought it had to do with the money he promised. I wrote to him and told him that it was fine if he could not help me send my son to Australia. I understand it.

In her humble apartment, where her son sleeps on the kitchen floor and her daughter sleeps on a cot in the living room, I am struck by the vivid inconsistency, if not paradox, between Truc's grand plan for migration to Australia and the reality of her family's current lifestyle. When probed about whether she knows how much Quang makes in America, or how he originally expected to assist her financially by supporting her son's studies abroad, Truc explains:

He has always been very generous with the family. He gave us money the few times we asked, like a few years ago he gave us $3,000 so my husband could buy a taxi license to work as a driver in the city. On the last trip, he said he would help us with his own money, but if he couldn't, he would get a loan from a bank in America. From what I understand, there should be no problem to get a loan from the bank. The interest from loans in America is much lower than in Vietnam, so I thought if Quang can help us with only one year, my son can start working in Australia while going to school, and we can take out loans from Quang if we need to do it.

Later when I visit Quang in Atlanta, I learn that he feels his sister has been making too many demands on him for money. He says he needs time to think through her request for such a large amount, and complains that his sister rushed into the matter too quickly. When Truc made the request for financial help during one of his visits, Quang felt pressured to acquiesce and ended up making a promise he was unable to keep. "The last time I visited, almost a year ago, just a few days before I needed to get ready to return to America, she

[Truc] asked me to go with her alone to a café. Her demeanor got very serious, and I thought something was wrong with the family," he begins the story. "I was worried, but suddenly she started to ask me for money. She gave a long list of all the things the family needed. I didn't say anything. I think that because I didn't say anything, maybe she got worried that I wouldn't help out at all." Quang elaborates on Truc's request for a large sum of money:

Suddenly, she talked about her son going to Australia to study, but I had never heard of the plan before that day. Because I know education is important, I felt pressured [ep buoc], and so I just said yes to the plan. But how can I help with $18,000 a year? It's impossible. I can't help with that much money. I can't take out loans that easily. I don't know how she knows, but she said people tell her that in America we can get personal loans very easily from the bank. I checked on it, and I'm not qualified for it. And what if she could never return the money? What would happen to me?

When I ask Quang what he plans to do about the situation, given what Truc told me about his not being in touch with them for a while, he says:

It's been a long time since I communicated with them. I think now over a year, and I don't plan to go back next year. I don't have the money to go. And if I were to go back next year, I need to save money for spending and to give them some money, too. I want to wait and see. I got her letters and e-mails, but I have not replied because I want to think about it. I want to wait to see if maybe she will forget about the money. But every time she writes me, she still talks about the money. She said it's fine that her son does not go to Australia, but she asks for money for other things. Something always comes up. The last time she asked if I could help her son go to the local university, and that cost more than $5,000 a year. It's not as much as Australia, but it's still a lot of money.

Although expectations from non-migrant families may appear rampant and unreasonable, another interpretation that carries important weight is that when migrants, such as Quang, give family members gifts and money, they grant them images of wealth, prosperity, and success. Mariano Sana argues that migrants sometimes send money even when they are in dire situations themselves because they want to sustain an image of success.[23] Furthermore, in an atmosphere of compensatory and excessive consumption among migrants, their non-migrant family members are often tempted to ask for money that they think their relatives, in fact, would have no problem spending or giving. The migrants themselves often cannot resist the temptation to make promises during the short periods they visit the country.

I have witnessed dozens of instances in which overseas family members cavalierly made promises to buy expensive commodities (e.g., motorbikes, durable goods, clothes, and other luxury items) on the spot, doing so happily, and thus demonstrating their (presumed) pecuniary strength. As Jose Itzigsohn and his colleagues note succinctly, when migrants expose their pecuniary strengths in the homeland, it is sometimes "the only way of enjoying the fruits of their hard work in the United States. It also allows people to enjoy their newly acquired status which they cannot enjoy in the United States."[24] Le Anh Tu Packard observes that "over time, stereotypical images of rich, ostentatious and arrogant Viet Kieu on the one side, and of ignorant, backward, and beggarly 'country bumpkins' on the other, have been replaced by more nuanced views."[25]

Yet my data reveal that most non-migrants have very limited knowledge about how their overseas relatives live, how much they make, and the extent of the purchasing power of their incomes. Quang once said, "The truth is that if you live in America, you have to show your family you can give them money. . . . If you don't give them money, they think you are failing." Moreover, he added, "As a family member living in America, you have to send money back home regularly to show your family you care for them and that you can afford to give them money." Thus, his broken promise and halted communications notwithstanding, Quang's pattern of sending money regularly to Vietnam, and of giving and spending it on return visits, established to his sister, Truc, that he had achieved the American Dream of prosperity and success.

THE BREAKING OF MORE THAN A PROMISE

Social frictions stemming from unfulfilled promises tend to conclude with family members minimizing communications, and subsequently monetary circulation, which is easy to do given the international distance and the time difference. This is a common exit strategy to an otherwise deep and affectionate transnational family relationship. However, some instances end in blowups. A case in point is the most heated blowup I witnessed, which occurred between thirty-six-year-old Dinh and his forty-eight-year-old uncle, Son. Dinh is the carpenter from Northern California who whenever he makes return visits to Saigon, spends excessively at bars and nightclubs, epitomizing the compensatory consumptive behavior discussed in Chapter 6. Son owns a small shop in Saigon, where he makes $1,000 a month, which puts him securely in the middle class in his cultural and local contexts, in which approximately two-thirds of the population make less than $350 per month.[26]

As I join Son and his wife for dinner one night at their house, Son reiterates some of the problems he has when Dinh returns to visit. Son is irritated with Dinh for spending excessively in Saigon, not because he wants to control Dinh's spending habits, but because Son feels he has to reciprocate occasionally by treating Dinh to meals, nights out, and excursions. Son also thinks Dinh engages in braggadocio that Son knows is inconsistent with his income level in the United States.[27] Furthermore, at some point, Dinh promised Son he would buy him a car, a promise Son knew was impossible for Dinh to fulfill. Even a cheap Honda Civic costs nearly $40,000 in Saigon, due to government taxes, and one must pay in cash because the credit market is available to only a few privileged individuals. This knowledge of an impossible promise can lead non-migrants to believe their overseas relatives are deceitful about their real incomes in order to gain social power. The centrality of money in his relationship with his nephew became a problem in Son's marriage, as he explains:

My wife is very frugal and responsible. Without her, we would never have gotten the shop and house that we bought. She saved money and managed to get help from her family. Even though I have a sister living in America, I was never able to get help from my relatives over there. All the things we have in the family we got through my wife's family, even though they don't have any family abroad. My wife wants me to be careful about spending too much money when Dinh comes to visit. She said Dinh is a big spender, he doesn't care about his future, he only spends to have a great time when he goes to Vietnam. She always tells me that I need to be less materialistic. She got mad at me for having high hopes that Dinh would buy us a car.

When I ask Son's wife in private about her perspective, she reiterates what Son described, while also explaining that she feels Dinh has negatively influenced Son. "I try to understand that it's a good time, it's for fun," she says. "I know they work hard over there [overseas], and so I can understand that when Dinh comes home to visit, he wants to treat his uncle, and they go out almost every night." Son's wife continues by describing how Dinh's spending habits are a burden for them:

But we can't afford to do all the stuff Dinh wants us to do, like go to expensive restaurants. He pays for us, it is true, but we have to repay him with nice meals, too, and not let him pay for us every time without treating him to something. The problem is that my husband tries to play on the same level as Dinh, and we can't do that. It's too expensive. Every time Dinh comes back here to visit, my husband spends almost all of our monthly income. He wants to spend so much of our money on Dinh. I don't know why. Maybe he thinks if he treats Dinh well, Dinh will buy us a car. But I told him Dinh does not have a lot of money. I know from other people that he doesn't make a lot of money. So how can he buy us a car? It is not good for us that Dinh tells us things like that [promising to buy a car].

On some level, Son and his wife subscribe to the Maussian model of gift giving,[28] which emphasizes that gift exchanges involve the obligation to return. From their viewpoints, Dinh's spending habits are gifts that must be reciprocated. Indeed, a long history of anthropological and sociological literature, beginning with Marcel Mauss, has captured the complex rules of gift exchanges.[29] Gifts can represent important aspects of social life, including status and social roles. But foremost, accepting a gift implies some obligation of social repayment. In some primitive societies, failure to reciprocate gifts can lead to loss of dignity by public shaming or, worse, can develop into warfare.[30] Of course, in modern societies, the same kinds of rules about reciprocity do not exist, but contemporary life does have certain "norms of reciprocity" that involve obligations and expectations.[31]

The complex relationship between expectations and norms of reciprocity embedded in the social relations between Dinh and Son was revealed one evening when I joined them at the 333 Bar. Dinh, like many migrant men, has the habit of inviting anyone and everyone he knows each time he goes out in Saigon. This evening out with Dinh, Son, and more than a dozen of Dinh's friends provides a vivid example of how a minor blowup can occur out of monetary exchanges, expectations, and the taboo of exposing a migrant's pecuniary weakness. The nightclub caters mostly to the local population, except for a few interspersed tables occupied by overseas men and their parties. As we begin to drink and order food, our group of fifteen men divides into small conversations of two to three people.

When the waiter arrives to take our order, Dinh wants several bottles of high-end cognac for the table, as he usually does, but this time Son objects. I hear Son say he wants to pay for this evening, and that maybe everyone should just order bottled beer, which is only a small fraction of what cognac would cost. This seems reasonable because Son can only afford to pay occasionally, and thus wants to keep the cost down. In fact, for this reason, he initially suggested that we go to a local bar, rather than one catering to the expat and foreigner population in a district across town. While the server waits for us to decide, the cacophonous background noise makes it difficult to hear Dinh's and Son's negotiations. Then, suddenly, I see Dinh push over the high table around which we are standing. All the glasses fall to the floor, and everyone has to clear out for the staff to clean up. As we all go our separate ways, everyone (including me) seems confused about what just transpired. I take a taxi home, leaving with many questions.

The next day I contact Son to see if we can meet for coffee, hoping he can tell me about what happened the previous night. We meet at a café near his house, and his wife joins us. Son starts the conversation by apologizing about what happened. I tell him it is not an issue for me, but that I hope he and Dinh can quickly repair their problems. Son's wife immediately responds to my comment: "Dinh has too much pride. He wants people to know he has a lot of money, all the time." Intrigued by her comment, I ask Son for his version of the story. Son begins as if he wants me to adjudicate the matter:

Before we decided to go out last night, my wife suggested I take everyone to the local bar, where it's less expensive. She said I should pay for the night out last night because Dinh treated us so many times and we are too busy to make him a nice dinner or take him out to a nice place. So I listened to my wife and decided to go to the cheap local bar. The drinks there don't cost as much and they don't even put the expensive stuff on the menu. They don't normally have the expensive cognac in stock, but if you order it, they will go somewhere to buy it and charge you for it. When I suggested to Dinh initially that we just order beer, we didn't have to buy the expensive items, he asked the waiter anyways to go and buy the expensive cognac for us.

I interject that from what I know about the situation, there didn't appear to be cause for such an explosion. "I guess it was my mistake mostly. I said something heavy [*nang ne*] to Dinh," Son replies. "I was also angry that he has to show off. He was boasting [*khoe khoang*] too much about money. He promised us several times he would buy us a car, but my wife convinced me and we believe that he cannot easily afford to buy us a car," He elaborates:

I wanted him to stop spending money and stop making promises to people. Because my wife said he had made promises to people in the village, too. So when I offered to pay, he made sure to order the most expensive items that were not on the menu so I would not pay for them. You know, once in a while, it's fine to do that. It's fine to show off once in a while that you are from over there [overseas]. But Dinh does it all the time. [*What "heavy" things did you say to him?*] I said I know how much money he makes in America, and I said, "You don't make that much money, why do you want to show off all the time?" That was when he pushed the table at the bar.

That evening was the last time I heard from Dinh. I made calls to him in the following days and weeks, but never heard back. However, Son continues to call and send me text messages on occasions when I return to the country. As of this writing, Son says Dinh still has not contacted him, but that he remains in constant communication with Dinh's mother (Son's sister) in Florida. At least three levels of analysis can be used to evaluate the blowup between Dinh and Son. First, the situation may have to do with Son and his wife. Feeling pressured by his wife to cool off his attempts to keep up with Dinh's spending behavior, Son may have been so anxious and stressed out about spending that he wanted to signal explicitly to Dinh to stop spending excessively. Second, perhaps Son, together with his wife, wanted to honor their belief in the principle of reciprocity, especially on the off chance that Dinh would eventually buy them a car. Because they were unable to adequately reciprocate for Dinh's long period of spending money, they may have felt somewhat uneasy and possibly powerless in the imbalanced relationship,[32] and maybe even irritated at the improbability of Dinh buying them a car. This may have prompted Son to put Dinh in his "rightful place" by telling him his income was, in fact, not good enough to boast so much and so frequently, and thus terminate any notion of a promise in their exchange. A third explanation is that Dinh felt humiliated because Son exposed his pecuniary weaknesses in public, something that is rarely put on display by transnational families. That public humiliation led Dinh to blow up at the bar, and subsequently to minimize, or even completely cut off, communications. Dinh felt humiliated because not only did Son question Dinh's ability to pay at the bar, but he denied Dinh the opportunity to display his success as a migrant relative living in the United States. He also revealed what was probably the truth: Dinh was in fact spending beyond his means and could never fulfill his promise to buy Son a car.

Among transnational families with monetary circulation, one of the taboos is to reveal the pecuniary weaknesses of migrants, either by questioning the migrants' ability to pay or by raising doubt about that ability in the public sphere. Doing so is to question the willingness of migrants to circulate money, or worse, exposes that they are unsuccessful migrants. Many studies have pointed out that migrants use their "spending displays to assert their success in the United States."[33] Empirical evidence of this, for example, has been documented for immigrants returning to the homeland in the Philippines,[34] Mexico,[35] and the Dominican Republic.[36]

· · ·

In the three transnational families described here, we see the complexity of social frictions transpiring from promises made by migrants. On the one hand, Cam wanted to maintain her social power over her younger sister by telling Lan for nearly a decade to defer entering a romantic relationship as well as to defer moving to the city. Lan hoped Cam would one day make good on the promise to arrange a marriage for Lan, which would enable her to migrate abroad, or to help her move to the city, where she would have more opportunities for upward mobility. On the other hand, Quang made the extemporaneous promise to help Truc's son study abroad in Australia, only to realize later (or even when he made the promise) that his low-wage work would never allow him to give such a large amount. His subsequent strategy was to avoid communication with Truc, which is perhaps the most prevalent strategy that migrant members of transnational families use to avoid the uncomfortable situation of revealing the limitations of their ability to help out financially, an approach that sometimes results in ending relationships. Finally, Dinh spent money excessively to belie his low status in the United States and to compensate for his inability to fulfill his promise to buy his uncle a car, a promise that itself was primarily boastful. This pattern of boasting was exposed by Son, leading to a blowup at the bar and the subsequent termination of all communication between the uncle and the nephew.

Against the backdrop of macroeconomic changes in post–market reform Vietnam, many non-migrant relatives of transnational families encounter overseas relatives with seemingly large amounts of capital, as evidenced, apparently, by their excessive and compensatory consumption. In the context of years of material deprivation, overseas family members suddenly return with promises of better lives and bright futures. Through these promises, migrant relatives manufacture acquisitive fantasies and mobility dreams among their non-migrant family members. The ostensible pecuniary strengths displayed by migrants also create a culture of raised expectations among non-migrants. Non-migrants thus occasionally make monetary requests to migrant families that appear on the surface to be ludicrous. But the complex entanglements of raised expectations and disappointments are as much about an emergent culture of emulative consumption as they are about the personal consequences experienced by left-behind family members whose overseas relatives have made tall promises within the material landscape of the new Saigon.

CONCLUSION

Special Money in Low-Wage Transnational Families

I NSUFFICIENT FUNDS has sketched an understanding of money in low-wage transnational families within the Vietnam–United States migration corridor. Testimonies from respondents reveal the geographically specific and asymmetric meanings associated with money, obligations, status, and worth in family life across transnational social fields. The study shows that money strengthens bonds of affection among some transnational family members, to be sure, but it can also have the real and dark consequences of alienating and separating others. Focusing on money in the homeland lucidly and significantly highlights the consequences of how and why the visible capital of returnees is set against their invisible labor. We have seen that the bleak realities of blocked mobility and financial precariousness are willfully obscured, if not buried, during return visits by migrants. The very explanation for the complexities, contradictions, and asymmetries pertaining to monetary circulation lies in the concealment of this precariousness, which is often done as a strategy to ignore migrants' failings and to retain social position at home.

How, through the juxtaposition of visible capital and invisible labor within the Vietnam–United States migration corridor, can we frame migrant money as special money?[1] The analytic of special money reveals, yet again, the context of blocked mobility within the indignities of U.S. capitalism. As Viviana Zelizer succinctly points out in her seminal work on money, "Not all dollars are equal . . . . Money is . . . routinely differentiated, not just by varying quantities but also by its special diverse qualities."[2] Her analysis provides the critical lens through which money has been seen as simply a "single, interchangeably absolutely impersonal instrument."[3]

Indeed, non-economic factors that shape and constrain the use of money include the allocation of money, the control of money, the users of money, and the sources of money.[4] Thus, as we have seen in the chapters on social frictions, although money is a medium of exchange on the market, it is not entirely a market phenomenon. And it is not always exchangeable. Furthermore, "money is not homogenous. There are multiple monies, existing in different contexts, and not all of them are the same."[5] Money is social in nature and culturally specific; it is embedded in relations of power and interacts with differences in gender, class, and other categories of differences. When money is not simply fungible, it is therefore appropriate only for specific uses. Money received from inheritances or weddings, for example, falls in the category of special money[6]—that is, money whose use has social and cultural significance.[7] In other words, money is not solely a financial affair. It shapes and is shaped by social relationships, cultural repertoires, and macrostructural determinants.[8]

Insufficient Funds demonstrates that migrant money is special money with variable personal and social meanings for different members of low-wage transnational families. Focusing on money "sent" across borders, Supriya Singh and her colleagues were the first to theorize about *transnational family money* as special money,[9] arguing that it "is transformed by family negotiations and meanings over cultural and physical distance across national borders."[10] My formulation of special money, in one sense, echoes their assertion that various members of transnational families have the "perception that the dollar sent is not the dollar received."[11] Prema Kurien likewise reports in her study of labor migrants in India that non-migrants view migrants' incomes as "serendipitous, easy money, one which is not fully earned. As such, community members [non-migrants] expect that the money will also be disbursed more freely."[12] Similarly, Lisa Åkesson, in her study of Cape Verdean transnationalism, points out that migrant money is special money because people put "particular kinds of money in particular places, and assign it to particular uses."[13]

Considering these various frameworks on special money, I depart from the analyses by Zelizer,[14] Singh et al.,[15] Kurien,[16] and Åkesson[17] in thinking of special money as an issue pertaining primarily or only to earmarking (i.e., part of a family economy of exchange). In my view, the analysis of special money in terms of earmarking within the context of transnational families tends to frame it as a matter upon which and through which recipients of money comply with the allocative and distributive decisions of givers and senders of money. As Åkesson argues, the earmarking of remittances can create conflicts in transnational families because migrants tend to take control over the money they give, while non-migrants claim they are better qualified to decide how money given to them is spent.[18] Thus, the notion of special money calls into question how the earners of money make decisions about its proper uses.[19]

I have shown iteratively in Chapters 3, 4, 8, and 9 the asymmetric conceptions regarding the earmarking of money held by different members of transnational families, which can contribute to potential diversions and conflicts within those families. Starting with perspectives from the homeland was an important research strategy because the spatiality of the homeland is a frontier of worth upon which and for which migrants use their overseas capital to articulate status. The engagement in compensatory consumption upon return visits is a magnified moment[20] that launches, without subtlety or disguise, the transnational expenditure cascade.[21] More concisely, the exposure of visible capital juxtaposed with invisible labor immediately and indubitably sets off manners of differentiation and determinants of hierarchies. These social differentiations and hierarchies are built into (new) reference systems that consumers within transnational families look toward for comparative spending, and that trigger acquisitive fantasies and mobility dreams among those on each level of the economic cascade. Unambiguous spending in leisure spaces and in the purchase of durable goods for left-behind relatives not only raises expectations but also displays relative affluence, even to the most transient observers within the new Saigon.

Significantly, money in transnational families, as special money, serves not only as an important currency of care, but also as a currency of status. This is true regardless of whether the realities behind such money are obscured or simply buried in return visits. I argue that money in transnational families is, most of all, special money because it is a currency that they, the migrants, allocate to themselves. It is special money indeed, to go against Jacques Derrida's conception about the "indecent mediocrity" and "impossibility" of the gift,[22] because it is gifted to the self. To gift money to oneself, a low-wage migrant devises coping strategies for difference, exclusion, and marginalization within the mendacious social contract of the American Dream[23]—a contract to low-wage laborers that disappoints at best, and punishes at worst, through first and foremost the absurdity of widening distributional imbalances.[24] Faced with limited economic opportunities in the United States, migrants turn to the sphere of consumption in the homeland as a source of buying power and self-valorization.

The temptation to give and spend money beyond utility, as shown in Chapters 6, 8, and 9, has set off a transnational expenditure cascade against the backdrop of accelerated economic reform in the homeland. This cascade has significantly altered standards and hierarchies with respect to consumption, leisure, and status signals and is a consequence of socioeconomic precariousness among migrants, who while barely eking out a life in the United States, find opportunities in the homeland to transnationalize their framework for identity, competence, esteem, worth, and status associated with their class position.[25] The homeland thus serves as a powerful (and perhaps the only) social space for expressing meaningful social citizenship within the framework of familial relations.[26] It has, in sum, evolved into the reference point upon which to draw a transnational class system. This reference point foregrounds that the homeland of the developing world, as a spatiality of memory and affection, no longer belongs to what Edward Said once called an "imaginative geography and history," that which helps "the mind to intensify its own sense of itself by dramatizing the difference between what is close to it and what is far away."[27]

This work extends the ongoing critique among migration scholars who object to structuralist explanations about migration[28] based on the spatial distribution of labor and capital in the new global economy.[29] Scholars such as Rhacel Salazar Parrenas and Caroline Brettell[30] object to these structuralist treatments of migrants as reactors manipulated by global capitalism through migration. In using the transnational perspective on migration, I join this objection by highlighting the agency of migrants and their non-migrant family members, and at the same time raise a severe limitation in ongoing studies of transnational practices.

The transnational perspective on migration, inaugurated in the early 1990s, focuses on the "the processes by which *immigrants* build social fields that link together their country of origin and their country of settlement [emphasis added]."[31] This perspective, with its focus on the viewpoints and social practices of those in motion, has fundamentally altered the ways scholars have analyzed the immigrant experience over the past two decades, but it has insufficiently addressed the experiences of those who stay put, yet are also fully embedded in transnational, global, and migratory processes.[32] Thus, a severe limitation in transnational migration studies is the paucity of scholars documenting how migrants interface with the homeland, and thus with their non-migrant relatives.[33] Attentive to this empirical gap, I have tried to model one way to think about transnationalism by underscoring the strategies and tactics—in short, the sense of agency—among different members of transnational families through the perspectives of those who migrate as well as those who stay put.

One problem in addressing the viewpoints of those who never leave their home countries stems from the systematic immobility imposed by Western nations,[34] which make it difficult for citizens of the developing world to travel and reunite with their families. Such transnational separation severely limits day-to-day and face-to-face interactions among family members divided by borders. To capture a more complete and complex view of variable experiences within the entire transnational social field, a strategic research procedure is to anchor more of our analytical gaze in the homeland.[35] Although many contemporary studies of migration invoke a transnational view, or at least refer to it, the field has done disappointingly little to offer perspectives from the homeland that view it not just as a space of identity but as a space within which migrants find meaning and live outside the domain of powerlessness experienced in the destination country.

"If anything," Ali Nobil Ahmad aptly asserts, "new theories of migration reflect the ongoing rational choice and utilitarian economism that pervade the mainstream of migration studies, a field in which the protagonists are only rarely discussed as complex social beings, willing and able to experience the full range of human emotions the rest of us take for granted."[36] Similarly, as Jorgen Carling notes, limited geographical mobility means that "most non-migrants have

never even been to the country where their migrant relatives lead their daily lives
. . . non-migrants relate to life abroad through their relatives, neighbors, and
friends, but have limited ability to verify patchy and sometimes contradictory
pieces of information."[37] The same can be said for scholars who capture experiences only from the vantage points of *immigrants* within transnational social
fields.[38] Precisely because of the structural barriers of legal and economic subordination that prohibit non-migrants from traveling to and exploring "the other
side," this work on transnationality is deliberately situated in the homeland.

MONEY ACROSS TRANSNATIONAL SOCIAL FIELDS

David Harvey writes that although money has universal properties in its exchange value, it is deeply associated with "a wide range of highly decentralized
and particularist decision making."[39] In this sense, Zelizer notes that money
"is not 'free' from social constraints but is another type of socially created currency, subject to particular networks of social relations and its own set of values
and norms."[40] As I have demonstrated, different constituents within transnational families interpret money in discrepant ways. From the standpoint of
non-migrant members, elaborated upon in Chapter 3, monetary distribution
from overseas relatives is a crucial way in which family members express their
affection and care for those left behind. Those who have money earn respect
and are valued as desirable family members, and giving and spending money
on relatives are ways to earn respect, affection, and love among the left-behind.
Money from overseas relatives is thus special money for non-migrants because
it is treated differently from money that belongs to relatives within the country. One reason, which reflects the conception of transnational family money
put forth by Singh et al., is that "people at home idealize the ease with which
money can be earned from overseas."[41]

    In contrast with the views of their left-behind relatives, as discussed in
Chapter 4, migrant members of transnational families aspire to provide for
their families through necessity-driven consumption. At first, they point to self-
sacrifice and altruistic motivations as the core reasons for giving to and spending
money on their non-migrant relatives (e.g., "My central responsibility is to my
family"; "I want them to have enough to live on"). Over time, however, upon
probes, inquiries, and observations of the returnee's social relationships in the

homeland, the picture appears more complicated, underlining the inadequacy of altruism as the central explanation for giving and spending money.

Evidence shows that monetary circulation stems not simply and only from altruistic motivations. It has emerged from consumption beyond calculations of utility, as well as within a deeper logic of self-making, which Anthony Giddens calls a "reflexivity of the self" in coping with "conditions of severe material constraints."[42] The need to fulfill altruistic motivations and the need to rebuff the indignities of low-wage work through consumption are intrinsically and unquestionably connected. Because many low-wage immigrants are unable to find outlets for competence, esteem, worth, and status under conditions of precariousness in the United States, spending money on themselves and on their left-behind relatives produces coherent identities that are perhaps otherwise unobtainable without a homeland to which to return. In the words of Daniel Miller, consumption is "the main arena in which and through which people have to struggle towards control over the definition of themselves and their values."[43] Similarly, Paul DiMaggio conceptualizes material goods as "cultural goods" that are "consumed for what they say about their consumers to themselves and to others as inputs into the production of social relations and identities."[44]

We have seen that Vietnamese immigrants subscribe wholeheartedly to the American Dream ideology and do it most apparently when they occupy multiple social spaces and make relative comparisons about their economic standing across transnational social fields, as shown in Chapter 5. Taking on a transnational optic is how they rationalize their altruistic behaviors and roles as accumulators of capital and their commitment to the material improvement of their lives and the lives of their families. By drawing on what is, in effect, a transnational status system from the homeland, they see the economic structure of the United States not as a disarticulation, but as a link between opportunity and outcome. This is demonstrated, as I have shown in Chapters 6 and 7, when we see the possibilities and pleasures of consumption, the importance of emotional and non-utilitarian meanings attached to commodities, and the relational feelings triggered by those who buy, give, and own those commodities.

We have seen, too, the importance of material acquisitions—a reflection of pecuniary strength—in defining standards of hierarchies and affective bonds among members of transnational families.[45] This ability to express economic standing transnationally is particularly salient when we consider studies that have shown that low-wage workers in the United States tend to experience greater stress about their sense of esteem stemming from their position in the occupational structure than do low-wage workers in other parts of the world (e.g., in Japan and Poland).[46] In the United States, too, we see more powerfully than in any other nation in the industrialized world that economic status plays the central role in people's measuring stick for social worth.[47] In this work, neither migrants nor their non-migrant relatives designated alternative non-economic measuring sticks for defining social status and worth.[48] The confluence of the recently marketized economy in Vietnam, the centrality of the new Saigon as the economic heartbeat of the country, and the mobility aspirations of respondents on both ends of the migration corridor indubitably create new terrains of judgments for social worth, wherein socioeconomic boundaries shape and are shaped by social relations.

Broadening the work of Bourdieu, Caplovitz, and Veblen to a transnational scale,[49] I have shown that compensatory consumption among low-wage migrant men and women, described in Chapter 6, illustrates a kind of status-driven consumption. Moreover, emulative consumption within the context of market reform, described in Chapter 7, challenges the view that consumption among the poor is exclusively tied to a taste for necessity. These patterns can be seen as distinct, but also confluent, where they interact in the transnational expenditure cascade. Return visits by migrants ultimately open up a sphere of consumption that, in most circumstances, is closed to them in the United States. Through emergent standards of hierarchies and differentiations, ideas and practices about money are both contradictory and complex.

Consumptive practices serve as a currency of care, providing the left-behind with daily needs that otherwise might not be met with state provisions from governments in the developing world in a climate of what Parrenas calls a "crisis in the political economy of care" in developing countries.[50] Yet, as discussed in Chapters 7, 8, and 9, consumptive practices reveal, if not reiterate, the importance of materiality among non-migrant respondents, whose material deprivation in the homeland is suddenly refashioned with the visibility of migrant capital. Although they serve as social instruments of care and bonding among families, monetary circulations do not occur without frictions and diversions, as seen in Chapters 8, 9, and 10.

Working overtime, spending, giving, and receiving money evolve as habits—in short, as a way of life for many migrants and their non-migrant relatives. Such habits of expenditure eventually become excessive, to the extent that some migrants enter the world of financial indebtedness in order to sustain the monetization of their social relationships. Others go to the point of making promises, simultaneously out of bonds of affection and to retain social positions, while remaining deluded about their financial capability. This financial bind, cast within the confluence of visible capital and invisible labor, demands that we turn to the unquestioned and yet false premise in the United States about notions of scarcity, rather than abundance and excess, used to justify the subjugation of the low-wage labor force. It is through this lens that we see, finally and in every respect, the special meanings of money to low-wage migrants in transnational families.

THE LOGIC OF EXCESS

The low-wage labor market proliferates precisely and unambiguously because of the waste and excess of the high-wage labor force. This waste and excess has generated demands in the consumption sphere as well as in the sphere of social reproduction (e.g., in the care industry).[51] The proliferation and costliness of high-end consumptive needs (e.g., expensive restaurants, luxury housing, gourmet shops, boutiques, and all types of cleaning and caring services) require the labor-intensive participation of low-wage workers.[52] The concentration of immigrant labor in cities in particular has made these kinds of exuberant spending, once luxuries for the wealthy, now available to the wider economic spectrum, with the exception of low-wage earners.[53] The migrant respondents in this study are clear examples of this labor force,[54] which includes retail sales workers, restaurant workers, cashiers, truck drivers, manicurists, mushroom pickers, and food preparers.[55] Simply put, they work for others to consume in spheres in which they are predominantly excluded from consuming. Privileging consumption as the site of critique and the site of empirical analysis, we can borrow from the work of Georges Bataille on the logic of excess within the political economy of labor to understand the logic of social subjugation within the immigrant low-wage labor force.[56]

Beginning with the anthropological analysis of gift giving by Mauss and taking the darker side of Veblen's investigation into consumption,[57] Bataille insists on the conceptualization and overlapping domains of waste, loss, utility, and expenditure in his "visions of excess."[58] Drawing on the Maussian work on gift giving among the Kwakiutl Indians of the American Northwest, Bataille theorizes that excess in gift giving communicates social rank.[59] Unlike Mauss, however, Bataille generalizes the logic of gift exchange into a universal logic of exchange in the economy. His interest in restoring an analysis of pleasure, of waste, and of loss leads him to push for the notion of "non-productive" expenditure in economic analysis.[60] Thus, Bataille's sociology represents an objection to the economist's refusal to acknowledge how dissipation is central to economic activities.[61] He argues against the "restricted economy" and utilitarian principles of classical liberal economics, and proposes instead a general theory of the economy that does not reduce exchange within the market as simply an arena of production. This contrasts with the theorem of economic liberalism that, as Guido Giacomo Preparata notes, "rationalized the prevailing distribution of wealth, which often tends to be skewed in favor of the elites: that restricted nucleus of financial bureaucratic and military interests commanding a vastly disproportionate share of the nation's wealth."[62]

Classical economics interprets poverty as a latent effect of the economy and holds that the poor must understand their condition as consequent frugality and scarcity in the macro system of economic exchange. This discourse on thrift, Bataille forcefully asserts, is "a miserable conception."[63] Bataille rejects the assumption that resources are scarce—an assumption that has been used to justify imbalances in wage distribution.[64] Instead, he insists on imagining and analyzing a society based on its consumption sphere. This means we need to underscore the pleasures of expenditure (i.e., the conditions around superfluous spending) as integral to the system that robs people of their time in the labor process. Thus, in his attempt to reverse the utility principle of classical economics, he interprets utility and excess as not binaries and mutually exclusive, but as part of a system that, in fact, must confront the question and the problem of abundance, rather than that of scarcity. "A society always produces on the whole more than is necessary to its subsistence," he argues. "It disposes of a surplus."[65]

Why, to follow up on Bataille, is surplus not the emphasis in economic analysis and the answer to macrostructural distributional imbalances? A Bataillean perspective allows us to grasp this fantastical problem because Bataille demands that we look at waste and excess in the general economy to view surplus as the problem, not scarcity. Once we understand that "it is not the store and the workshop, the bank and the factory, that hold the key from which the principles of the economy can be deduced,"[66] we can see through a Bataillean frame how dissipations explain the general law of the economy. This perspective reveals that waste among the elites (e.g., in expensive art, couture clothing, and the boutiqueness of anything) is celebrated and justified, but waste among the poor is seen as useless. In fact, Bataille goes so far as to argue that a huge portion of society's surplus, the "accursed share," goes into violent dissipation; this can occur through war, and also through the symbolic violence of conspicuous and excessive consumption by the rich as a means of putting the poor in their place.[67] After all, for Bataille, a big portion of life is about wasting away, wasting time, and spending money without calculated aims; in short, about superfluous pleasures that are supposed to be enjoyed only among members of a certain class.[68] He writes that surplus in a community "*is the cause of disturbances, changes of structure, and of its entire history* [emphasis added]"; reading more closely, we see that Bataille establishes that the way a community uses its surplus reflects its "fundamental division."[69]

The masters, who act as if they were the expression of society itself, are preoccupied—more seriously than with any other concern—with showing that they do not in any way share the abjection of the men they employ. *The end of the workers' activity is to produce in order to live, but the bosses' activity is to produce in order to condemn the working producers to a hideous degradation* [emphasis in original]—for there is no disjunction possible between, on the one hand, the characterization the bosses seek through their modes of expenditure, which tend to elevate them high above human baseness, and on the other hand this baseness itself, of which this characterization is a function.[70]

Clearly, Bataille is speaking about the darker side of what Veblen criticized half a century earlier and termed "conspicuous consumption";[71] for Bataille, the notion of expenditure is not a status game among the rich, but a mode of domination that symbolically puts the poor in their place through the articulation of scarcity as the principle of the economy.

THE WORTH OF LOW-WAGE WORK

Paula Chakravartty and Denise Ferreira da Silva call the economic crisis of early-twenty-first-century capitalism a product of the "architectures of U.S. Empire and apparatuses of social subjugation."[72] Reading through a Bataillean lens, we see how the logic of excess, as a function of distributional imbalances, generates wage variability on the consequent hourglass economy that has established low-wage capitalism in the United States.[73] This variability is specific to the United States, given the severe lack of regulatory apparatuses in terms of social provisions for the disenfranchised, which, to be sure, as articulated by a number of scholars, is distinct to the country.[74] The hourglass economy, "characterized by a proliferation of jobs at the top and the bottom of the wage distribution for those with high and low educations, but few jobs in the middle for those with modest educational attainments,"[75] disproportionably relies on immigrant labor at the bottom of the economic pyramid.[76] As Sassen-Koob succinctly notes, "The availability of immigrant labor reduces the pressure on backward sectors of capital to change techniques to production or to improve working conditions unacceptable to national workers."[77]

While economic restructuring over the past several decades has decreased wages in real terms for their indispensable,[78] and often preferred, labor,[79] the demand for immigrants in the productive sphere of the low-wage labor force has increased dramatically, and yet it simultaneously excludes them from the consumption sphere. The important research program by Saskia Sassen has shown that the casualization and informalization of work in the new economy have created new conditions of growth, such that immigrants continue to fulfill the "ongoing demand for a low-wage labor supply even in the most advanced economic sectors."[80]

Rather than viewing the decline of manufacturing work as obsolescence, as scholars such as William Wilson have done,[81] firms proliferate in their escape from regulatory apparatus as a form of adaptation by "downgrading" numerous dimensions of work at the bottom of the economic pyramid.[82] This adaptation, which rests on a "particular form of powerlessness" among immigrants,[83] has necessarily incorporated them into low-wage labor.[84] Chapter 6 specifically underscored the paradox of this international division of labor that relies on immigrants in the low-wage market and yet excludes them, through wage suppression, from the sphere of consumption. For example, Vietnamese migrants, who help sustain the high-wage sector in the United States through the many services they provide, cannot participate as consumers in the spaces in which they serve, but do so volubly in the homeland as a way of rebuffing conditions of precariousness.

The recruitment and retention of immigrant labor unquestionably helps advanced countries flourish,[85] while at the same time deepening the subordination of the low-wage labor force through restricted and blocked mobility as well as through the segregation of these workers from the rest of the working class.[86] State apparatuses sustain these low wages, not only by establishing unlivable benchmarks for minimum-wage earners but also through outdated assumptions about expenditures used to classify poverty levels.[87] These state apparatuses of social subjugation increase the precariousness of the low-wage labor force in the productive sphere.[88]

To succinctly underscore the peripheralization of low-wage work in the absence of regulatory apparatuses in this country, consider that surveys of poverty rates across the world,[89] after adjusting for taxes and government transfers,[90] show that the United States has the highest poverty rate among all Western European, Nordic, and Anglophone countries.[91] Furthermore, it is well known that the definition of the U.S. poverty level, a baseline used to determine eligibility for government transfers, is severely outdated and grossly underestimates how much it takes to meet basic needs to simply survive, let alone participate in the pleasures of consumption.

Studies[92] have shown that, on average, to meet basic minimum needs (e.g., adequate food and shelter),[93] families need an income equal to about two times the federal poverty level, which in 2012 was $13,970 for a single worker and $23,050 for a family of four.[94] For instance, a two-income household with two children, and the adults working full-time at the prevailing federal minimum wage of $7.25, would have a total income of about $30,160 a year,[95] a severely insufficient amount to meet basic needs for a family of four in cities such as New York or Houston; suburban towns such as Aurora, Illinois; and rural areas such as Decatur County, Iowa.[96] This income, in fact, barely meets half of the basic expenses to survive in these regions of the country. As I have shown throughout, most migrant respondents must creatively strategize if they are to survive and to accumulate enough for return visits to the homeland. They do so by living in shared housing, working overtime, or denying themselves some of the basic standards of decency that their middle-class counterparts enjoy.

Such descriptions, of course, capture only the baseline of adequate living, according to an absolute measure of poverty level that is distinct to the United States.[97] The picture is more complicated when we consider that minimum-wage earners, and certainly some members of the low-wage labor force (i.e., those earning any more than 100 percent of the poverty-level income) are not part of the poor and thus are disqualified from government assistance. This is because full-time work places minimum-wage earners (slightly) above the poverty rate, yet with earnings that fulfill barely *half* of the basic needs for decent survival in most parts of the country.[98] Furthermore, the low-wage labor force includes any worker who makes less than 200 percent of the prevailing minimum wage, which at the maximum ceiling translated to about $30,000 in 2012.[99] These statistics highlight the state as a real financial usurer in U.S. capitalism. Yet these quantitative typologies about the poor and near poor do not capture *poverty* as a relative experience and an identity that cannot simply be a category or classification according to the government's dollar designation. David K. Shipler astutely notes, "More people than those officially designated as 'poor' are, in fact, weighted down with the troubles associated with poverty."[100]

Low-wage workers can be viewed as the "major philanthropists of our society."[101] They endure great sacrifices—through the donation of their time in the form of physical, emotional, and even intimate labor—that permit the richest economy of the world to flourish.[102] Yet the U.S. economy is distinct among those of industrialized nations in its severely deficient public care provisions for the low-wage labor force. These workers must therefore make sense of the social subjugation they endure by devising personal strategies for the flow of their hard-earned money so they can attain a sense of competence, esteem, worth, and status. If the conventions of U.S. capitalism force members of this labor market to earn less than what is required to meet basic needs, then perhaps they should take up the habit of keeping a healthy distance from the American Dream ideology. Most of all, it should be routine, and profoundly justified, for low-wage workers to engage in "fiscal disobedience," including indebtedness as a form of social protest.[103] Only through this kind of disobedience can some low-wage workers recuperate from and even thrive in what otherwise would be a permanent life of insufficient funds. Perhaps eventually more of them—and more of us—will engage in this and other forms of social protest that could lead to a more balanced distribution of resources as a matter of decency rather than one of equality.

APPENDIX

Methodology and Interviewees

The analysis for this study is based on three specific sets of data collected mostly in Saigon. The first set of data is based on separate, but overlapping, phases of in-depth interviews with 98 individuals in transnational families, including low-wage Vietnamese immigrants from the United States and their non-migrant relatives in Saigon. I interviewed each respondent more than once, and many of them several times, during a span of seven years that began in May 2004 and ended in September 2011. These participants were drawn from an initial list of migrant respondents whose eligibility was determined by the combined regularity of their return visits and their low-wage work status. After I sampled the migrant respondents, I obtained a sample of their non-migrant relatives. Respondents represent transnational families from all of the nineteen urban districts of Saigon.

The second set of data comprises field notes I collected systematically while based in Saigon for a total of thirty-five discontinuous months. The notes were gathered at distinct intervals, including fifteen research trips during each summer and winter between 2004 and 2011,[1] as well as two intensive phases of fieldwork. The first phase was a ten-month stint conducted from May 2004 through March 2005. The second phase was a seven-month stint from January through July 2009. A third set of data comprises twenty-three exploratory interviews I conducted in 2009 with a group of local individuals in Saigon who have no association with migration, transnational actors, or relatives abroad.

In sum, the final analysis includes interviews and participant observations with 121 individuals in Saigon: 46 migrant and 52 non-migrant members of transnational family networks, as well as 23 locals. Twenty-four of the migrant interviewees are women and 22 are men. The age range is twenty-eight to fifty-three, with an average age of about thirty-nine.[2] Among the non-migrant respondents, 28 are women and 24 are men. They range in age from twenty-one to seventy-three, with an average age of about forty-one.[3] Of the locals I interviewed, 13 are women and 10 are men, ranging in age from nineteen to fifty-one, with an average age of about thirty-five.[4] (The migrant and non-migrant interviewees are listed by gender, occupation, and age in Tables 1–4, located at the end of this appendix).

DEFINING THE SAMPLE: DESTINATION COUNTRY,
LOW-WAGE STATUS, AND FREQUENCY OF RETURN VISITS

I began the study with three related questions: How do social ties develop among transnational families in the homeland when immigrants make return visits? Why are return visits significant for transnational families? Why and how are homeland family dynamics significant for immigrants living abroad?

At a general level, I was interested in the reunification process between immigrants and their left-behind family members in light of the fact that many of the immigrants had just begun to make return visits in the mid-1990s, when Vietnam and the United States reestablished diplomatic relations after a twenty-year hiatus. Return visits intensified in the late 1990s for many living in the diaspora, and have become a way of life for some immigrants in the twenty-first century. I began anchoring my conceptual ideas for this project in 2004, although it is worth noting that at that time I had just completed another book on international marriages linking women in Vietnam and overseas Vietnamese men, for which I spent more than thirty discontinuous months in Saigon between 1996 and 2004.[5] At a more specific level, I was interested in the dynamics of transnational families from the standpoint of the homeland. My aim was to investigate the ways in which overseas relatives affected family life when they returned. I initially thought of money as only one aspect of the reunification process for transnational families, but it became the dominant theme as I conducted fieldwork, and ultimately became the focus of this book.

My original plan was to interview migrant returnees from different countries of the Vietnamese diaspora, but after interviewing more than a dozen migrants from several countries, I realized that the differing economic contexts of these countries made it impossible to compare the experiences of low-wage migrants from the United States with those of low-wage migrants elsewhere. One could design a project to make these comparisons, but considering the questions I sought to answer, comparing cross-national experiences of migrants was not feasible for a project of this scope. I came to this realization when I considered international disparities in economic opportunity structures and social welfare systems.

For example, the low-wage labor markets in France and Australia, two countries with large Vietnamese immigrant populations, have meanings and consequences that are very different from those of the low-wage labor market in the United States. This is particularly true when we compare different health care systems and social benefits provided by the respective governments.[6] Most of the migrant respondents in this study do not have health care insurance, for example, although I did meet migrants who worked in low-paid menial jobs solely because such jobs provided health care insurance for their families and who had opted for this reason to forgo better-paying jobs with, for instance, co-ethnic employers. In contrast, Vietnamese-origin nationals of Australia and France enjoy universal health care benefits provided by their governments. The issue of health care and other social benefits (i.e., benefits that are provided by various countries of the developed world to all their citizens, but that some citizens in the United States do not enjoy) is paramount to the migrant respondents' sense of class precariousness.

I also quickly realized that the Vietnamese have devised a hierarchical way of ranking migrants of the diaspora according to their destination countries, with the United States at the top, for reasons that are easy to understand. First, more than half of overseas Vietnamese reside in the United States. Second, the United States has a particular and painfully intimate history with Vietnam, as well as having the status of a global economic superpower. The American influence, especially through the return visits of Vietnamese American immigrants, is much more visible than the influence of immigrants from other parts of the globe. In some ways, the American Dream ideology, a topic of Chapter 5, is stronger among some migrants and their non-migrant relatives in Vietnam than it is in the United States. Finally, I met many local respondents who thought migrants from the United States were more ostentatious with their spending than were migrants from other parts of the world. This view of migrants from the United States was sometimes positive and sometimes negative, depending on the context of evaluation.

Although further investigation (which I do not provide in this book) is needed, the initial phase of research pertaining to different parts of the diaspora yielded enough differences that I decided to isolate the experiences of overseas Vietnamese from the United States and the experiences of their non-migrant relatives. I believe that isolating the specific experiences of transnational family members in the Vietnam–United States migration corridor produced analytical clarity and underscored the importance of transnational (rather than global) social fields that link specific nation-states with particular historical relationships. I should note that it is possible that some family members in Vietnam have overseas relatives in multiple countries. Likewise, some Vietnamese Americans may have family members in different parts of the diaspora. This global dispersion is a fascinating history, but one I cannot adequately address in this book, so I abstain from it.

After I decided to isolate the experiences of Vietnamese migrants from the United States, low-wage status was the second criterion used to generate the sample of migrants in order to understand a specific experience of social class and how it assumes different social and economic meanings in the homeland. I define low-wage workers as non-college-educated, hourly paid workers who, because of their lack of a college degree, face barriers to stable employment and to the benefits that many college-credentialed jobs offer. In demographic terminology,[7] these workers earn 200 percent or less of the prevailing minimum wage, which ranged from $5.15 to $7.25 per hour between 2004 and 2011. Notably, 15 percent occupy jobs with full health benefits, which might put them closer to lower-middle-class status in the United States.[8] About 20 percent of the migrant respondents work for co-ethnic employers, and 10 percent own businesses that generate higher wages than those earned by hourly paid workers, but because such businesses tend to be unstable, their incomes are unpredictable and fluctuate greatly from month to month.

To ensure clear measurements, I did not include any worker whose reported annual income is greater than $35,000. The average reported annual income of all respondents is about $26,000, with more than a quarter of them making less than $20,000. There are a few self-employed individuals who make more than $35,000 annually, but those incomes are household incomes, which means they involve the labor of more than one individual, even though the person I interviewed sometimes thought of the income as his or hers alone. For example, one woman I interviewed owns a small nail salon that earns about $50,000 a year. Thus, when I asked her how much income she generated, she said she makes that amount yearly. However, upon close inspection, I found out that her husband helps at the salon almost every day and does not have a job apart from his "help" at the nail salon. Thus, the income is a household income.

I deliberately focused on low-wage workers for several reasons. Census data reveal that Vietnamese Americans are overwhelmingly concentrated in the low-wage labor market. In 2010, only about a quarter of Vietnamese Americans had at least a bachelor's degree, while among the other five major Asian American groups nearly half of the Japanese, more than half of the Chinese, Filipinos, and Koreans, and 75 percent of Asian Indians had at least a bachelor's degree.[9] Correspondingly, Vietnamese immigrants had the lowest rate of workers in management, professional, and related occupations. Only slightly more than a quarter (27 percent) of Vietnamese workers in the United States had professional and management jobs, compared with 43 percent of Filipinos, 47 percent of Koreans, 53 percent of Chinese, 55 percent of Japanese, and 68 percent of Asian Indians. At the other end of the occupational spectrum, nearly a third (32 percent) of all Vietnamese workers were in service occupations, compared with 20 percent of Filipinos, the next-largest group.[10] Another justification for my focus on low-wage workers across different ethnic groups is the surprising fact that low-wage migrants are more likely than their high-wage counterparts to give money to the homeland. Not only do they send a larger proportion of their incomes than do high-wage migrants, but they also send more in absolute terms, as documented by economist Michele Wucker.[11] Consequently, a central aim of this study is to capture how low-wage workers redefine, or convert, their low-wage status in the United States to a higher-status position in the homeland. This is an important task because a significant portion of low-wage migrants' incomes is spent in the homeland, and their incomes represent a chief portion of all the macroeconomic indicators used to measure economic well-being in developing countries.

As a third criterion for the sample, to understand the lives of individuals who have regular transnational ties to their homeland, I restricted eligible respondents to migrants who made at least five return trips to Vietnam during the decade from 1995 to 2005. Furthermore, no eligible respondent was absent from Vietnam for more than thirty months at a time during that period. With a few exceptions, migrant respondents had to have stayed in Vietnam for at least one month on each of their visits to qualify for the sample. Meeting this criterion never became a problem because virtually every low-wage migrant I met on return visits comes for longer periods in order to make the high cost of passage worth their while. Because most work in hourly paid jobs that can easily be performed by their coworkers, it is not difficult for them to take extensive time off from work, as long as they can afford to forgo the pay. As mentioned, many take on overtime work or additional jobs, depending on shifting financial circumstances, when they return home as a strategy to make up for wages lost during their absence.

ELIGIBILITY, AVAILABILITY, AND INTERVIEW PROCEDURES

Because no roster of transnational families exists, the first step was to create a pool of eligible respondents from which to draw a sample. During the first phase of intensive fieldwork, between May 2004 and March 2005, four full-time research assistants, supervised by Hanh Nguyen, a graduate student in sociology at Vietnam National University, helped me recruit eligible respondents who were on return visits to Saigon during that period. We recruited through personal social networks from my previous book project and through various spaces (e.g., health clubs, real estate agencies, and upscale cafés) that cater to overseas Vietnamese—almost exclusively migrant returnees. The upscale cafés and health clubs were where we met more than a quarter of the low-wage migrants. Merchants in Vietnam no doubt understand the spending habits of overseas Vietnamese and have established high-end venues to cater to them. For example, I could easily walk into any number of large cafés in Saigon on any particular afternoon and identify dozens, if not hundreds, of overseas Vietnamese migrants as potential respondents. These cafés include any branch of the popular Windows Café and the hip Central Café, located under the Citibank Tower in the city, both of which are popular gathering places in the evenings for overseas Vietnamese returnees. Because of the gendered nature of these spaces, two of my research assistants also went to more femininized commercial spaces, such as beauty salons, to recruit overseas migrant women for the study.

Through the process of meeting these overseas migrants at various hubs across the city, and by way of supplemental snowball sampling, we ended up with 324 *eligible* migrant interviewees by December 2004, a process of recruitment that effectively took eight months. Because I originally set out to interview migrant returnees from many parts of the diaspora, this pool of 324 eligible interviewees included migrants from such diverse places as France, Taiwan, and Australia.

To avoid the problems of self-selection and systematic bias, I selected 100 potential respondents from among these 324 migrants by using a random-number table to generate a simple random sample. From this procedure, I ended up with 83 migrants from all over the diaspora, of whom 46 were from the United States. It is important to note again that we met overseas Vietnamese from different parts of the diaspora, but I decided to focus on migrants from the United States because of the distinct nature of the transnational ties between the United States and Vietnam, as discussed in Chapter 2. I conducted interviews with 21 Vietnamese migrants from France, Canada, and Australia, as well as 10 from South Korea, Taiwan, Cambodia, and Laos. However, the interviews with non-U.S. overseas Vietnamese are not included in the analysis, for reasons that I have already discussed.

Next, we had to assess the availability of respondents, because the visiting migrants had a limited amount of time in Vietnam. About one-third of the initial interviews were conducted during the first half of 2005, after our initial determination of eligibility. The remaining interviews were administered from 2005 through 2011, when I conducted fieldwork during periods that coincided with the migrants' return. Except for one summer and one winter, I spent every summer and winter from 2004 through 2011 in Saigon, so meeting up with the eligible respondents, with whom we maintained long-distance contact, was easy. Also helpful was the fact that I got to know the migrants' left-behind family members in Vietnam during their return visits, as well as in their absence.

I interviewed non-migrants in overlapping phases with the interviews conducted with migrant returnees. As noted earlier, I found that genealogical information does not always reflect depth or closeness of relationships. For example, it is not unusual for migrants to provide monetary support to their non-migrant first cousins more readily than to their own siblings. Thus, I identified non-migrant relatives who were recipients of money, rather than assumed the importance of their genealogical relations to the migrants. Åkesson notes that monetary support plays "a crucial role not only for relations between those who have left and those who have stayed, but also for relations between those remaining at home."[12]

The unit of analysis for this study is the transnational family. As mentioned, the initial entry into each transnational family network began with migrant respondents. However, for logistical reasons, interviews with migrants and non-migrant family members were not conducted sequentially. Consequently, sometimes I interviewed non-migrant relatives before interviewing the migrants. In four cases, I interviewed one side of the transnational family but not the other side, for several reasons, including unavailability or unwillingness on one side of the transnational family to participate in the study, and logistical reasons that impeded coordination of the interviews.

For example, in Chapter 3, I tell the story of Linh, a non-migrant, and her cousin, Gloria, a migrant from Orange County, California. Even though I met Gloria, talked to her informally, and then formally interviewed Linh several times, I did not have the opportunity to formally interview Gloria. Therefore, I did not include Gloria in my sample of migrant interviewees in Table 1. Likewise, in Chapter 9, I report on the story of Vu, a migrant from Southern California and his sister, Trieu, a non-migrant from Saigon. Even though I got to know Vu and Trieu well, I had the opportunity to conduct a formal interview with only Vu. Therefore, I excluded Trieu from the sample of non-migrants in Table 3. Because this study is more interview-based than ethnographic, I note these rare exceptions to convey procedural clarity.

In addition to the interviews in Saigon, I visited fourteen of the overseas migrants in various locations in the United States: ten in and around Los Angeles or San Francisco, and two each in Atlanta and Boston. The non-California visits were brief and occurred when I incidentally visited those cities to deliver lectures. The visits to the Californians were regular. These visits allowed me to understand the contexts of migrants' lives in their communities in the United States, which more often than not were quite different from their lifestyles in Saigon.

The interviews focused on the formation of transnational ties, experiences of return activities and reconnections in Vietnam and the diaspora, spending habits, consumption patterns, monetary decisions and behaviors, evaluations of others' use of money, and future plans for sustaining transnational households. My goal was to capture the activities of giving, spending, and receiving money before, during, and after migrants' return visits. I asked family members to describe as much as possible their perceptions of economic behaviors and the cultural and social meanings they assign to those behaviors. In addition, I wanted to understand how these family members judge one another and themselves with respect to their viewpoints on money, especially how they define their mutual obligations and social worth across transnational social fields.

All respondents had at least one formal, recorded, semi-structured, in-depth interview with me, and with a few exceptions, I interviewed respondents several times over several years.[13] More than three-quarters of the respondents gave more than four interviews each.

All the initial interviews lasted from ninety minutes to four hours, with the modal ones lasting about two hours. Some of the subsequent interviews were not recorded, and most were shorter than the original interviews. All interviews were held at times and in places requested by the respondents, who chose cafés, restaurants, their homes, and other spaces. Most of the time, I invited respondents to my apartment to be interviewed because I had an office; about 30 percent of the interviewees took me up on that offer. All the respondents agreed to additional interviews, and more than half allowed my assistants and me to contact them for participant observations with little or no prior notice. On such occasions, we often dropped by their house or invited them to gatherings in public spaces. These stints of participant observation were mostly extemporaneous and involved daily routines that allowed me to informally probe for information that had come up during the interviews.

Interviews were conducted and recorded with the permission of respondents. I have native fluency in the Vietnamese language, which allowed me to conduct most interviews in Vietnamese, and to use English whenever respondents preferred to speak English. Surprisingly, no clear pattern distinguished non-migrants and migrants with respect to their preferred language. I conducted every interview for this project, and my four research assistants in Vietnam, two of whom are fluent in English, transcribed all the interviews verbatim. Two of my research assistants translated half of the Vietnamese transcripts into English, and I translated the rest myself. I listened to and cross-checked each interview for accuracy of both transcription and translation. Interview and ethnographic data were analyzed in the tradition of the grounded theory approach,[14] using the constant comparative method of generating themes and categories for analysis. This approach to data analysis allowed me to read interviews and determine whether to conduct additional interviews and follow up with respondents.

Overall, the analysis relies much more on interview data than on fieldwork. Even though I provide ethnographic data from my fieldwork, open-ended, in-depth interview data are far superior to ethnographic data in capturing individuals' worldviews, specifically pertaining to judgments about monetary circulation within family life. Interviews allow respondents to describe, narrate, and evaluate their worlds, which permits the researcher to develop analytical categories that are relevant to the issues at hand.[15] On some occasions, witnessing the economic behaviors of respondents allowed me to generate analytical categories. However, because respondents rarely had difficulty talking in a straightforward fashion about money (i.e., unlike comparable discussions in Western cultures), I never felt social or emotional barriers to asking questions about money. Simply put, it is rare to meet someone in a social setting in Saigon where issues of money do not come up in the first encounter. Likewise, I do not believe the respondents ever felt awkward asking me about my financial life (or about many other dimensions of my life, for that matter). Readers interested in my experiences doing interviews and conducting transnational research as a Vietnamese immigrant in relation to questions about the "insider/outsider role" in terms of ethnicity, class, and age can consult the research appendix of my previous book, where I elaborate on issues of entry and rapport.[16]

Name	Occupation	Age
1. An	Restaurant worker	46
2. Bay-Huong	Factory worker	29
3. Bich	Clerical worker	38
4. Cam	Supermarket cashier	38
5. Chi	Restaurant worker	52
6. Cuc	Hair stylist	47
7. Dao	Nail salon worker	51
8. Doan	Retail clerk	34
9. Duc	Restaurant worker	53
10. Giang	Warehouse packaging worker	41
11. Han	Amusement park worker	45
12. Hien	Nail salon worker	43
13. Hoa	Supermarket cashier	46
14. Hong	Eyeglass factory worker	46
15. Hue	Hair salon worker	29
16. Luu	Food preparer	34
17. Nga	Restaurant server	29
18. Ngan	Restaurant worker	36
19. Ngoc	Assistant manager of hair salon	32
20. Phung	Typist	34
21. Siu	Clerical worker	39
22. Thao	Department store cashier	35
23. Trinh	Nail salon worker	42
24. Tuyet	Amusement park worker	42
Average age		40

Name	Occupation	Age
1. Chanh	Construction worker	37
2. Chinh	Car mechanic	38
3. Cong	Taxi driver	42
4. Dai	Car mechanic	28
5. Dinh	Carpenter	36
6. Hiep	Mushroom farm worker	52
7. Khang	Machine operator	43
8. Kiet	Truck driver	38
9. Loc	Retail clerk	31
10. Loi	Convenience store cashier	34
11. Long	Car mechanic	37
12. Luc	Produce market handler	42
13. Mach	Hotel maintenance worker	38
14. Phong	Furniture deliveryman	32
15. Phuc	Supermarket stock clerk	47
16. Quang	Airplane cabin cleaner	42
17. Quoc	Hotel maintenance worker	43
18. Quy	Electrical maintenance worker	41
19. Sang	Retail sales worker	37
20. Trai	Department store clerk	36
21. Vinh	Gas station owner	36
22. Vu	Supermarket butcher	39
Average age		39

TABLE 3: OCCUPATION AND AGE OF
FEMALE NON-MIGRANT INTERVIEWEES

Name	Occupation	Age
1. An-Phi	Unemployed	34
2. Diep	Secretary	26
3. Dieu	Unemployed	43
4. Ha	Drugstore cashier	38
5. Kieu	Lightbulb merchant	56
6. Kim-Le	Unemployed	39
7. Ky	Department store clerk	49
8. Lan	Tailor	27
9. Lien	Textiles merchant	62
10. Linh	Teacher	30
11. Loan	Unemployed	32
12. Mai	Retail store sales	28
13. Mai-Van	Unemployed	34
14. My-Chi	Unemployed	55
15. Ngon	Data-entry clerk	41
16. Nhi	Unemployed	32
17. Ninh	Unemployed	61
18. Nu	Unemployed	52
19. Phuong	Restaurant worker	31
20. Quyen	Office worker	25
21. Thanh	Bookkeeper	31
22. Thu	Owner of a small café	35
23. Tien	Lightbulb merchant	51
24. Trieu	Restaurant worker	32
25. Truc	Unemployed	54
26. Vy	Unemployed	36
27. Xuan	Unemployed	26
28. Yen	Unemployed	22
Average age		39

TABLE 4: OCCUPATION AND AGE OF
MALE NON-MIGRANT INTERVIEWEES

Name	Occupation	Age
1. Bao	Retail clerk	32
2. Canh	Hotel receptionist	36
3. Chung	Unemployed	73
4. Duoc	Nightclub attendant	43
5. Duong	Hotel receptionist	30
6. Hai	Lightbulb merchant	53
7. Hoang	Unemployed	51
8. Khoi	Owner of small shop	32
9. Lam	Food hawker	47
10. Manh	Unemployed	55
11. Nhan	Unemployed	58
12. Quach	Unemployed	64
13. Son	Owner of small shop	48
14. Ta	Unemployed	28
15. Tan	Student	24
16. Thang	Construction worker	44
17. Thinh	Unemployed	43
18. Tin	Bartender	40
19. Tong	Manuel worker (pipe installation)	46
20. Trong	Student	22
21. Tung	Electrician	29
22. Tuong	Student	21
23. Vien	Owner of small shop	68
24. Vuong	Machine port operator	39
Average age		43

NOTES

CHAPTER I

1. Except for instances in which I wish to magnify the meanings of the term "immigrant," I will generally use the terms "migrants" and "non-migrants," instead of the crystallized term "immigrants." I do so to underscore the nature of migration as a process, rather than to label migration as a uni-directional status that characterizes the term "immigrants." For discussion of this distinction, see Mahler 1995, 5.

2. I will go into more detail about this history in Chapter 2.

3. Regarding note 1, the terminology gets even more complicated when we refer to labels such as "transnational migrants" and "transmigrants." I will rarely use these terms in this book because they are meaningless to my respondents, who only call themselves migrants, immigrants, overseas migrants, or non-migrants, even if they lead transnational lives. I am aware, however, of the literature that uses the term "transmigrants"; see, for example, Schiller 1999; Schiller, Basch, and Blanc 1995.

4. I have changed all real names to protect the confidentiality of respondents.

5. Although the metric system prevails in Vietnam, I have converted all measurements to the imperial (standard) measuring system for clarity to readers in the United States.

6. All four of her siblings work in garment factories nearby, one of the largest labor niches in Thu Duc. Only one sister, Lan, moved to the city to work in a tailor shop.

7. For a lengthy treatment of the situation among unaccompanied refugee minors who were part of the exodus after the Vietnam War, and who were later either sponsored to the West or repatriated to Vietnam, see Freeman and Huu 2003.

8. I have chosen to retain the real names of all public spaces I refer to throughout the book. Some of them, such as the Monaco Club, have closed down since I began the field-

work, but others have stayed in business. Readers familiar with Saigon will recognize these places as central sites of leisure for the overseas Vietnamese population.

9. All dollar amounts refer to U.S. dollars unless designated "VND," which refers to Vietnamese dongs. In late 2011, $1 was equivalent to about 20,000 VND.

10. As I will elaborate in Chapter 6, when foreigners and overseas Vietnamese talk about "locals," they mean the local population. By using this label, they also refer to spaces within the city that cater to different segments of the population, with three distinct groups: "locals," overseas Vietnamese, and foreigners (by which most mean white Americans and Europeans) living in the city.

11. "Viet Kieu" refers to "overseas Vietnamese." See Chan and Tran 2011.

12. Divergent viewpoints exist with respect to classification of the American class structure. For example, some studies differentiate between the "working poor," "the near-poor," "the underclass," and the "working class." To complicate the picture further, other studies refer to the "truly disadvantaged" and the "precariat class." In this work, I refer to the Vietnamese American respondents as "low-wage workers." Most of these workers' incomes are above the poverty level, but they make 200 percent of or less than the minimum wage. The majority of the respondents are part of the working class because, by Lamont's definition, these workers have relatively stable employment, but since they lack college degrees, they face severe barriers to obtaining better jobs. Yet the respondents in this study are more heterogeneous than the descriptions provided by Lamont in her study of the working class because of the immigration factor. Some respondents, for example, work for co-ethnics who pay them relatively high wages (e.g., as nail salon workers earning $2,500 per month), but their jobs can be unstable and unpredictable. For more detailed discussions on these variations, see Gilbert 2010; Lamont 2000; Newman 1999; Newman and Chen 2008.

13. For a discussion of conditions of low-wage work, see Gautie and Schmitt 2010.

14. In Chapter 10, I return to and elaborate on the problem of this categorical system of wages, especially pertaining to the poverty level in the United States.

15. Capps et al. 2003, 1.

16. Newman and Chen 2008; for information about the poverty level, see Federal Register 2012.

17. Newman and Chen 2008, 8.

18. I discuss the significance of return visits in detail in the next chapter.

19. Donor Working Group 2012, 10.

20. Abrego 2009; Åkesson 2009; Dreby 2010a; McKenzie and Menjivar 2011; Singh 2006, 2009; Thai 2006, 2009, 2012a.

21. For example, see Fajnzylber and Lopez 2007; Funkhouser 1995; Lucas and Stark 1985; Orozco 2002; Russell 1986; Stark 1986; Stark and Lucas 1988; Taylor 1999; Terry and Wilson 2005; Vanwey 2004; Yu 1979; Zarate-Hoyos 2004.

22. The Vietnam–United States migration corridor is the twentieth-largest migration flow in the world; see Ratha, Mohapatra, and Silwa 2011, 5.

23. The phrase "monetary circulation" has been used in macroanalysis of the economy, particularly in economic history. To the best of my knowledge, however, it has not been used in the study of migrant money and transnational families. Moreover, and importantly,

I have not seen giving, spending, and receiving analyzed as related processes. On monetary circulation and macroeconomic analysis, see Kuroda 2008.

24. See Chapters 8 and 10 for coverage of large purchases.

25. In rare cases, migrants helped with house renovations or businesses, but money was generally given or spent on daily consumption. The modal amounts given to non-migrants ranged from $125 to $300 per month.

26. The amount migrants sent generally accounted for at least 10 to 25 percent of their net incomes.

27. Wucker 2004, 1.

28. Safri and Graham 2010, 109.

29. This is based on 2006 data; Safri and Graham 2010, 108–9.

30. Safri and Graham 2010, 111.

31. For recent studies that tackle the topic of money among low-wage workers living across two countries, see Abrego 2009, Dreby 2010a, and Schmalzbauer 2008. Scholars cite sturdy evidence that contemporary global capitalism has produced new "employment regimes," whereby the labor of immigrants in the low-wage sector has become a necessary companion to the emergence of markets for highly skilled labor, especially in global cities. See, for example, the work of Saskia Sassen (1994, 1995, 1998).

32. The argument I make here, to be clear, does not ignore the scholarly efforts that have documented the ways in which non-migrants spend money, such as on daily expenditures and durable goods. See, for example, Itzigsohn 1995 and Itzigsohn et al. 1999.

33. Exceptions to this include, for example, Abrego 2009; Grasmuck and Pessar 1991.

34. Basch, Glick Schiller, and Szanton-Blanc 1994.

35. Goldring 1998, 2003; Levitt 2001b; Schmalzbauer 2005b, 2008.

36. Waters 1999, 102.

37. Capps et al. 2003, 1.

38. Zelizer 1989.

39. Wimmer and Schiller 2002, 2003.

40. For more details on the research procedures, including sampling, see the Appendix.

41. Although Saigon's name was changed to Ho Chi Minh City when the South surrendered to Northern Vietnamese military troops in 1975, most people I met in contemporary Vietnam still refer to the city as "Saigon" or simply "Thanh Pho" [The City]. I echo their frames of reference by using the name "Saigon," and "Saigonese" to refer to the locals there.

42. For studies that look at social changes since the Doi Moi economic reform, see Kokko 1998; Nghiep and Quy 2000; Pelzer 1993; Thai 2009; Turner and Nguyen 2005; Waller and Cao 1997; Werner and Belanger 2002.

43. Furthermore, Carruthers notes that the official 300th-year celebration of the city in 1998 was titled "Saigon 300 Years" (Carruthers 2008a, 83, note 1).

44. The official estimate in 2007 indicates that Saigon has about 6.6 million people, but the official estimate does not account for internal migrants and others who are not registered with the city and thus are excluded from census reports. The United Nations estimates that the city has about 8.7 million people when we consider the latter groups (Dapice and Gomez-Ibanez 2009, 10).

45. Freeman 1989, 1995; Kibria 1993; Zhou and Bankston 1998.

46. Dapice and Gomez-Ibanez 2009, 11.

47. About half of all remittances were sent to Saigon in 2001, and one-third in 2004. The numbers declined partly because of the out-migration of individuals from diverse regions of the country (i.e., mainly through labor migration), who then sent money to places outside Saigon. Still, Saigon continues to receive the largest share of remittances (Anh 2005); see also Pfau and Giang 2009.

48. The latest available data refer to 2008; see Cuong and Mont 2012, 150, table 1.

49. Between May 2004 and September 2011.

50. These two phases included ten months from May 2004 through March 2005 and seven months from January 2009 through July 2009.

51. Prior to conducting fieldwork for this book, I spent more than thirty months, also in distinct intervals, in Saigon from 1996 through 2004 to conduct the research for my previous book (Thai 2008).

52. For the tables listing the migrant and non-migrant interviewees by gender, occupation, and location (either migrants in the United States or non-migrants in Vietnam), see Tables 1–4 in the Appendix.

53. The period from 1995 to 2005.

54. In the immigration literature, "second generation" generally refers to immigrant children who were born in the United States or who came to the country before the age of twelve. However, the four immigrants in this study who came to the United States before the age of twelve came after the age of eight and identify themselves as first generation, so I do not distinguish between the first and second generations; see Kibria 1997, 2002.

55. It is important to note here that these are reported individual incomes, not household incomes.

56. For a lengthy treatment of the economic diversity among Vietnamese immigrants in the United States since 1975, see Zhou and Bankston 1998, chapters 1 and 2.

57. Scholars in Vietnam report that 80 percent of the overseas Vietnamese population is concentrated in ten destination countries, the most significant being the United States, Australia, France, Canada, and more recently, Taiwan, Korea, Malaysia, and Russia (Anh et al. 2010, 6, 14).

58. Postwar Vietnamese migrants first came as refugees directly to the United States as part of the airlift effort that evacuated more than 130,000 Saigonese, mostly from the urban middle class. Subsequent waves of refugees and immigrants included a large number of "boat people" from various regions of Vietnam, who spent time in refugee camps in other Asian countries (most notably Hong Kong, Thailand, and the Philippines) before they were sponsored by a country in the West; see Thai 2008, introduction.

59. Pham 2002.

60. Thai 2008, introduction.

61. Thai 2008, introduction.

62. Lan Anh Hoang 2011.

63. For notable works on the flight of Vietnamese refugees, immigrants, and transmigrants over the past four decades, see Cargill and Huynh 2000; Dorais 1998; Freeman 1989, 1995; Freeman and Huu 2003; Kelly 1977; Kibria 1993; Liu, Lamanna, and Murata 1979; Montero 1979; Rutledge 1992; Thai 2008; Zhou and Bankston 1998. For excellent

discussions and critical analyses on the "refugee figure" as a trope in the construction of Vietnamese immigration, see Espiritu 2006 and, more recently, Nguyen 2012.

64. Espiritu 2006; Nguyen 2012.

65. Carruthers 2002, 2004, 2008a, 2008b; Hoang forthcoming; Schwenkel 2009; Small 2012a, 2012b; Thomas 1997, 1999a, 1999b; Thu-Huong 2008; Truitt 2013; Valverde 2012.

66. For a close examination of the different types of emigrants from contemporary Vietnam, see Anh et al. 2010. These emigrants include immigrants and refugees, labor migrants, international students, and marriage migrants.

67. As Mahler aptly notes, "Heterogeneity exists even among those who occupy the lowest rung of the economic ladder" (1995, 5).

68. Lowe 1996, chapter 6.

69. Cuong and Mont 2012, 148.

70. These five other Asian American groups are Chinese, Filipino, Japanese, Korean, and Asian Indian.

71. For a recent study of Vietnamese Americans in the labor market, particularly dealing with discrimination issues, see Yamane 2012.

72. Allard 2011; see also my discussion in the Appendix.

73. Pew Social and Demographic Trends Research Group 2012, 8.

CHAPTER 2

1. This figure amounts to about 3 percent of the world's population. The latest data are from 2011 (Ratha, Mohapatra, and Silwa 2011).

2. World Bank 2012a.

3. This is the latest amount of remittances sent in 2012 by migrants (World Bank 2012a).

4. Cohen 2011.

5. Cohen 2011.

6. World Bank 2007, 1.

7. Buencamino and Gorbunov 2002, 5.

8. For recent general theoretical discussions on the nature and extent of transnational families, see Bryceson and Vuorela 2002a; Chamberlain and Leydesdorff 2004; Dreby 2010b; Huang, Yeoh, and Lam 2008; Lima 2001; Skrbis 2008; Zentgraf and Chinchilla 2012.

9. Dreby 2010a, 33.

10. Åkesson 2009; Dreby 2010a; Gamburd 2000, 2004; Hondagneu-Sotelo and Avila 1997; Parrenas 2001a, 2001b, 2005; Schmalzbauer 2004, 2005a, 2005b, 2008.

11. A few scholars have begun to examine the situation of Vietnamese labor migrants, who are temporary and contractual workers with no prospect for settlement in the country in which they work; see, for example, Lan Anh Hoang 2011.

12. A few studies have broadened the definition of transnational families to include siblings and other kin; see, for example, Carling 2008; McKay 2007.

13. Rouse 1991, 14.

14. See, for example, Carling and Åkesson 2009; Schmalzbauer 2005b.

15. Allen, Blieszner, and Roberto 2011; Thorne and Yalom 1992; Wilson and Pahl 2011.

16. For an excellent theoretical analysis on this point, see the classic piece by Zinn (1994).

17. A number of cases in this study are of elderly parents who live in the United States

and who have adult children living in Vietnam. However, very few of these elderly parents have surplus income to financially support their adult children in Vietnam.

18. Survey data reveal that money sent by parents constitutes only 30 percent of all monetary flows into Vietnam from the diaspora, and virtually all of this amount comes from labor migrants (Cuong and Mont 2012; Pfau and Giang 2009).

19. For recent studies documenting social change at the family level in the post-market reform period, see Barbieri and Belanger 2009.

20. For recent discussions on the salience of extended kinship in Vietnamese transnational families, see Hoang 2011; Poon, Thai, and Naybor 2012; Tingvold et al. 2012.

21. The first major evacuation of Vietnamese refugees occurred when the U.S. military organized an airlift out of Saigon, days before April 30, 1975, when Northern troops moved into the city. For a discussion of this history, see Zhou and Bankston 1998, chapter 1.

22. Freeman 1995; Zhou and Bankston 1998.

23. It is important to note here that overseas Vietnamese in other parts of the diaspora were returning to the country before Vietnam and the United States resumed diplomatic relations in 1995. For a discussion of this matter, see Anh et al. 2010; Dorais 1998.

24. Communications and the flow of money occurred between 1986 and 1995, but Vietnamese Americans did not begin to return to the country until after diplomatic relations were resumed in 1995. For a discussion of the 1986–1995 interim period, see Anh et al. 2010.

25. Thai 2008.

26. For a recent discussion of the impact of these macroeconomic changes, see Migheli 2012.

27. It is important to note that Vietnam did not close its economy to all countries after the war ended in 1975. For example, it continued diplomatic relations with the Soviet Union and other socialist countries; see Waller and Cao 1997.

28. Hugo 2005.

29. Sassen 1988.

30. For a discussion of destination countries and labor niches of recent Vietnamese labor migrants, see Anh et al. 2010, 14–18.

31. For an analysis of different state policies on the two groups of diasporic Vietnamese subjects (i.e., labor migrants and returnees), see Small 2012a.

32. Anh et al. 2010, 12.

33. Anh et al. 2010; Ratha, Mohapatra, and Silwa 2011; Thao 2009.

34. The latest comparative data available indicate that in 2006, of the $4.8 billion that was sent to Vietnam, $1.6 billion was sent by labor migrants, mostly Vietnamese migrant workers in the Asian region, primarily South Korea, Taiwan, and Malaysia. Vietnamese-origin permanent residents and citizens living in Western countries sent most of the rest of the remittances (Anh et al. 2010).

35. Cuong and Mont 2012.

36. Ratha, Mohapatra, and Silwa 2011, 253.

37. Donor Working Group 2012, 2, note 1.

38. Donor Working Group 2012, 10.

39. Glewwe 2004.

40. Donor Working Group 2012, 10.

41. World Bank 2012b, 1–3.

42. For an excellent analysis on the origin of this postwar economic success, see Fforde 2009.

43. See, for example, Adams and Tran 2010; Arkadie and Mallon 2003; Hiebert 1996; Homlong and Springler 2012.

44. Anh et al. 2010; Cuong and Mont 2012.

45. Cuong and Mont 2012, 145.

46. Nguyen 2002; Ratha, Mohapatra, and Silwa 2011; World Bank 2012a.

47. The eight top-receiving countries, in descending order, are India ($70 billion), China ($66 billion), the Philippines ($24 billion), Mexico ($24 billion), Nigeria ($21 billion), Egypt ($18 billion), Pakistan ($14 billion), and Bangladesh ($14 billion). These numbers are estimates as of November 2012; see World Bank 2012a, 2.

48. Buencamino and Gorbunov 2002; Thai 2008, 2009, 2012a, 2012b.

49. It is significant to note that Vietnamese from abroad can bring in an unlimited amount of cash upon their return visits to the country, but are limited to taking out $7,000 when they depart.

50. See Frank 2007, chapter 5.

51. Frank (2007, 43–47) presents an interesting case study of the size of Americans' homes and shows how the notion of adequate size changed dramatically over the second half of the twentieth century.

52. Schor 1998.

53. Although the empirical data for this study do not speak directly to the research on money and the psychology of happiness, some of the ideas I present are related to the emotional costs associated with spending money, which are addressed in research that raises questions about the psychological costs of buying goods for status; see, for example, Kasser 2012; Roberts 2011; Schor 1998.

54. Frank 2007; Frank and Cook 1997.

55. Frank 2007.

56. Frank 2007, 2010; Frank and Cook 1997; Schor 1998.

57. See, for example, Campbell 1987; Kasser 2012; Schor 1998.

58. A few studies report that the local Vietnamese population is engaged in impulse and luxury purchases in ways that did not exist before market reform; see Mai et al. 2001; Mai and Smith 2011; Mai and Tambyah 2011.

59. For theoretical discussions on the logics of valuation and pricing of marketized goods, see Beckert and Aspers 2011.

60. Connell 1995; Wright 1997.

61. Bourdieu 1990, 1986, 1984; Weber [1922] 1978.

62. Frank 1967; Wallerstein 1974.

63. Radhakrishnan 2011, 17.

64. This is based on 2008 data; see Ohno 2009, 25.

65. As Peggy Levitt and Nina Glick Schiller state: "Social scientists often use national income statistics to assess the socioeconomic status of migrants without considering the other statuses that they occupy. But when society differs from polity and is made up of sets of social relationships in intersecting and overlapping national and transnational social

fields, individuals occupy different gender, racial, and class positions within different states at the same time" (2004, 1005).

66. For recent figures, see Chan and Tran 2011; for older figures, see Thomas 1997.

67. Lamb 1997; Larmer 2000; Nguyen 2002; Nhat 1999; Tran 2000; *Vietnam News* 2002. For past scholarly work on overseas Vietnamese return activities, see Long 2004; Packard 1999. For recent analyses, see Thai 2008, 2012a, forthcoming and Small 2012a, 2012b.

68. Mandy Thomas (1997, 1999a, 1999b, 2001) has done some important work on the case of Vietnamese Australians who return to visit family members in Hanoi.

69. Pickles and Smith 1998.

70. Lascu, Manrai, and Manrai 1994, 92.

71. Lascu, Manrai, and Manrai 1994, 89.

72. Shultz et al. 1998, 247.

73. Levine 1997.

74. Currently, the Vietnam–United States migration corridor is the twentieth-largest migration corridor worldwide; see Ratha, Mohapatra, and Silwa 2011, 5.

CHAPTER 3

1. *Lo* means "to care," but many use the term *lo lang*, which also means "to care."

2. For a lengthy treatment of this point, see Thai (forthcoming) and Truitt 2006, 2013.

3. Zelizer 1994, 2005.

4. Zelizer 1994, 2005.

5. Marx and Engels 1988; Simmel [1900] 2004; Weber 1947.

6. In his philosophical analysis of money, Simmel recognized early on the problem of quantifying money: "The calculative exactness of practical life which the money economy has brought about corresponds to the ideal of natural science: to transform the world into an arithmetic problem, to fix every part of the world by mathematical formulas. Only money economy has filled the days of so many people with weighing, calculating, with numerical determinations, with a reduction of qualitative values to quantitative ones" (1950, 412).

7. Weber 1947, 86.

8. Davidson 1972; Scitovsky 1969.

9. Dodd 1994; Ingham 1996; Parry and Bloch 1989; Singh 1997, 2006, 2009; Zelizer 1989, 2000, 1998.

10. Parry and Bloch 1989, 22.

11. Almost twenty years ago, Zelizer (1994) published her seminal piece, which established a significant argument for looking at the social meanings of money in economic sociology. In later years, and more recently, Zelizer (2005, 2012) expanded her perspective into what she dubs "relational economic sociology."

12. Delaney 2012.

13. Delaney 2012, 6.

14. Belk 1999.

15. Parrenas 2005.

16. McKenzie and Menjivar 2011; Schmalzbauer 2005a, 2008.

17. Coe 2011.

18. Åkesson 2009 2011; Carling and Åkesson 2009.

19. Peter 2010.

20. Suro 2003, 5.

21. Coe 2011.

22. Coe 2011.

23. Coe 2011, 8.

24. Coe 2011, 21.

25. See, for example, Cuong et al. 2000 and Knodel et al. 2000.

26. On this point, see Fleming 1997 and Singh 2006.

27. For a discussion about sibling financial responsibilities, see also McKay 2007.

28. Thomas 1999a; Truitt 2006.

29. Thomas 1999a, 148.

30. Thomas 1999a, 148.

31. Shohet 2010.

32. For a discussion about sacrifice as a sign of love in Vietnamese cultural repertoires, see Shohet 2010.

33. Thai 2012a.

34. Dreby 2009.

35. Dreby 2009, 35.

36. Arlie Russell Hochschild discusses the commodity frontier in globalization as referring to the place where market and the self meet in the negotiation of subjective meanings of objects and possessions. "In the past, on the commodity frontier the fantasy of a perfect purchase might more often center on some feature of external reality," Hochschild writes. "But today, as more elements of intimate and domestic life become objects of sale, the commodity frontier has taken on a more subjective cast. So the modern purchase is more likely to be sold to us by implying access to a 'perfect' private self" (2000, 49).

37. On the point of gossip and exaggeration of monetary flows, see also Brennan 2004.

38. On this point, see Calder 1999 and Hyman 2012b.

39. Cheal 1987, 164.

40. Singh 1997.

41. Cuong et al. 2000; Johnson 2003; Knodel et al. 2000.

42. Truitt 2006, 295.

43. Truitt 2006, 295.

44. Teigen, Olsen, and Solas 2005; Webley and Wilson 1989.

CHAPTER 4

1. Anh et al. 2010.

2. It is important to note that the new Saigon is an international city that has witnessed a tremendous rise in cost of living in the past two decades. Yet the cost of living for local citizens is still relatively inexpensive when compared with costs in other urban centers in Asia and when compared with costs in the United States, partly because of a tiered system of "standards" and pricing of goods, services, and housing. For in-depth analysis of differential costs of living within the city, see Harms 2011; Thu and Perera 2011.

3. For the Vietnamese wages, see Donor Working Group 2012. For the American wages, see Seskin and Smith 2011. According to the World Bank (2011), when adjusted for pur-

chasing power parity in 2010, the per capita incomes for Vietnam and the United States, respectively, were $2,910 and $47,020.

4. For a lengthy treatment of what the author calls contradictory class mobility under transnational and migratory forces, which refers to how low-wage migrants experience social dislocations through the shifting identities and experiences of social class across transnational social fields, see Parrenas 2001b, chapter 1.

5. Here and elsewhere, I have theorized and provided empirical evidence for thinking about processes of "economic convertibility" for immigrants who live across transnational social fields; see Thai 2006, 2009.

6. For an assessment of this point, see Agarwal and Horowitz 2002.

7. Luis Guarnizo (2003) notes that it is necessary to distinguish between monetary and non-monetary remittances.

8. Lucas and Stark 1985; Stark and Lucas 1988.

9. Agarwal and Horowitz 2002; Åkesson 2011; Cohen 2011; Hugo 2005; Russell 1986; Stark 1986.

10. Cohen 2011.

11. Taylor 1999.

12. For studies that make a case for this "pessimistic" perspective, see Lipton 1980 and Reichert 1981, 1982.

13. For studies that make a case for this "optimistic" perspective, see Durand et al. 1996; Durand, Parrado, and Massey 1996; Keely and Tran 1989; Ratha, Mohapatra, and Silwa 2011; Taylor 1999.

14. For an excellent recent review of these competing perspectives, see Cohen 2011.

15. Cohen 2011, 955.

16. For recent discussions of this point, see Agarwal and Horowitz 2002; Cohen 2011; Vanwey 2004.

17. Carling 2008; Singh, Robertson, and Cabraal 2012.

18. I do not deny the exploitative nature of low-wage work in the United States, especially for immigrants. However, the point I make here is an emic one, from the migrant perspective. Scholars of labor note the severe deregulatory nature of contemporary low-wage work in the United States; see, for example, Sassen 1988, 1989a, 1989b, 1995, 2002.

19. In Vietnam, I met one respondent who makes about $50 per month working in a restaurant. Among the migrant respondents, I met a woman from Florida who said her net income is about $1,200 per month as an assembly line worker in an eyeglass factory. Some respondents actually make less than this amount in the United States. One woman from Texas makes only $5 per hour as a restaurant worker, but I did not count her as the lowest-wage worker because her work is generally unpredictable and unreliable; she also works in a number of part-time jobs to make ends meet, with her income being highly variable from month to month.

20. In both situations, the workers help with general kitchen support at the restaurants.

21. Most of the migrant respondents who give consistent monthly support give in the range of $50 to $300, with no one giving more than $300 per month.

22. Some respondents take on part-time jobs with ethnic employers for "under the table" wages, for which they do not pay taxes. They work in these extremely low-paid jobs for a number of reasons. Some cannot find work in their vicinity; others take on the extreme

low wages because such jobs are conveniently located near them. Others lack the skills and experience that would qualify them for other kinds of jobs that might pay low wages as well, but that would pay higher wages than do some ethnic enterprises.

23. In interviews, migrant respondents often said, "Lam bao nhieu an bao nhieu" [I eat whatever I work], meaning they pay their expenses on a paycheck-to-paycheck basis. Also, the amount of savings considered adequate varied widely among respondents.

24. Comparative housing circumstances are important factors, although beyond the scope of this analysis. In some instances, non-migrant respondents live in a home they inherited from migrant members who left the country. In other instances, non-migrant respondents live in homes that are much cheaper than any house one could buy in the United States, as in the case of one non-migrant respondent who lives in (and owns) a house with a dirt floor. These complexities and differences mean that non-migrants are generally cash poor, even though they have assets (e.g., land and properties) that they either inherited or purchased with minimal capital.

25. Waters 1999.

26. Goldring 1998.

27. Smith 2006.

28. Espiritu 2001.

29. Espiritu 2001, 425.

30. As Espiritu reports: "I met Filipinos/as who toiled as assembly workers but who, through the pooling of income and finances, owned homes in middle-class communities . . . I encountered individuals who struggled economically in the United States but owned sizable properties in the Philippines. And I interviewed immigrants who continued to view themselves as 'upper class' even while living in dire conditions in the United States" (2001, 425).

31. For a theoretical discussion on the differences between "households" and "families," see Thorne 1992.

32. For an excellent discussion of social patterns and analytics as ideal types, see Hekman 1983.

33. Grasmuck and Pessar 1991; Hondagneu-Sotelo 1994; Levitt 2001b.

34. Folbre 1986.

35. Kibria 1990, 1993, 1994.

36. Kibria 1993, 1994.

37. Kibria 1994, 82.

38. Kibria 1994.

39. Kibria 1994, 87.

40. Singh 2006, 2009.

41. As Singh, Cabraal, and Robertson note, tensions often develop among transnational families when those who send money feel that those who receive the money do not attach the same value to it that the senders attach (2010, 253).

42. Akuei 2005; Baldassar, Baldock, and Wilding 2007; Schmalzbauer 2008.

43. Family sponsorship to the United States is based on a complicated preference system according to specific relations between the sponsor and the potential immigrant. Siblings over the age of twenty-one, for example, rank near the bottom of the preference system. For a discussion of this preference system, see Wasem 2010.

44. Peter 2010); Schmalzbauer 2008; Singh 2006.

45. Future research might also consider the internal heterogeneity (e.g., variations in gender, age, and marital status) within each group of transnational providers.

CHAPTER 5

1. Numerous studies report that children of immigrants and immigrant children take part in wage labor to help with the immigrant household economy. For a few examples of research on this topic over the past two decades, see Estrada and Hondagneu-Sotelo 2010; Orellana 2001; Song 1999; Valenzuela 1999.

2. A number of studies argue that it is through material goods, especially those that bear status, that low-wage migrants make sense of their precariousness in their daily worlds in the United States; see, for example, Goldring 1998; Peter 2010; Schmalzbauer 2005b.

3. Katherine S. Newman and her colleague (1999; Newman and Chen 2008) report that despite what most Americans think, long-range mobility occurs less often in the United States than in other industrialized nations (e.g., among minorities in Western Europe).

4. Hochschild 1995.

5. Lamont 2000, 103.

6. Here, I do not explicate the many political and scholarly debates on the ideology of the American Dream. In this chapter, I only interpret what migrants say about what they believe in terms of their views about achievement and mobility in the United States. For studies that deal with the debates on the American Dream discourse, see Clark 2003; Hochschild 1995; Louie 2012; Mahler 1995; Zia 2000.

7. For a recent critical and groundbreaking analysis of the notion of gratitude to the U.S. national identity among Vietnamese refugees, see Nguyen 2012.

8. Prior to and during the early years of market reform, it was extremely difficult for Vietnamese citizens to obtain Western goods, particularly medicine. Since market reform, supermarkets and malls have proliferated, especially in the city. Many respondents report that prices for imported goods are now comparable to prices in the West, so migrants have fewer economic incentives to bring back supplies than they had during the early years of return visits. For a discussion about the rise of supermarkets and imported commodities, see Maruyama and Trung 2007.

9. Schmalzbauer 2005a, 2005b, 2008.

10. Schmalzbauer notes: "I learned that my respondents are rugged individualists, loyal to family and few others, and they believe passionately that hard work brings success . . . their work ethic has roots in Honduras where the poor engage in hard labor beginning at a young age" (2005b, 5).

11. Newman and Chen report that intergenerational mobility is lower in the United States than it is in France, Germany, Canada, and a host of other high-income countries (2008); for a recent in-depth analysis of the structure of mobility according to income groups, see Mishel et al. 2012.

12. Other studies also point to the American Dream ideology among immigrants, but I single out the work of Schmalzbauer because she uses data from the United States and Honduras to provide evidence for how migrants actually execute their transnational status system. For other works in the past decade that analyze views of the American

Dream ideology by immigrants, see Clark 2003; Louie 2012; Mahler 1995; Park 1997; Waters 1999.

13. Schmalzbauer 2005b, 5.

14. Schmalzbauer notes that the American Dream "appears more plausible when it is interpreted in a transnational context" (2005b, 18).

15. Most Southeast Asian refugees who arrived before the 1990s were provided a maximum of eighteen months of government assistance. For analyses of the plight of Vietnamese refugees in the early period of refugee migration in the 1970s and 1980s, see Bankston and Zhou 1997 and Montero 1979; for a critical analysis, see Tang 2000.

16. For a classic comprehensive analysis of the effects of deindustrialization on the U.S. labor market, see Wilson 1987, 1996. For perspectives on race and ethnic relations pertaining to deindustrialization, see Lin 1998; Lipsitz 1995; McCall 2001; Wilson and Pahl 2011.

17. Some migrant respondents in this study work multiple jobs to make ends meet. In the list of interviewees I provide in the appendix, I include only the primary job of each respondent.

18. Zhou and Portes 1992, 116.

19. There are, of course, various systems of oppression confronted by racialized, gendered, and classed minorities, including patriarchy, homophobia, and ageism, which are collectively beyond the scope of this analysis. Here, I speak to the political economy of capitalist modes of production that situate low-wage immigrants at the bottom of the economic pyramid in the United States. For extensive discussions of intersecting systems of oppression, see Bonacich, Alimahomed, and Wilson 2008; Sacks 1989.

20. A number of scholars report that migrant minorities cope with structural barriers, such as discrimination, by retaining the belief that despite earning menial wages, they enjoy a better life in the United States than they ever could in the country of origin. These scholars argue that non-migrant minorities do not have this same sort of coping strategy. The work of anthropologist John Ogbu best represents this comparative view; see, for example, Ogbu 1987 and Ogbu and Simons 1998.

21. A good comparative case analysis of minorities within the same racial category is the study of black immigrants by Mary Waters (1999), who shows that black immigrants tend to have a more optimistic view about the American economic opportunity structure than do native-born African Americans.

22. Levitt and Schiller 2004, 1003.

23. Levitt and Schiller (2004, 1015) forcefully point to the limits of measuring income and status within a national boundary.

24. It is not uncommon among some respondents to work for co-ethnic employers who pay them in cash, a strategy that mutually benefits both parties because it allows both to avoid taxes. However, employers take advantage of the (un)employability of some migrants by paying extremely low wages.

25. Louie 2012; Park 1997; Schmalzbauer 2005b; Waters 1999.

26. In a fascinating singular case study of a Mexican immigrant family, Smith argues that success among the second generation under difficult circumstances can be made possible by "how children keep the immigrant bargain and their role vis-à-vis parents and siblings. In this sense, I suggest that parents mediate that bargain by upholding a strong sense of the American Dream ideology to facilitate success" (2008, 273).

27. A number of studies report no statistical differences with respect to the influence of marital status and parental status on migrants' perspectives on mobility, particularly pertaining to the American Dream ideology; see, for example, Khairullah and Khairullah 1999; Kim, Hurh, and Kim 1993; Kitano and Sue 1973. The robust literature on second-generation immigrants shows, however, some discrepant views on mobility among children and their parents when, for instance, children do not keep the immigrant bargain their parents embrace; see, for example, Kasinitz et al. 2008; Waters 1999; Zhou and Bankston 1998.

28. As Heather Beth Johnson (2006) reports, most parents across the economic spectrum vehemently defend their beliefs in key premises of the American Dream ideology, such as principles of individualism, equal opportunity, and meritocracy. Yet, in focusing on the experiences of children from different social classes, Johnson empirically shows the disparate trajectories of children's achievement, based on their respective economic backgrounds.

29. Two respondents hope their children start businesses rather than go to college. These are exceptions to the rule because the rest of respondents have extremely optimistic views about education as the primary route for mobility; notably, most respondents view self-employment as inferior to educational attainment, at least for the younger generation.

30. One way Vietnamese immigrants continue to take on this tour of duty and to cope with it is to devise ethnic capital within their communities. For example, in economically repressed regions in the United States, immigrants are particularly active in community organizations. For a case study of this analysis among poor Vietnamese immigrants in New Orleans, see Zhou and Bankston 1998.

31. Zhou and Bankston 1998.

32. Zhou and Bankston (1998) note that while Vietnamese immigrant parents view their positions in American society as tenuous and marginal, they "emphasize opportunities rather than discrimination" (40). Furthermore, in close-knit ethnic communities, the social networks of the community can "provide an essential adaptive mechanism for survival and a means of maintaining consistent standards, establishing role models, and ensuring parental authority and effective social control over children" (55).

33. Mary Waters (1994) argues that second-generation black immigrants from the West Indies sometimes share their parents' optimistic view of opportunity in the United States, but are much more critical of discrimination and blocked mobility than are their parents.

34. Zhou and Bankston 1998.

35. Elsewhere, I focus extensively on how migrant men gain a sense of self-esteem precisely through homeland visits; see, for example, Thai 2006, 2008.

36. The phrase *huong thu* translates as "to enjoy," but when used in the context of consumption, it means "to indulge and/or to pamper." I wish to acknowledge Hoang Lan Anh for this clarification.

37. Clark 2003; Hochschild 1995; Johnson 2006; Mahler 1995; Park 1997; Waters 1999.

CHAPTER 6

1. Veblen [1899] 1994.

2. Veblen notes: "Conspicuous consumption of valuable goods is a means of reputability to the gentleman of leisure" ([1899] 1994, 64).

3. Veblen [1899] 1994, 43.

4. Furthermore, Veblen notes that in touting their wealth, consumers demonstrate that they need not worry about earning a wage. As he explains, "If, in addition to showing that the wearer can afford to consume freely and uneconomically, it can also be shown in the same stroke that he or she is not under the necessity of earning a livelihood, the evidence of social worth is enhanced in a very considerable degree" (105).

5. For some excellent recent analyses and applications of Veblen's idea of conspicuous consumption, see Bird and Smith 2005; Dwyer 2009; Ordabayeva 2011; Reisman 2012; Schor 1998; Trigg 2001; Urry 2010; Watson 2012.

6. In her study of labor migrants from rural India, Prema A. Kurien (2002) reports on the conspicuous consumption of returnees through ostentatious spending. In my work, I do not view such spending behavior as "conspicuous" per se, as in Veblen's formulation, but rather as "compensatory" for blocked mobility. I see conspicuous consumption as a kind of spending pattern among the wealthy, or leisure, class, as Veblen points out.

7. Caplovitz 1967.

8. Caplovitz 1967, 13.

9. Chinoy 1952, 459.

10. The idea behind compensatory consumption, as Caplovitz notes, originated with studies published in the 1930s by Robert and Helen Lynd (1937) on the "Middletown" of the United States, which were later elaborated upon by their student Eli Chinoy (1952), who used the idea to talk about the situation of automobile workers. Caplovitz, however, coined the term "compensatory consumption" under the advice of his mentor, Robert K. Merton. Caplovitz also was the first to explicitly address minority consumers, who accounted for nearly 80 percent of the sample in his study in New York City (1967, 8–13).

11. Veblen notes: "Beyond the priestly class, and ranged in an ascending hierarchy, ordinarily comes a superhuman vicarious leisure class of saints, angels, etc." ([1899] 1994, 207).

12. In a fascinating study of inner-city race relations in New York and Philadelphia, Jennifer Lee shows how poor inner-city African Americans spend excessive amounts of money on clothing, sneakers, and jewelry to buffer their low status in the U.S. stratification system (2002, 57).

13. Robert Hollands (2002) notes that segmented consumption occurs among youths in the night economy of Britain, although he does not look specifically at the process of compensatory consumption.

14. Social visibility is immensely important for compensatory consumption to be successful because it relies on an "audience" to validate the status claims, which "are made with statements, behaviors, and symbols that indicate to others one's membership in one particular status group" (Pellerin and Stearns 2001, 1).

15. Pellerin and Stearns also observe that "people in non-dominant relatively deprived positions (minority, lower-income, or lower education) are likely to experience threats to their status honor. Because of these threats, they will experience a more critical need to make status claims than those in dominant, relatively advantaged positions" (2).

16. On the notion of modality of action, see Camic 1986, 1046.

17. Caplovitz points out that non-whites are more likely than whites to engage in compensatory consumption because when "they have comparatively few opportunities to

improve their social standing in the community . . . the sphere of consumption is one of the few that is open to them" (1967, 127).

18. Elsewhere, I show how immigrants convert their low wages from "low incomes from the United States" to relatively "high incomes in Vietnam" through spending on leisure for public display; see Thai 2006, 2009, 2012b.

19. For recent research on intimate labor in the new Saigon, see Hoang 2010, 2011a.

20. Young 1999, 71.

21. The phrase *an choi* conveys a range of meanings pertaining to the consumption of leisure. It is used colloquially to convey "eat for fun" or "eat and play." Variations include "hanging out" and "playing." In many contexts, such as in this example I give, people use the term along with *xa lang* to denote that they want to "eat and play extravagantly or with no limits." I wish to thank Hoang Lan Anh and Phan Van Chanh for help with this clarification.

22. Chao and Schor 1998, 111.

23. In Vietnam, they are called "Viet Kieu *dom*" [fake overseas Vietnamese]. Journalist Andrew Lam (2005) discusses the typology of overseas Vietnamese migrants from the view of those in the homeland.

24. Here I point to and agree with Lisa Drummond's reminder in her analysis of urban space in Vietnam that "feminist analyses are particularly critical of the patriarchal character of these concepts, where public is associated with men/masculinity and private with women/ femininity" (Drummond 2000, 2380).

25. I discuss this aspect of consumption in more detail elsewhere; see Thai 2009.

26. Osella and Osella 2000, 122.

27. I do not suggest here that Saigon is a global city. Global cities have specific financial and technological apparatuses. For discussions on the characteristics of global cities, see Sassen 2001.

28. Chao and Schor 1998, 111.

29. Guarnizo and Smith 1998, 13.

30. Caldeira notes that in developing countries, new models of spatial segregation have transformed the quality of life in many cities. She aptly points out that new segregation schemes in cities in the developing world make it "difficult to maintain the principles of openness and free circulation that have been among the most significant organizing values of modern cities" (1996, 303).

31. Caldeira 1996, 303.

32. For an excellent analysis of spatiality within the local working class in the new Saigon, see Chae 2003.

33. As I discuss in the appendix, my fieldwork data suggest that many in Vietnam have a stratified view of migrants from different parts of the diaspora. Most see migrants from the United States as more ostentatious than those from other parts of the diaspora. This is also reflected in the movie *14 Days*, which specifically portrays the experience of migrants from the United States.

34. By "durable goods," I mean commodities, such as furniture and appliances, that generally last three or more years; see Waldman 2003.

35. Freire (2009) notes that motorbikes are the new "consumption icon" of Saigon. Truitt (2008) also discusses the importance of motorbikes as a signal of mobility in the country.

36. Georges 1990; Grasmuck and Pessar 1991; Hondagneu-Sotelo 1994.

37. Sana 2005, 239.

38. Young 1999, 70.

39. Coleman 1990; Frank 1985.

40. Pels, Hetherington, and Vandenberghe 2002.

41. Appadurai 1986; Engestrom and Blackler 2005; Miller 1998a; Pels, Hetherington, and Vandenberghe 2002.

42. Hirschman and Holbrook 1982; Holbrook 1986; Woods 1960.

43. For in-depth theoretical analysis of symbolic meanings attached to material goods, see Appadurai 1986; Csikszentmihalyi and Halton 1981.

44. Weber 1946.

45. Studies conducted during the 1960s and 1970s of social stratification in the United States point to the purchase of a "standard set" of goods as an important signal for entering the middle class; see, for example, Coleman and Rainwater 1978.

46. On the nature of gendered allocative systems, see Acker 1988; Kenney 2006.

47. Burgoyne 1990; Deutsch, Roksa, and Meeske 2003; Osella and Osella 2000; Prince 1992, 1993; Singh 1997, 2006; Smelt 1980; Thai 2006; Zelizer 1989, 1998.

48. Prince 1992, 1993; Rudmin 1992.

49. Goldberg and Lewis 1978; Knight 1968; Lindgren 1980; Prince 1992, 1993.

50. Yablonsky 1991.

51. Datta et al. 2009; Osella and Osella 2000; Thai 2006, 2009.

52. Hochschild 2002; Yeates 2004.

53. Veblen [1899] 1994.

CHAPTER 7

1. For theoretical and empirical discussions of this idea, as derived from Veblen and Simmel, see Ackerman 1997; Blumberg 1974; Dwyer 2009; Hoyt 1956.

2. Although emulative consumption is generally understood as a process by which lower-income groups emulate higher-income groups, some arguments assert that it is not just a "trickle-down" process, but also a "trickle-up" process. For example, research on how the middle and upper classes appropriate urban fashion suggests a "tendency of fashionable practices to percolate upward from lower to higher status groups" (Ramstad 1998, 13).

3. Simmel 1904; Veblen [1899] 1994.

4. This is particularly true because Veblen's main idea applies to wealth formation, and primarily to the consumption of luxury goods, with no regard for utility to display wealth; see Trigg 2001, 99.

5. Simmel 1904.

6. Veblen [1899] 1994, 71.

7. In his analysis of fashion as part of his formulation of the trickle-down theory, Simmel points to the ways in which fashion changes constantly due to the emulative motives of the lower class, which then drive the strata above to create new trends. Simmel writes, "Every fashion is essentially the fashion of a social class; that is, it always indicates a social stratum which uses similarity of appearance to assert both its own inner unity and its outward differentiation from other social strata. As soon as the lower strata [*sic*] attempts to imitate the upper strata and adopt their fashion, the latter create a new one" ([1900] 2004, 466).

8. Duesenberry 1949.

9. Nurkse 1957.

10. Nurkse 1957, 59.

11. For recent studies on consumption and distinction among the urban middle class in contemporary Vietnam, see Nguyen-Marshall, Drummond, and Belanger 2012.

12. See also Truitt 2013.

13. Goffman 1951.

14. Bourdieu 1980, 1984, 1986.

15. Bourdieu 1984, 6.

16. On the point of relative deprivation that drives emulative consumption, see Frank 2011.

17. Morey and Luthans 1984; Pelto 1970.

18. Recent research calls for a comprehensive theoretical model of analyzing a global class system with respect to transnational actors in developing countries who never migrate abroad but have ties to global and transnational processes, such as capital from overseas relatives. To do this would mean to move away from the pervasive methodological nationalism that pervades social science research. For example, national incomes may not be sufficient for an analysis of class structure when considered within transnational contexts. For a discussion of this point, see Levitt and Schiller 2004, 1015.

19. As I have shown, monetary circulation in the homeland simultaneously improves the lives of some members of the homeland and also exacerbates social inequality.

20. Cohen 2001, 2011; Lucas and Stark 1985; Osella and Osella 2000; Sana 2005; Stark and Lucas 1988.

21. Other scholars report convincingly how money from migrants undermines the national balance of payments by increasing demand for imported goods, and in the long run increases inflation in the developing world. At a local level, migrant money changes the price of land and housing for the local population. For a discussion of these factors, see Grasmuck and Pessar 1991; Itzigsohn 1995; Martin 1991.

22. Bourdieu 1984.

23. Bourdieu 1980, 1984, 1986.

24. Bourdieu contends that understanding modes of sophistication and style vis-à-vis consumption is in some ways like understanding a language. It helps to communicate one's logic and mastery of a certain kind of lexicon of power. Analytically, the comparison of consumption to a form of communication also means considering the coded language of consumption. Bourdieu writes that consumption is "a stage in a process of communication, that is, an act of deciphering, decoding, which presupposes practical or explicit mastery of a cipher or code" (1984, 2).

25. Ustuner and Holt 2010, 52.

26. Bourdieu states that "cultural consumption are [sic] predisposed, consciously and deliberately or not, to fulfill a social function of legitimating social differences" (1984, 7).

27. Dwyer 2009, 332.

28. Ustuner and Holt 2010, 52.

29. For a critique of Bourdieu's theory of social class in analyzing less affluent societies, see Ustuner and Holt 2010.

30. For the study on the upper class, see Bourdieu 1992. For the study on the working class, see Bourdieu 2000.

31. Schiller 2005, 442.

32. Bourdieu 1984, 6.

33. Bourdieu 1984, 6–7.

34. Thus, central to Lamont's critique is Bourdieu's elision of the possibility that individuals can gain social standing by using other measures besides cultural capital to evaluate, assert, and maintain social standing.

35. Lamont 1992, 9.

36. Lamont further argues that Bourdieu's sampling procedures produced a limited argument. She writes: "Bourdieu's work relies too heavily not just on French attitudes but on Parisian attitudes, thereby exaggerating the importance of cultural boundaries. Finally, while Bourdieu argues that worldviews are primarily defined by habitus (via proximate environmental factors), my analysis illustrates the importance of considering the roles of macrostructural determinants and cultural repertoires in shaping tastes and preferences" (1992, 181).

37. Lamont points out that Bourdieu implies that "those who value morality do so because they have no alternative, no resources other than their moral purity and asceticism to offer on the market" (1992, 184).

38. See Lamont 2000, chapter 1.

39. Lamont argues that the working class is concerned with "keeping the world in moral order," and that "morality is a more important criterion of worth for workers than for professionals and managers who stress socioeconomic status instead" (2000, 53).

40. Lamont 1992, 10.

41. Truitt 2013.

42. Mai and Smith 2011; Mai and Tambyah 2011.

43. For a lengthy treatment of how money is used as a standard for measuring moral and social worth, see Truitt 2013.

44. Among the non-migrants, fourteen respondents were fifty and over.

45. Ustuner and Holt 2010, 52.

46. Ustuner and Holt 2010, 53.

47. Ustuner and Holt 2010, 42.

48. Ustuner and Holt 2010, 42–47.

49. Bourdieu 1984, 6.

50. Ustuner and Holt argue that respondents with low cultural capital "are able to continually bracket out Western consumers as a point of comparison and constantly reinforce that their peers are only other Turks" (2010, 53). In some sense, these respondents reject the "orthodox portfolio of consumption practices" (Ger and Belk 1996a, 52–53).

51. Until the accelerated changes following market reform, surveys indicated that morality was the most important criterion for status; see Mai and Tambyah 2011, 80.

52. Mai and Tambyah 2011, 80.

53. Freire 2009.

54. Freire notes, "Motorbikes served as the central component of a material and pleasure-seeking culture that emerged with the implementation of the renovation policies in 1986 and served the stability of the social order. . . . If motorbikes remain an object of social classification, an 'investment of economic value' for some, a simple fashion item for others,

the forms of social distinction and the consumerism significations have also evolved in urban areas. For sure, the price, the brand, and the model count" (2009, 72, 78).

55. Truitt 2008, 3.

56. Truitt 2008, 6.

57. Ger and Belk 1996b, 291.

58. Campbell 1987; Heilbroner 1956.

59. Belk 2011, 50.

60. Belk 1999.

61. Frank 2000; Twitchell 2003.

62. Belk 1999, 41.

63. Frank 2011.

64. On the psychological fulfillment of material objects, see Csikszentmihalyi and Halton 1981.

65. Ma 2001, 447.

66. Ger and Belk (1996a) use the term "consumptionscape" in their analysis of less affluent societies. They draw on Arjun Appadurai, who talks about the "transnational constructions of imaginary landscape" (1996, 33) in global flows of capital and labor. Appadurai does not refer to a consumptionscape, but rather to five other landscapes of the mind: ethnoscape, technoscape, financescape, mediascape, and ideascape. These dimensions share the same suffix, which "allows us to point to the fluid, irregular shapes of these landscapes, shapes that characterize international capital" (33).

67. In the words of Belk, "the social comparison to those in more affluent countries continues to provide an engine for further consumption aspirations among transitional consumers. . . . When everyone has something it is no longer a luxury" (1999, 52).

68. Ger and Belk 1996a, 278.

69. Juliet Schor points out that a reference group is a "mental category, a comparison concept a person carries around in his or her head, not something we can measure directly" (2004, 28).

70. In their discussion of local-level consumption in less affluent societies against the backdrop of global processes, Ger and Belk write: "What appears to be emulation and senseless pastiche when looking from the outside is seen as sensemaking synthesis, and meaningful and coherent symbiosis when looking from the inside. It is a gradual, unexplicated, and largely undetected symbiosis from the local perspective" (1996a, 296).

71. In her research on the "overspent" Americans, Juliet Schor discusses the mass competitive and comparative spending that leads to numerous consumption problems (1998, 8).

72. Arnould 1989; Campbell 1987; McCracken 1986.

73. Coleman and Rainwater 1978; Rainwater 1974.

74. See also Pellerin and Stearns 2001, 2.

75. For a discussion of the new development of shopping malls in the new Saigon, see Chae 2003. For a discussion of the nature of shopping malls as "public parks" in the developing cities of Southeast Asia, see Young 1999.

76. It is important to note here that Saigon has many "floating" migrants, totaling nearly 20 percent of the city's population. These residents are not registered with the city, which means they are not accounted for in census calculations. State policies in Vietnam

require the registration of all residents in every city and town, and internal migration requires approval from the state. See Dapice and Gomez-Ibanez (2009); for further details,
see Chapter 2 of this book.

77. Maruyama and Trung 2007.

78. Ger and Belk 1996a, 281.

CHAPTER 8

1. We briefly met Kiet in Chapter 5.

2. Salary differentials for office staff, such as secretaries, vary tremendously between local
and foreign firms in Saigon. At the time of my fieldwork, I learned from human resource
agencies that local firms paid about $150 per month for a full-time secretary, whereas foreign
firms paid about five to ten times that amount. I note this to indicate the enormous disparity in wages when one has English competence in Saigon. But because English classes range
widely in quality, having foreign capital to pay for them can make a difference in people's
access to relatively higher-end employment and wages.

3. Kiet arrived in the United States ten years before we did the interview.

4. Dwyer 2009, 331.

5. In dealing with the notion of habit, I highlight the dynamics of monetary circulation as
"conventional action even without an initially deliberate emulative move" (Dwyer 2009, 336).

6. Giddens 1979, 218.

7. James [1890] 1950, 107.

8. Camic 1986, 1046.

9. Guarnizo 2003. For use of the language of "remittance habits" and "spending habits,"
see, for example, Abrego 2009; Kolb and Egbert 2008; Lindley 2010; Pluiss and Kwok-Bun
2012; Sampson 2003; Terry and Wilson 2005.

10. Sana 2005, 240.

11. Miller 1995, 1998a, 1998b.

12. See for example, de Certeau 1988.

13. Peter 2010, 231.

14. Goldring 1998, 2003; Levitt 1998, 2001b; Peter 2010; Pribilsky 2012; Schmalzbauer
2005b, 2008.

15. Carling, for example, documents how in Cape Verde, non-migrants see many returnees touting their success, and thus the non-migrants cannot believe it when their migrant
relatives tell stories of hardship in their life abroad. As Carling observes, "The issue here, of
course, is not what the life of emigrants is 'really' like, but that non-migrants' inability to
see for themselves is a key inequality in transnational relationships" (2008, 1467).

16. Although I do not deal with issues of mental health or psychological problems
associated with the stress of responsibilities, I did encounter a few migrant respondents
who said they lost sleep or turned to alcohol when they faced stress about money in their
families. Future research should explore these dimensions of monetary circulation in transnational families.

17. As I noted in Chapter 3, non-migrant relatives often articulate more respect for family members who distribute money than for those who do not, reflecting the importance of
materiality as a form of care. I described the different social evaluations made toward Han

and her sister, Tuyet, because of the different levels of monetary support they distribute in the homeland.

18. Smith (2006, 50); for other works that talk about the rise of a remittance bourgeoisie, see Dreby 2010a and Schmalzbauer 2008.

19. See especially chapters 2 and 3 in Smith 2006.

20. Schmalzbauer 2008.

21. See especially chapter 1 in Dreby 2010a.

22. Mahler 1995, 2.

23. Spivak 1996.

24. McCracken 1988.

25. Ma 2001, 448.

26. Ma 2001, 448.

27. Diderot 1956, 309–10.

28. Shove 2003.

29. Weber [1922] 1978.

30. Biggart and Beamish 2003.

31. Duesenberry 1949; Frank 2000; Schor 1998.

32. Dwyer 2009, 337.

33. Shove 2003.

34. Veblen noted early on that "for the great body of the people in any modern community, the proximate ground of expenditure in excess of what is required for physical comfort is not a conscious effort to excel in the expensiveness of their visible consumption, so much as it is a desire to live up to the conventional standard of decency in the amount and grade of goods consumed" ([1899] 1994, 102).

CHAPTER 9

1. Among all migrant respondents who regularly send money (usually monthly) monetary support, $300 was the highest amount reported.

2. In some instances, I found that migrants who came to the United States before adulthood and who left siblings behind in Vietnam returned with the notion that time had not changed things. This pattern is an interesting topic for future research, but is beyond the scope of my data.

3. Their grandparents had asked that Phuoc stay in Vietnam because they did not want to leave the country, and Hue's father was the last of their adult children to migrate to the United States. Thus, if Phuoc had gone abroad, the grandparents would not have had any children or grandchildren staying back with them.

4. At the time Hue bought the Dylan motorbike, it was actually the top-of-the-line motorbike on the market. The SH model arrived on the scene two years later.

5. Credit cards, to be clear, are financial tools that allow cardholders to make purchases or take out cash advances. The amount allowable for borrowing or to make purchases is generally predetermined, set by the card issuer. If the money is paid in full within a grace period (normally three to four weeks after the closing date of a statement, which occurs monthly), then no interest accrues on the purchase or cash advance, although a one-time fee is usually associated with a cash advance. Otherwise, a financial charge, including fees and

interest, is levied on the card, according to the terms of the "cardholder agreement." Cash advances tend to have much higher interest rates than do purchases of goods and services. For further details, see Peterson 2003.

6. According to Hue, this payment is more than the minimum payment and she plans to pay it off in five years.

7. Drawing on psychological as well as sociological studies on consumer debt, this chapter makes a key point in recognizing that personal consumer debts are, in fact, relational; on this point, see DiMaggio and Louch 1998; Livingstone and Lunt 1992.

8. Numerous scholars report that migrants routinely take on debt in order to migrate in the first place; see, for example, Dreby 2010a; Mahler 1995; Parrenas 2001b; Smith 2006. For work specific to migrants in Asia, see Afsar 2005; Jones and Findlay 1998; Pertierra 1992; Yeoh and Rahman 2005.

9. Recent research on the consumption dilemmas of Ecuadorian migrants in New York City touches on some dimensions of debt among migrant men who informally borrow from each other (Pribilsky 2012). Also, Katherine S. Newman and Victor Tan Chen (2008), in several chapters of their recent book on near-poor Americans, focus on immigrants who use credit cards to make return visits to their homeland; see specifically chapter 3.

10. In her comparative study of parents in different economic strata, Pugh reports that parents buy material goods for children not so much for status-driven motives, but to claim a sense of belonging in their communities. She argues that "my use of 'dignity' refers less to 'envy' than to the 'esteem' of others, the goal of joining the circle rather than one of bettering it" (2009, 7).

11. In general, migrant respondents were brutally honest about their debts, mostly because I had gotten to know them for several years before I broached the issue, and also sometimes because they were in such dire circumstances that they had little to lose by talking about their indebtedness. Without doubt, people sometimes withhold such personal information because debt is about the management of shame. In some instances, respondents asked me to help them find ways to reduce their debts through debt consolidation programs. More frequently, however, they were interested in getting more credit cards and/or higher credit limits.

12. Geertz 1973, 353.

13. Although credit cards are free of stigma at the time consumers obtain them, they can turn into stigmatized identities when borrowers are unable to pay them off. For a discussion of this aspect of credit cards among low-income consumers, see Littwin 2007.

14. Godwin (1997, 1996).

15. As I note in Chapter 2, only 20 percent of the migrant respondents were homeowners.

16. This respondent was only able to take out amounts under $500 each time, which he paid off diligently because of the exorbitant fees he had to pay to secure and maintain those loans.

17. Payday loans, in particular, bear extremely high interest rates, even when compared with the high interest rates of cash advances on credit cards. The one respondent who took out payday loans paid an interest rate of more than 40 percent on the loan. For a discussion of this kind of loan, see Rivlin (2011).

18. Journalist Gary Rivlin (2011, 22) coined the phrase "the poverty industry" to explain

the rise of financial institutions (e.g., payday loan centers and pawnshops) that prey on the vulnerability of the poor who need access to cash. See especially chapter 1.

19. A few respondents also had access to rotating credit associations, common in many immigrant communities, especially in Asia. These credit associations rely on installments from members who take out loans and pay back the money with interest. Although some of my respondents paid into credit associations, it was not a common method for obtaining capital for transnational journeys to Vietnam or for expenditures while there because such associations have strong social control over repayments, and respondents generally do not want to risk exploiting those conditions. For discussions of these credit associations, see Granovetter 1985; Portes and Sensenbrenner 1993.

20. For succinct and excellent analyses of the history of consumer and credit card debts since the turn of the twentieth century, see Hyman 2012a, 2012b.

21. Credit scores serve as a powerful method for financial exclusion in the world of low-wage workers. For an excellent discussion of financial exclusion and what they call "financial abandonment" in the new economy, see Leyshon and Thrift 1995.

22. For an extensive discussion of the impact of credit scores on financial well-being, see Levinger, Benton, and Meier 2011.

23. For lengthy treatments of the legal consequences of credit card defaults, see Lea, Webley, and Walker 1995; Manning 2000; Peterson 2003; Sullivan, Warren, and Westbrook 1989.

24. Newman and Chen note that rates of credit card ownership have risen at a faster pace for Americans in the income bracket of $20,000 to $40,000 than for any of the other four income groups in the United States. They report that six of ten families in this income bracket had at least one credit card in 2001, a large increase from one of ten in 1970 (2008, 68).

25. Credit cards are not only easy to obtain, but it is easy to withdraw money from them. Some credit cards can be used like an ATM card associated with a personal checking and savings account. In Vietnam, there is a black market that makes it possible to withdraw cash from a credit card for a fee without having to pay cash advance surcharges to a financial institution. Typically, black market merchants ring up a cash advance as if it is a purchase and charge the cardholder an additional 2 percent for the purchase. In this way, both the merchant and the credit card holder benefit from the transaction.

26. In the words of Newman and Chen, "Part of the reason this segment of the market is so profitable is that many near-poor households simply lack the financial acumen to deftly juggle and dispose of their debt" (2008, 68).

27. Many low-income individuals use credit cards to buffer future income. For a discussion of this point, see Medoff and Harless 1996; Nocera 1994; Sullivan, Warren, and Westbrook 2000.

28. Calder 1999; Hyman 2012b; Manning 2000.

29. Rivlin 2011.

30. Rivlin 2011, 23.

31. In Newman and Chen's study, one respondent had 17 credit cards and an annual income of $16,895 (2008, chapter 3, note 2).

32. The issue of debt and credit cards did not emerge until one respondent brought it up with me, and so I had not talked about debt in the early part of the research. Yet, even though I decided to include this dimension of monetary circulation later in the fieldwork,

my tally is that 60 percent reported this number of credit cards. This number excludes nine respondents with whom I did not broach the topic of debt.

33. One respondent told me he had a credit line of $50,000. He said he had religiously paid his monthly payments for years, and the credit card company always increased his credit limit on a yearly basis.

34. In this sense, I echo much of what Newman and Chen (2008) argue in chapter 3 of their book on the near poor. They aptly illustrate how examining people's economic pasts, particularly those of low-wage immigrants, in the context of mobility helps to explain their current spending habits. In appraising their lives over time, we obtain a better picture of why and how seemingly excessive spending is about purchasing dignity and worth.

35. Here and elsewhere I discuss how low-wage immigrants occasionally view themselves as social betters compared with their low-wage peers in Vietnam, and how much of this evaluation depends on context and sense of class across transnational social fields.

36. Katrak 1996, 125.

37. For an extensive discussion of subsidized housing policies in the United States, including the Section 8 housing voucher program, see Schwartz 2006.

38. For a recent look at the immigrant bargain debate, see Louie 2012.

39. Numerous studies point to immigrant parents' expectations for and investment in their children's education. For general empirical statements, see notable studies on mobility and the second generation, such as Gans 1992; Portes and Rumbaut 2001; Waldinger and Feliciano 2004. For an in-depth examination of the Vietnamese experience, see Zhou and Bankston 1998.

40. On the opposite end of the economic spectrum, one recent provocative study documents the unprecedented rate of middle- and upper-middle-class earners who have "gone solo," living alone for a large part of their adult lives. Klineberg (2012) argues that economic security among the privileged means that many are opting to live alone, in contrast with the past, when relationships were formed largely for economic reasons.

41. Ehrenreich 2001.

42. Newman and Chen 2008, 69.

43. See Chapter 5 in this book, where I discuss the immigrant bargain; also see Louie 2012.

44. Hue told me she wanted to seek therapy at one point, but she could not afford it.

45. Indeed, a number of studies report that credit use begins with small amounts and the intention to repay within the grace period. The seduction of consumption and the marketization of the lending industry, however, subsequently drive many of the problems associated with high credit card spending. For a psychological perspective on this point, see Lea, Webley, and Walker 1995; Manning 2000; Peterson 2003.

46. These were the three most common expenditures migrants took on debt to pay.

47. In the words of Elizabeth Warren and Amelia Warren Tyagi, "Credit card issuers make their profits from lending lots of money and charging hefty fees to families that are financially strapped" (2003, 139).

48. Indeed, most respondents said going to Vietnam was the first flight they took, not including the flight to the United States when they migrated. Furthermore, for most, it is the only airplane ride they ever take.

49. By this, I mean that migrant respondents generally did not have large expenses in

their day-to-day lives in the United States. The very process of going to Vietnam requires a substantial amount of money, and then they must confront the expenditures for themselves and their relatives while they are visiting.

50. Some scholars report that consumers have different psychological detachments for credit card purchases than for the use of personal cash or savings, mostly because consumers who pay with credit do not immediately associate the economic cost with the merchandise; those who pay with cash, on the other hand, have to part with actual money at the time of purchase. For a discussion of this point, see Hirschman 1979; Hyman 2012a.

51. As Newman and Chen report, for low-wage workers "running up card balances is not so much about acquiring things as seeking what everyone else seems to have" (2008, 61).

52. The highest interest rate reported to me was 30 percent, although several respondents said that if they defaulted on the cards, they would have to pay higher rates still. Some credit card companies charge up to 70 percent in interest rates for delinquent accounts; see Peterson 2003.

53. For an excellent discussion on Orange County as the capital of Vietnamese America, see Juan 2009.

54. Vu told me fried rice with salted fish lasts longer because the fermented salted fish serves as a preservative for the rice.

55. As mentioned in the previous chapter, Vu had bought Trieu a $500 bed during one of his visits because she had complained about having back pain.

56. Vu said he estimated the final total cost of the house was about $35,000.

57. He had never heard of debt consolidation programs until I suggested one to him; in fact, I only suggested it to him when he asked if I knew of ways for him to increase his credit limits or to get additional credit cards.

58. Using an amortization schedule, I calculated that if he were to pay about $640 per month on a $30,000 credit card balance with a 25 percent interest rate, it would take him 15 years to pay off the amount. This calculation assumes he pays on time every month. Adding to the equation, however, are his five cards, one of which carries a 29 percent interest rate—which means that after all is said and done, it might take longer for him to pay off the credit card balance.

59. Anthropologists have reported on the difficulties of communications in transnational families. For a good review of this line of inquiry, see Mahler 2001. Economists have analyzed the significance of information asymmetries in transnational household finances; see, for example, Ashraf 2009; Lundberg and Pollack 1993; Seshan and Yang 2012.

60. Because debt is a sensitive topic, even though migrant respondents were blunt to me about it, I did not feel it prudent to talk about the migrants' debts to their non-migrant relatives; thus a limitation to the analysis of debt here is that I did not get the perspective of the non-migrant family members.

61. A long-standing argument in economic sociology demonstrates that "personal debts" are most often embedded in the context of social relationships. For a number of studies documenting the impact of social relationships on personal consumer debt, especially of credit cards, see Livingstone and Lunt 1992; Manning 2000; Medoff and Harless 1996; Nocera 1994; Sullivan, Warren, and Westbrook 1989, 2000.

62. Dew 2011.

63. Dew 2011, 554.

64. The subprime crisis that began in 2007 affected numerous low-income minorities, but it was mostly irrelevant to the migrant respondents in this study because none were involved in buying property during that period. Furthermore, none of those who owned a home had taken out an equity loan on it. For a thorough discussion of the consequences of the subprime crisis, which led to the so-called great recession, on low-income racial and ethnic minorities, see Chakravartty and Silva 2012; Heintz and Balakrishnan 2012.

65. They were, therefore, not involved in the mortgage downfall that principally contributed to the subsequent economic recession.

66. Newman and Chen (2008) point out the reality for the American working class of living under "asset-poor" conditions, arguing that many near-poor individuals face a range of financial vulnerabilities because they do not have assets to turn to as a cushion. For a critical analysis of the subprime crisis, see Chakravartty and Silva 2012.

CHAPTER 10

1. In an excellent assessment of the interpersonal levels of transnationalism, Jorgen Carling proposes to focus on the problem of "asymmetries" of long-distance closeness among transnational networks (2008, 1453). In this study, he looks at multiple levels of asymmetries in transnational relationships among Cape Verdean migrants in the Netherlands, with some references to money. I have shown throughout that asymmetry in the social and personal meanings of money plays a crucial role in the dynamics of expectations and consumptive practices, but here I highlight that asymmetries are especially important vectors of analysis for the prevalence of making promises among migrant members of transnational families.

2. Because of the mobility and material inequality inherent in transnational relationships, social frictions are rife. For a case study assessment of social frictions between spouses pertaining to money in Sri Lanka transnational families, see Gamburd 2000. For an assessment of parent-child social frictions pertaining to money in the Philippines, see Parrenas 2005.

3. Carling reminds us that a key problem in the asymmetries of transnational relationships is the very fact that both sides do not know what goes on at the other end of their transnational social fields (2008, 1465).

4. For studies on the boasting behaviors of transnational migrants in their homelands in various parts of the world, see Kim 2010; Phillips and Potter 2009; Shen 2008; Suksomboon 2008; Valenta and Strabac 2011.

5. As McKenzie and Menjivar observe, "Although those who stay are not merely passive recipients, significant power asymmetries between migrants and those who stay have been found, though not always in the direction of the migrants" (2011, 65).

6. Bryceson and Vuorela, in their discussion about transnational families as a new category within transnational studies, note that social conflicts are inevitable in the transnational family, even as migrants and non-migrants develop "modes of materializing the family as an imagined community with shared feelings and obligations" (2002b, 14).

7. Kankonde Bukasa Peter points out that migrants often conceal their true earnings from non-migrant families because they "feel a compelling need to be perceived as financially 'successful' as well as 'valid' and 'good' family members not only in their communities of origin, but also among other migrants" (2010, 226).

8. Indeed, as I have shown, visible pecuniary display is a form of communicating status because the meanings of consumption can be interpreted tacitly and prosperity implied through articulation of a purchase. As Luin Goldring notes, "Spending practices and other status claims made in the context of transnationalized localities offer individuals and families an opportunity for social mobility within a local stratification scheme, and at the same time help to alter the prevailing stratification scheme by introducing new elements into the status lexicon" (1998, 183).

9. In the words of Peggy Levitt, "In the receiving country and at home, their social lives continue to be so entwined with one another that those who do not send money to their families or do not 'do right' by the community feel the consequences. . . . Many migrants still use their sending community as the reference group against which they gauge their status" (2001a, 198).

10. Goldring 1998; Mahler 1995; Sana 2005; Schmalzbauer 2008.

11. A number of studies report that in addition to projecting an image of success by avoiding discussions about wages, migrants avoid talking about their real wages because they do not want to worry their families about money; see, for example, Goldring 1998; Levitt 2001b; Schmalzbauer 2005b.

12. Mahler 1995.

13. As Levitt and Schiller point out, "People living in transnational social fields experience multiple loci and layers of power and are shaped by them, but they can also act back upon them" (2004, 1013).

14. Carling notes three different kinds of "relational asymmetries" in migrant transnationalism: (1) transnational moralities, (2) information and imagination, and (3) transnational resource inequalities (2008, 1453).

15. Carling 2008.

16. Smith 2006.

17. Although in this chapter I focus only on the six respondents we met in Chapter 1, blowups happened in other cases as well, resulting in migrants' not returning to visit or severing ties with their non-migrant relatives. The cases in this chapter provide analytical clarity for these processes of transnational family conflict.

18. As I discussed in Chapter 1, Lan and her husband were given a total of $4,000 by a number of relatives when they got married, which they used to buy their plot of land.

19. Motorbikes in Saigon generally run between six and ten miles per hour, and with traffic, it takes them that long to get home, even though the distance is only seventeen miles.

20. For the social organization of shame in transnational families, see Peter 2010.

21. Sarah Mahler writes on the unequal power relations between migrant and non-migrant members of transnational families. She argues that differential access to communications "both reflects and translates to unequal power and corresponding dependency" (2001, 610). I note here that technologies of communication play a role in who initiates communication, but migrants do not always have greater access to technology than do non-migrants. Access is unevenly divided in both the homeland and the United States, with no uniform pattern of who has regular access. Distance and time play a role in how someone could ignore a phone ringing, avoid replying to an e-mail message, or not respond to Skype. In other words, just because technology exists does not mean social actors want to sustain communication.

22. For an in-depth look at the social pressures that deter migrants from making return visits to their home countries because they feel too ashamed of their economic inadequacy, see Carling 2002.

23. Sana writes: "Many migrants send money to their home communities simply to help family members pay everyday expenses. These remittances show altruism, moral commitment, or simply emotional attachment. They also transmit the news of the migrant's success in the United States. Yet this message may be deceptive: it is not unusual that migrants in dire financial situations still send money home to keep their families from suspecting the truth" (2005, 238).

24. Itzigsohn et al. 1999, 335.

25. Packard 1999, 82.

26. Mai et al. 2001.

27. Although rare, in some instances non-migrants find out through networks about the buying power of their migrant relatives' incomes.

28. Mauss 2000.

29. Carrier 1995; Levi-Strauss 1965; Malinowski 1932; Mauss 2000.

30. Codere 1950.

31. Gouldner 1960.

32. In the words of Peter Blau, "A person can establish superiority over others by overwhelming them with benefits they cannot properly repay and thus subduing them with the weight of their obligations to him . . . Imbalances of obligations incurred in social transaction produce differences of power. Unreciprocated, recurrent benefits obligate the recipient to comply with the requests of the supplier and thus give the latter power over the former" ([1964] 2009, 113, 140).

33. Sana 2005, 239.

34. Espiritu 2003.

35. Goldring 1998.

36. Georges 1990.

CONCLUSION

1. See the initial argument in Chapter 1 about the topic of special money.

2. Zelizer 1989, 343.

3. Zelizer 1994, 1.

4. Zelizer 1989, 344.

5. Singh 2006, 379.

6. For a discussion on wedding and inheritance money within transnational families, see Singh 2006.

7. Zelizer 1989.

8. Zelizer 1989, 1994, 1996, 1998, 2000.

9. Supriya Singh and her colleagues (2012) coined the term "transnational family money." They argue that transnational family money is "special monies." Here I draw on their insights, but my own formulation of migrant money is different from their analysis in three ways. First, I examine extended families, whereas they focus on nuclear families. Second, I explore the case of low-wage Vietnamese migrants, whereas they look at middle-class Indian

migrants. Finally, I assert that special money is about gaining status and returning to the homeland for consumption, whereas they do not look at this feature.

10. Singh, Robertson, and Cabraal 2012, 484.

11. Singh, Robertson, and Cabraal 2012, 464.

12. Kurien 2002, 38.

13. Åkesson 2011, 342.

14. Zelizer 1994.

15. Singh, Robertson, and Cabraal 2012.

16. Kurien 2002.

17. Åkesson 2011.

18. Åkesson 2011, 344.

19. A good body of research exists on the problems of monetary allocations in marriage that are separate from the kind of earmarking I discuss here; see, for example, Burgoyne 1990 and Pahl 2000.

20. I discuss elsewhere the importance of return visits as a "magnified moment" for Vietnamese immigrants; see Thai 2011.

21. Return visits are important magnified moments because they are, as Hochschild defines them, "episodes of heightened importance, either epiphanies, moments of intense glee or unusual insight, or moments in which things go intensely but meaningfully wrong. In either case, the moment stands out; it is metaphorically rich, unusually elaborate and often echoes" (1994, 4).

22. Derrida 1994, 64.

23. For a discussion on downward mobility as it relates to the American Dream ideology as a social contract for the American working class, see Newman 1993.

24. For a recent analysis of the social contract, particularly how shifts in the implicit contract embedded in American ideologies have evolved due to macrostructural changes, see Rubin 2012.

25. Lamont also documents the importance of competence as a "particular piece of evidence of equality" among black blue-collar workers. Furthermore, she shows that some black blue-collar workers stress consumption over production as a criterion for cultural membership (2000, 74–77).

26. For a discussion of Asian American identities, social citizenship, and consumption, see Park 2005.

27. Said 1979, 55.

28. For example, Parrenas advocates for a "subject level analysis" of migration that "moves beneath the structural and Institutional bases of social processes to deconstruct their minute effects on the subject" (2001b, 31).

29. See, for example, Harvey 1995, 2010; Sassen 1988, 1998.

30. Brettell and Hollifield 2008; Parrenas 2001b.

31. Schiller, Basch, and Blanc-Szanton 1992, 1.

32. For recent notable exceptions, see Dreby 2010a; Smith 2006.

33. In terms of return visits, Loretta Baldassar (1997, 1998, 2001) writes extensively on the theoretical and empirical importance of documenting homeland return visits and how such visits engender various forms of care regimes and identities.

34. Another problem, which is important to note here, is that language barriers among researchers based in the West impede their study of migration from the migrants' homeland; on this point see, for example, Boccagni 2011; Wimmer and Schiller 2003.

35. For a recent theoretical discussion on avoiding the paradigm of methodological nationalism in transnational studies in migration, see Amelina and Faist 2012. For a discussion of sampling procedures and studying floating populations, see Meeus 2012.

36. Ahmad 2009, 310.

37. Carling 2008, 1465.

38. Here I note the groundbreaking work of Espiritu (2003), who demonstrates a critical view of transnationalism through the experiences of the Filipino/a community in San Diego. While this work on transnational lives adds to our understanding of the immigrant experience, I take the analysis further by bringing into focus the perspectives of those in the homeland.

39. Harvey 1996, 362.

40. Zelizer 1997, 19.

41. Singh, Robertson, and Cabraal 2012, 484.

42. Giddens 1991, 6–7.

43. Miller 1995, 277.

44. DiMaggio 1991, 133.

45. For a discussion of standards of hierarchies as they relate to socioeconomic boundaries, see chapter 1 in Lamont 1992.

46. Kohn 1987.

47. See the concluding chapter in Lamont 2000.

48. Lamont (2000, chapters 1 and 2) found that some working-class individuals, such as blacks, identified measuring sticks other than economic success for validating self-esteem.

49. Bourdieu 1984; Caplovitz 1967; Veblen [1899] 1994.

50. By a "crisis in the political economy of care," we mean the depletion of care from the private home due to the nonparticipation of men in household work as more women enter the workforce locally or globally. We also mean that the crisis involves the depletion of care from the state in many forms, mostly in social services. Because of obligations to fulfill debts to international financial organizations, many developing nations cannot afford to provide basic needs for their citizens, prompting a migration culture among the poor. For a discussion of this point, see chapter 1 in Parrenas (2005). For an in-depth discussion of the evolution of the term "culture of migration," see Cohen 2004. For an analysis of a depletion of state care in Vietnam, see Cuong et al. 2000; Friedman et al. 2003; Knodel et al. 2000.

51. For an elaboration of this point, see, for example, Ehrenreich and Hochschild 2003; Parrenas 2001b.

52. For an in-depth treatment of the evolution of this demand, see Munger 2007.

53. Pierrette Hondagneu-Sotelo (2001) demonstrates this point most vividly in her work on housecleaners in Los Angeles. She argues that the concentration of Latinas in this occupational sector has cheapened the cost of labor to such an extent that even apartment dwellers can hire cleaners, whereas historically only the wealthy could afford such services.

54. As Sassen-Koob notes, "the use of immigrant labor reduces the cost for employers

directly through lower wages and indirectly through lower costs for the organization of production" (1981, 72).

55. For a discussion of the growth of these occupational classifications, see Sassen 1996a, 585–86.

56. Bataille [1932] 1985.

57. Mauss 2000; Veblen [1899] 1994.

58. Bataille [1932] 1985.

59. Bataille [1932] 1985, 121.

60. Bataille says, "If a part of wealth is doomed to destruction or at least to unproductive use without possible profit, it is logical, even inescapable, to surrender commodities without return" ([1949] 1988, 25).

61. For a lengthy treatment of this point, see Preparata 2008.

62. Preparata 2008, 175.

63. Bataille [1932] 1985, 117.

64. Indeed, Bataille writes: "In so-called civilized societies, the fundamental obligation of wealth disappeared only in a fairly recent period. . . . Everything that was generous, orgiastic, and excessive has disappeared" ([1932] 1985, 123).

65. Quoted in Goux 1990, 207. This entire issue of the journal focuses on Bataille's intellectual impact on theories of the economy.

66. Goux 1990, 206.

67. Symbolic power and symbolic violence were introduced by Bourdieu to analyze the tacit ways power and class are legitimated in society, wherein domination is accomplished invisibly. In the words of Bourdieu, "The distinctiveness of symbolic domination lies precisely in the fact that it assumes, of those who submit to it, an attitude which challenges the usual dichotomy of freedom and constraint" (1991, 51).

68. On this point, for an analysis of the "rationality of irrational behavior," see Jantzen and Ostergaard 1999.

69. Bataille [1932] 1985, 126.

70. Bataille [1932] 1985, 125–26.

71. Veblen [1899] 1994.

72. Chakravartty and Silva 2012, 364.

73. The hourglass economy has proliferated in many countries, especially in urban centers, but the distinction of the United States is the lack of state care, with the deepest form of deregulation in the industrial world. For an analysis of this point, see Sassen 1996b and Sassen-Koob 1981. For a theoretical discussion on the hourglass economy and immigrant incorporation, see Portes and Zhou 1993. For a historical look at the development of the hourglass economy over the second half of the twentieth century, see Massey and Hirst 1998.

74. See, for example, Glickman 1999; Gradin 2010; Harvey 2005, 2010.

75. Massey and Hirst 1998, 51.

76. Sassen-Koob (1981) notes that the hourglass economy has become a reality not only in the United States but in many major urban centers across the globe.

77. Sassen-Koob 1981, 72.

78. Wages for the low-wage labor force have declined over the past three decades when

we control for inflation; see Appelbaum, Bernhardt, and Murnane 2003; Capps et al. 2003; Munger 2007; Sassen 2002.

79. For example, studies have shown that migrant women are preferred over other women for jobs in the caring industry; see Glenn 1992, 2002; Hondagneu-Sotelo 2001; and Parrenas 2001b.

80. Sassen 1996a, 590.

81. See, for example, Wilson 1996, 1987.

82. Sassen 1996a, 580.

83. Sassen-Koob 1981, 81.

84. For elaborations on this point, see Sassen 1988, 1993, 1996a, 2002.

85. Here, I note Sassen-Koob's reminder that, given the prevalence of immigrants in the low-wage labor force, "it is important to point out that not all immigrants are at the bottom of the wage scale and that it is not simply through their low wages that they [firms] have a cost-lowering effect on production" (1981, 72).

86. As Sassen-Koob notes, "Their status as foreigners (often as temporary labor), their lack of familiarity with union politics, and their frequent segregation from native workers on the job and in neighborhoods, all combine to make immigrants unusually dependent on employers and difficult to recruit to working-class struggles" (1981, 72).

87. The current means of classifying the poverty level in the United States was devised more than forty years ago and assumed that families spend a third of their income on food. Multiplying food costs by three, then, set the official poverty rate. That number has been updated annually only to adjust for inflation. This method is severely flawed because food counts for far less than a third of family expenses today (because costs for housing and child care, for example, have increased). Compounding the problem is the fact that income is counted before subtracting payroll taxes; see Betson, Citro, and Michael 2000.

88. Capps et al. 2003.

89. This comparison refers to Australia, Austria, Canada, Denmark, Finland, Germany, Ireland, Luxembourg, the Netherlands, Norway, Sweden, Switzerland, and the United Kingdom. When we compare the U.S. poverty rate with poverty rates internationally, American children are more than twice as likely to be poor than are children in eight of these countries; see Gornick and Jantii 2011.

90. Gornick and Jantii 2011; Rainwater and Smeeding 2005.

91. In 2010, about 15 percent of Americans were living below the poverty rate; see Cauten and Fass 2008.

92. Berstein 2007; Betson, Citro, and Michael 2000; Cauten and Fass 2008.

93. For comparative expenditures for minimal basic needs, see Cauten and Fass 2008, 3.

94. These figures are for the forty-eight contiguous U.S. states and the District of Columbia. Hawaii and Alaska have separate guidelines; see Federal Register 2012, 4035.

95. I calculated this amount based on the federal minimum wage of $7.25 per hour, set in 2009. States, however, set their own minimum wage levels, and some states have higher minimum wages than the prevailing federal rate. A few states (e.g., Georgia and Wyoming) do not follow the federal minimum wage law; for instance, in Georgia, businesses with fewer than six employees do not have to apply the federal minimum law; see U.S. Census Bureau 2012.

96. To meet basic needs in New York, Houston, Aurora, and Decatur, a family of four needs, respectively, $66,840, $50,624, $57,998, and $42,748; see Cauten and Fass 2008.

97. Poverty levels in the United States are determined in absolute terms, with a baseline established by the federal government. In contrast, most advanced industrialized countries use a relative measure of poverty for social welfare provisions. As an example of what this means, the poverty level in the United States is about a quarter of the median income, whereas in Germany the poverty level is about two-thirds of the national median income; see Gautie and Schmitt 2010.

98. Appelbaum, Bernhardt, and Murnane 2003; Cauten and Fass 2008; Ehrenreich 2001; Gautie and Schmitt 2010.

99. This figure is based on the prevailing federal minimum wage of $7.25 and assumes fifty-two weeks of work at forty hours a week, which amounts to $30,160.

100. Shipler 2004, x–xi.

101. Ehrenreich 2001, 221.

102. Parrenas and Boris (2010) underscore intimate labor, such as the work of care and affection, particularly in the low-wage labor market. In doing so, they theorize intimate labor in relation to other forms of labor.

103. Roitman 2005.

APPENDIX

1. I did not go into the field in the summer of 2010 and winter 2011.

2. The average was precisely 39.3.

3. The average was precisely 40.5.

4. The average was precisely 34.6.

5. Thai 2008.

6. Gautie and Schmitt 2010.

7. Capps et al. 2003; Gautie and Schmitt 2010.

8. Newman and Chen 2008.

9. Whereas 28 percent of Vietnamese Americans had a bachelor's degree, the figures were, respectively, 53 percent, 52 percent, and 56 percent for the Chinese, Filipinos, and Koreans. For the Japanese and Indians, the figures were, respectively, 47 percent and 75 percent. These figures are based on census data for adults ages 25 and older; see table 1 in Allard 2011, 5.

10. Allard 2011, 12–13.

11. Wucker 2004.

12. Åkesson 2004, 153.

13. I employed strategies of the in-depth interview method, as discussed by Weiss 1995.

14. Charmaz 1983; Glaser and Strauss 1967; Strauss and Corbin 1997.

15. Other studies have commented on the use of interview data versus ethnographic field notes. See Lamont 1992, 2000; Rubin 1976, 1985; Waters 1999.

16. Thai 2008.

BIBLIOGRAPHY

Abrego, Leisy. 2009. "Economic Well-Being in Salvadoran Transnational Families: How Gender Affects Remittance Practices." *Journal of Marriage and the Family* 71 (November): 1070–85.

Acker, Joan. 1988. "Class, Gender, and the Relations of Distribution." *Signs: Journal of Women in Culture and Society* 13 (3): 473–97.

Ackerman, Frank. 1997. "Consumed in Theory: Alternative Perspectives on the Economics of Consumption." *Journal of Economic Issues* 31 (3): 651–64.

Adams, F. Gerard, and Anh Le Tran. 2010. "Vietnam: From Transitional State to Asian Tiger." *World Economics* 11 (2): 177–97.

Afsar, Rita. 2005. "Conditional Mobility: The Migration of Bangladeshi Female Domestic Workers." In *Asian Women as Transnational Domestic Workers*, edited by Shirlena Huang and Brenda Yeoh, 115–45. Singapore: Marshall Cavendish Academic.

Agarwal, Reena, and Andrew W. Horowitz. 2002. "Are International Remittances Altruism or Insurance? Evidence from Guyana Using Multiple-Migrant Households." *World Development* 30 (11): 2033–44.

Ahmad, Ali Nobil. 2009. "Bodies That (Don't) Matter: Desire, Eroticism, and Melancholia in Pakistani Labour Migration." *Mobilities* 4 (3): 309–27.

Åkesson, Lisa. 2004. "Making a Life: Meanings of Migration in Cape Verde." Ph.D. diss., University of Gothenburg, Gothenburg.

———. 2009. "Remittances and Inequality in Cape Verde: The Impact of Changing Family Organization." *Global Networks* 9 (3): 381–98.

———. 2011. "Remittances and Relationships: Exchange in Cape Verdean Transnational Families." *Ethnos: Journal of Anthropology* 76 (3): 326–47.

Akuei, Stephanie Riak. 2005. "Remittances as Unforeseen Burdens: The Livelihoods and Social Obligations of Sudanese Refugees." Global Migration Perspectives Working Paper #18. Geneva: Global Commission on International Migration.

Allard, Mary Dorinda. 2011. "Asians in the U.S. Labor Force: Profile of a Diverse Population." *Monthly Labor Review* (November): 3–22.

Allen, Katherine R., Rosemary Blieszner, and Karen A. Roberto. 2011. "Perspectives on Extended Family and Fictive Kin in Later Years." *Journal of Family Issues* 32 (9): 1156–77.

Amelina, Anna, and Thomas Faist. 2012. "De-naturalizing the National in Research Methodologies: Key Concepts of Transnational Studies in Migration." *Ethnic and Racial Studies* 35 (10): 1707–24.

Anh, Dang Nguyen. 2005. "Enhancing the Development Impact of Migrant Remittances and Diaspora: The Case of Vietnam." *Asia-Pacific Population Journal* 20 (3): 111–22.

Anh, Dang Nguyen, Tran Thi Bich, Nguyen Ngoc Quynh, and Dao The Son. 2010. "Development on the Move: Measuring and Optimising Migration's Economic and Social Impacts in Vietnam." In *Vietnam Country Report*, edited by Ramona Angelescu, Laura Chappell, Alex Glennie, George Mavrotas, and Dhananjayan Sriskandarajah. Delhi: Global Development Network and Institute for Public Policy Research.

Appadurai, Arjun. 1986. *The Social Life of Things: Commodities in Cultural Perspective.* Cambridge, UK: Cambridge University Press.

———. 1996. *Modernity at Large: Cultural Dimensions of Globalization.* Minneapolis: University of Minnesota Press.

Appelbaum, Eileen, Annette D. Bernhardt, and Richard J. Murnane. 2003. *Low-Wage America: How Employers Are Reshaping Opportunity in the Workplace.* New York: Russell Sage.

Arkadie, Brian Van, and Raymond Mallon. 2003. *Vietnam: A Transition Tiger.* Canberra: Asia Pacific Press.

Arnould, Eric J. 1989. "Toward a Broadened Theory of Preference Formation and the Diffusion of Innovations: Cases from Zinder Province, Niger Republic." *Journal of Consumer Research* 16 (2): 239–67.

Ashraf, Nava. 2009. "Spousal Control and Intra-Household Decision Making: An Experimental Study in the Philippines." *American Economic Review* 99 (4): 1245–77.

Baldassar, Loretta. 1997. "Home and Away: Migration, the Return Visit and 'Transnational' Identity." In *Communal Plural: Home, Displacement, Belonging*, edited by Ien Ang and Michael Symonds, 69–94. Sydney: RCIS.

———. 1998. "The Return Visit as Pilgrimage: Secular Redemption and Cultural Renewal in the Migration Process." In *The Australian Immigrant in the 20th Century: Searching Neglected Sources*, edited by Eric Richards and Jacqueline Templeton, 127–56. Canberra: Research School of Social Sciences, Australian National University.

———. 2001. *Visits Home: Migration Experiences between Italy and Australia.* Melbourne: Melbourne University Press.

Baldassar, Loretta, Cora Vellekoop Baldock, and Raelene Wilding. 2007. *Families Caring across Borders: Migration, Ageing, and Transnational Caregiving.* New York: Palgrave.

Bankston, Carl L., and Min Zhou. 1997. "The Social Adjustment of Vietnamese American Adolescents: Evidence for a Segmented Assimilation Approach." *Social Science Quarterly* 78 (2): 508–26.

Barbieri, Magali, and Daniele Belanger. 2009. *Reconfiguring Families in Contemporary Vietnam*. Stanford: Stanford University Press.

Basch, Linda, Nina Glick Schiller, and Cristina Szanton-Blanc. 1994. *Nations Unbound: Transnational Projects, Postcolonial Predicaments, and Deterritorialized Nation-States*. Amsterdam, The Netherlands: Gordon and Breach Publishers.

Bataille, Georges. [1932] 1985. "The Notion of Expenditure." In *Visions of Excess: Selected Writings, 1927–1939*, edited by Allan Stoekl, 116–29. Minneapolis: University of Minnesota Press.

———. [1949] 1988. *The Accursed Share*. New York: Zone Books.

Beckert, Jens, and Patrik Aspers. 2011. *The Worth of Goods: Valuation and Pricing in the Economy*. Oxford: Oxford University Press.

Belk, Russell W. 1999. "Leaping Luxuries and Transitional Consumers." In *Marketing in Transitional Economies*, edited by Rajeev Batra, 39–54. Boston: Kluwer Academic Publishers.

———. 2011. "Benign Envy." *Academy of Marketing Science Review* 1 (3/4): 117–34.

Berstein, Jared. April 2007. *More Poverty Than Meets the Eye*. Washington, DC: Economic Policy Institute.

Betson, David M., Constance F. Citro, and Robert T. Michael. 2000. "Recent Developments for Poverty Measurement in U.S. Official Statistics." *Journal of Official Statistics* 16 (2): 87–111.

Biggart, Nicole Woolsey, and Thomas D. Beamish. 2003. "The Economic Sociology of Conventions: Habit, Custom, Practice, and Routine in Market Order." *Annual Review of Sociology* 29: 443–64.

Bird, Rebecca Bliege, and Eric Alden Smith. 2005. "Signaling Theory, Strategic Interaction, and Symbolic Capital." *Current Anthropology* 46 (2): 221–48.

Blau, Peter M. [1964] 2009. *Exchange and Power in Social Life*. New Brunswick: Transaction Publishers.

Blumberg, Paul. 1974. "The Decline and Fall of the Status Symbol: Some Thoughts on Status in a Post-Industrial Society." *Social Problems* 21 (4): 480–98.

Boccagni, Paolo. 2011. "Rethinking Transnational Studies: Transnational Ties and the Transnationalism of Everyday Life." *European Journal of Social Theory* 15 (1): 117–32.

Bonacich, Edna, Sabrina Alimahomed, and Jake B. Wilson. 2008. "The Racialization of Global Labor." *American Behavioral Scientist* 52 (3): 342–55.

Bourdieu, Pierre. 1980. *The Logic of Practice*. Stanford: Stanford University Press.

———. 1984. *Distinction: A Social Critique of the Judgement of Taste*. Cambridge, MA: Harvard University Press.

———. 1986. "The Forms of Capital." In *Handbook for Theory and Research for the Sociology of Education*, edited by John G. Richardson, 241–58. New York: Greenwood Press.

———. 1990. "Social Space and Symbolic Power." *Sociological Theory* 7 (1): 14–25.

———. 1991. *Language and Symbolic Power*. Translated by Gino Raymond and Matthew Adamson. Cambridge, UK: Polity Press.

Brennan, Denise. 2004. "Women Work, Men Sponge, and Everyone Gossips: Macho Men and Stigmatized/ing Women in a Sex Tourist Town." *Anthropological Quarterly* 77 (1): 705–33.

Brettell, Caroline B., and James F. Hollifield. 2008. *Migration Theory: Talking across Disciplines*. New York: Routledge.

Bryceson, Deborah, and Ulla Vuorela. 2002a. *Transnational Families in the Twenty-First Century*. Oxford: Berg.

———. 2002b. "Transnational Families in the Twenty-First Century." In *The Transnational Family: New European Frontiers and Global Networks*, edited by Deborah Bryceson and Ulla Vuorela, 3–30. Oxford: Berg.

Buencamino, Leonides, and Sergei Gorbunov. 2002. *Informal Money Transfer Systems: Opportunities and Challenges for Development Finance*. New York: United Nations.

Burgoyne, Carole B. 1990. "Money in Marriage: How Patterns of Allocation Both Reflect and Conceal Power." *Sociological Review* 38 (4): 634–65.

Caldeira, Teresa. 1996. "Fortified Enclaves: The New Urban Segregation." *Public Culture* 8 (2): 303–28.

Calder, Lendol. 1999. *Financing the American Dream: A Cultural History of Consumer Credit*. Princeton, NJ: Princeton University Press.

Camic, Charles. 1986. "The Matter of Habit." *American Journal of Sociology* 91 (5): 1039–87.

Campbell, Colin. 1987. *The Romantic Ethic and the Spirit of Modern Materialism*. Oxford: Basil Blackwell.

Caplovitz, David. 1967. *The Poor Pay More: Consumer Practices of Low-Income Families*. New York: Free Press.

Capps, Randy, Michael Fix, Jeffrey S. Passel, Jason Ost, and Dan Perez-Lopez. 2003. "Immigrant Families and Workers: A Profile of the Low-Wage Immigrant Workforce." Facts and Perspectives Brief #4. Washington, DC: Urban Institute.

Cargill, Mary Terrell, and Jade Quang Huynh. 2000. *Voices of Vietnamese Boat People*. Jefferson, NC: McFarland.

Carling, Jorgen. 2002. "Return and Reluctance in Transnational Ties under Pressure." Paper presented at the Conference on the Dream and Reality of Coming Home, University of Copenhagen.

———. 2008. "The Human Dynamics of Migrant Transnationalism." *Ethnic and Racial Studies* 31 (8): 1452–77.

Carling, Jorgen, and Lisa Åkesson. 2009. "Mobility at the Heart of a Nation: Patterns and Meanings of Cape Verdean Migration." *International Migration* 47 (3): 123–55.

Carrier, James. 1995. *Gifts and Commodities: Exchange and Western Capitalism since 1700*. New York: Routledge.

Carruthers, Ashley. 2002. "The Accumulation of National Belonging in Transnational Fields: Ways of Being at Home in Vietnam." *Identities* 9 (4): 423–44.

———. 2004. "Cute Logics of the Multicultural and the Consumption of the Vietnamese Exotic in Japan." *Positions: East Asia Cultures Critique* 12 (2): 401–30.

———. 2008a. "Saigon from the Diaspora." *Singapore Journal of Tropical Geography* 29 (1): 68–86.

———. 2008b. "The Trauma of Synchronization: The Temporal Location of the Homeland in the Vietnamese Diaspora." *Crossroads: An Interdisciplinary Journal of Southeast Asian Studies* 19 (2): 63–91.

Cauten, Nancy K., and Sarah Fass. 2008, June. "Measuring Poverty in the United States." Fact Sheet. New York: National Center for Children in Poverty, Columbia University, Mailman School of Public Health.

Chae, Suhong. 2003. "Contemporary Ho Chi Minh City in Numerous Contradictions: Reform, Foreign Capital, and the Working Class." In *Wounded Cities*, edited by Jane Schneider and Ida Susser, 227–48. New York: Berg.

Chakravartty, Paula, and Denise Ferrera da Silva. 2012. "Accumulation, Dispossession, and Debt; The Racial Logic of Global Capitalism." *American Quarterly* 64 (3): 361–85.

Chamberlain, Mary, and Selma Leydesdorff. 2004. "Transnational Families: Memories and Narratives." *Global Networks* 4 (3): 227–41.

Chan, Yuk Wah, and Thi Le Thu Tran. 2011. "Recycling Migration and Changing Nationalisms: The Vietnamese Return Diaspora and Reconstruction of Vietnamese Nationhood." *Journal of Ethnic and Migration Studies* 37 (7): 1101–17.

Chao, Angela, and Juliet B. Schor. 1998. "Empirical Tests of Status Consumption: Evidence from Women's Cosmetics." *Journal of Economic Psychology* 19 (1): 107–31.

Charmaz, Kathy. 1983. "The Grounded Theory Method: An Explication and Interpretation." In *Contemporary Field Research*, edited by Ralph Emerson, 109–26. Boston: Little, Brown.

Cheal, David. 1987. "'Showing Them You Love Them': Gift Giving and the Dialectic of Intimacy." *Sociological Review* 35 (1): 150–69.

Chinoy, Ely. 1952. "The Tradition of Opportunity and the Aspirations of Automobile Workers." *American Journal of Sociology* 57 (5): 453–59.

Clark, William A. V. 2003. *Immigrants and the American Dream: Remaking the Middle Class*. New York: Guilford Press.

Codere, Helen. 1950. *Fighting with Property: A Study of Kwakiutl Potlatching and Warfare, 1792–1930*. Seattle: University of Washington Press.

Coe, Cati. 2011. "What Is Love? The Materiality of Care in Ghanaian Transnational Families." *International Migration* 49 (6): 7–24.

Cohen, Jeffrey H. 2001. "Transnational Migration in Rural Oaxaca, Mexico: Dependency, Development, and the Household." *American Anthropologist* 103 (4): 954–67.

———. 2004. *The Culture of Migration in Southern Mexico*. Austin: University of Texas Press.

———. 2011. "Migration, Remittances, and Household Strategies." *Annual Review of Anthropology* 40: 103–14.

Coleman, James S. 1990. *Foundations of Social Theory*. Cambridge, MA: Belknap.

Coleman, Richard P., and Lee Rainwater. 1978. *Social Standing in America: New Dimensions of Class*. New York: Basic Books.

Connell, R. W. 1995. *Masculinities*. Berkeley: University of California Press.

Csikszentmihalyi, Mihaly, and Eugene Halton. 1981. *The Meaning of Things: Domestic Symbols and the Self*. Cambridge, UK: Cambridge University Press.

Cuong, Bui The, Si Truong Anh, Daniel Goodkind, John Knodel, and Jed Friedman. 2000. "Older People in Vietnam amidst Transformations in Social Welfare Policy." In *Ageing in the Asia-Pacific Region: Issues, Policies, and Future Trends*, edited by David Phillips, 360–75. London: Routledge.

Cuong, Nguyen Viet, and Daniel Mont. 2012. "Economic Impacts of International Migration and Remittances on Household Welfare in Vietnam." *International Journal of Development* 11 (2): 144–63.

Dapice, David, and Jose A. Gomez-Ibanez. 2009. "Ho Chi Minh City: The Challenges of Growth." Vietnam's WTO Accession and International Competitiveness Research

Series, Policy Dialogue Paper #2. Ho Chi Minh City: United Nations Development Programme in Vietnam and Harvard Kennedy School.

Datta, Kavita, Cathy McIlwaine, Yara Evans, Joanna Herbert, Jon May, and Jane Wills. 2007. "From Coping Strategies to Tactics: London's Low-Pay Economy and Migrant Labour." *British Journal of Industrial Relations* 45 (2): 404–32.

Datta, Kavita, Cathy Mcilwaine, Joanna Herbert, Yara Evans, Jon May, and Jane Wills. 2009. "Men on the Move: Narratives of Migration and Work among Low-Paid Migrant Men in London." *Social and Cultural Geography* 10 (8): 853–73.

Davidson, Paul. 1972. "Money and the Real World." *Economic Journal* 82 (325): 101–15.

de Certeau, Michel. 1988. *The Practice of Everyday Life*. Berkeley: University of California Press.

Delaney, Kevin J. 2012. *Money at Work: On the Job with Priests, Poker Players, and Hedge Fund Traders*. New York: New York University Press.

Derrida, Jacques. 1994. *Given Time: I. Counterfeit Money*. Chicago: University of Chicago Press.

Deutsch, Francine M., Josipa Roksa, and Cynthia Meeske. 2003. "How Gender Counts When Couples Count Their Money." *Sex Roles* 48 (7/8): 291–304.

Dew, Jeffrey. 2011. "The Association between Consumer Debt and the Likelihood of Divorce." *Journal of Family Economic Issues* 32 (4): 554–65.

Diderot, Denis. 1956. "Regrets on Parting with My Old Dressing Gowns, Or, a Warning to Those Who Have More Taste than Money." In *Rameau's Nephew and Other Works by Denis Diderot*, edited by Denis Diderot, 309–17. New York: Hackett.

DiMaggio, Paul. 1991. "Social Structure, Institutions, and Cultural Goods." In *Social Theory for a Changing Society*, edited by Pierre Bourdieu and James S. Coleman, 133–55. Boulder, CO: Westview Press.

DiMaggio, Paul, and Hugh Louch. 1998. "Socially Embedded Consumer Transactions: For What Kinds of Purchases Do People Most Often Use Networks?" *American Sociological Review* 63 (5): 619–37.

Dodd, Nigel. 1994. *The Sociology of Money: Economics, Reason, and Contemporary Society*. Cambridge, UK: Polity Press.

Donor Working Group. 2012. *Vietnam Development Report 2012: Market Economy for a Middle-Income Vietnam*. Hanoi: Vietnam Development Information Center.

Dorais, Louis-Jacques. 1998. "Vietnamese Communities in Canada, France, and Denmark." *Refugee Studies* 11 (2): 108–25.

Dreby, Joanna. 2009. "Gender and Transnational Gossip." *Qualitative Sociology* 32 (1): 33–52.

———. 2010a. *Divided by Borders: Mexican Migrants and Their Children*. Berkeley: University of California Press.

———. 2010b. "Inequalities in Transnational Families." *Sociology Compass* 4 (8): 673–89.

Drummond, Lisa B. W. 2000. "Street Scenes: Practices of Public and Private Space in Urban Vietnam." *Urban Studies* 37 (12): 2377–91.

Duesenberry, James S. 1949. *Income, Saving, and the Theory of Consumer Behavior*. Cambridge, MA: Harvard University Press.

Durand, Jorge, William Kandel, Emilio A. Parrado, and Douglas S. Massey. 1996. "International Migration and Development in Mexican Communities." *Demography* 33 (2): 249–64.

Durand, Jorge, Emilio A. Parrado, and Douglas S. Massey. 1996. "Development: A Reconsideration of the Mexican Case." *International Migration Review* 30 (2): 423–44.

Dwyer, Rachel E. 2009. "Making a Habit of It." *Journal of Consumer Culture* 9 (3): 328–47.

Ehrenreich, Barbara. 2001. *Nickel and Dimed: On (Not) Getting By in America*. New York: Metropolitan Books.

Ehrenreich, Barbara, and Arlie Russell Hochschild. 2003. *Global Woman: Nannies, Maids, and Sex Workers in the New Economy*. New York: Metropolitan Books.

Engestrom, Yrjo, and Frank Blackler. 2005. "On the Life of the Object." *Organization* 12 (3): 307–30.

Espiritu, Yen Le. 2001. "We Don't Sleep Around Like White Girls Do: Family, Culture, and Gender in Filipina American Lives." *Signs: Journal of Women in Culture and Society* 26 (2): 415–40.

———. 2003. *Home Bound: Filipino American Lives across Cultures, Communities, and Countries*. Berkeley: University of California Press.

———. 2006. "Toward a Critical Refugee Study: The Vietnamese Refugee Subject in U.S. Scholarship." *Journal of Vietnamese Studies* 1 (1–2): 410–33.

Estrada, Emir, and Pierette Hondagneu-Sotelo. 2010. "Intersectional Dignities: Latino Immigrant Street Vendor Youth in Los Angeles." *Journal of Contemporary Ethnography* 40 (1): 102–31.

Fajnzylber, Pablo, and J. Humberto Lopez. 2007. *Close to Home: The Development Impact of Remittances in Latin America*. Washington, DC: World Bank.

Federal Register. 2012. *Annual Update of the Health and Human Services Poverty Guidelines*. Washington, DC: Department of Health and Human Services.

Fforde, Adam. 2009. "Economics, History, and the Origins of Vietnam's Post-War Economic Success." *Asian Survey* 49 (3): 484–504.

Fleming, Robin. 1997. *The Common Purse: Income Sharing in New Zealand Families*. Auckland: Auckland University Press.

Folbre, Nancy. 1986. "Hearts and Spades: Paradigms and Household Economics." *World Development* 14 (2): 245–55.

Frank, Andre Gunder. 1967. "The Development of Underdevelopment." *Monthly Review* 18 (4): 17–31.

Frank, Robert H. 1985. *Choosing the Right Pond: Human Behavior and the Quest for Status*. New York: Oxford University Press.

———. 2000. *Luxury Fever: Money and Happiness in an Era of Excess*. Princeton, NJ: Princeton University Press.

———. 2007. *Falling Behind: How Rising Inequality Harms the Middle Class*. Berkeley: University of California Press.

———. 2010. "Relative Deprivation, Inequality, and Consumer Spending in the United States." In *Beyond the Consumption Bubble*, edited by Karin M. Ekstrom and Kay Glans, 165–73. New York: Routledge.

———. 2011. "Relative Deprivation, Inequality, and Consuming Spending in the United States." In *Beyond the Consumption Bubble*, edited by Karin M. Ekstrom and Kay Glans, 165–73. New York: Routledge.

Frank, Robert H., and Philip Cook. 1997. *The Winner-Take-All Society*. New York: Penguin Books.

Freeman, James M. 1989. *Hearts of Sorrow: Vietnamese-American Lives*. Stanford: Stanford University Press.

———. 1995. *Changing Identities: Vietnamese Americans, 1975–1995.* Boston: Allyn and Bacon.

Freeman, James M., and Nguyen Dinh Huu. 2003. *Voices from the Camps: Vietnamese Children Seeking Asylum.* Seattle: University of Washington Press.

Freire, Alexandre Dormeier. 2009. "Motorbikes against Ho Chi Minh? Or the Consumption Icons of a Social Transformation in Vietnam." *Copenhagen Journal of Asian Studies* 27 (1): 67–87.

Friedman, Jed, John Knodel, Bui The Cuong, and Truong Si Anh. 2003. "Gender Dimensions of Support for Elderly in Vietnam." *Research on Aging* 25 (6): 587–630.

Funkhouser, Edward. 1995. "Remittances from International Migration: A Comparison of El Salvador and Nicaragua." *Review of Economics and Statistics* 77 (1): 137–46.

Gamburd, Michele Ruth. 2000. *The Kitchen Spoon's Handle: Transnationalism and Sri Lanka's Migrant Housemaids.* Ithaca, NY: Cornell University Press.

———. 2004. "Money That Burns Like Oil: A Sri Lankan Cultural Logic of Morality and Agency." *Ethnology* 43 (2): 167–84.

Gans, Herbert. 1992. "Second Generation Decline: Scenarios for the Economic and Ethnic Futures of Post-1965 Immigrants." *Ethnic and Racial Studies* 15 (2): 173–92.

Gautie, Jerome, and John Schmitt. 2010. *Low-Wage Work in the Wealthy World.* New York: Russell Sage Foundation.

Geertz, Clifford. 1973. *The Interpretation of Cultures.* New York: Basic Books.

Georges, Eugenia. 1990. *The Making of a Transnational Community: Migration, Development, and Cultural Change in the Dominican Republic.* New York: Columbia University Press.

Ger, Guliz, and Russell Belk. 1996a. "I'd Like to Buy the World a Coke: Consumptionscapes of the 'Less Affluent World.'" *Journal of Consumer Policy* 19 (3): 271–304.

———. 1996b. "Cross-Cultural Differences in Materialism." *Journal of Economic Psychology* 17: 55–78.

Gerth, Hans H., and C. Wright Mills. 1946. *From Max Weber: Essays in Sociology.* New York: Oxford University Press.

Giddens, Anthony. 1979. *Central Problems in Social Theory.* Berkeley: University of California Press.

———. 1991. *Modernity and Self Identity: Self and Society in the Late Modern Age.* Stanford: Stanford University Press.

Gilbert, Dennis. 2010. *The American Class Structure in an Age of Growing Inequality.* Thousand Oaks, CA: Sage.

Glaser, Barney G., and Anselm L. Strauss. 1967. *The Discovery of Grounded Theory: Strategies for Qualitative Research.* New York: Aldine de Gruyter.

Glenn, Evelyn Nakano. 1992. "From Servitude to Service Work: Historical Continuities in the Racial Division of Paid Reproductive Labor." *Signs: Journal of Women in Culture and Society* 18 (1): 1–43.

———. 2002. *Unequal Freedom: How Race and Gender Shaped American Citizenship and Labor.* Cambridge, MA: Harvard University Press.

Glewwe, Paul. 2004. "An Overview of Economic Growth and Household Welfare in Vietnam in the 1990s." In *Economic Growth, Poverty, and Household Welfare in Vietnam,* edited by Paul Glewwe, Nisha Agrawal, and David Dollar, 1–26. Washington, DC: World Bank.

Glickman, Lawrence. 1999. *A Living Wage: American Workers and the Making of Consumer Society*. Ithaca, NY: Cornell University Press.

Godwin, Deborah D. 1996. "Newlywed Couples' Debt Portfolios: Are All Debts Created Equally?" *Financial Counseling and Planning* 7 (1): 57–70.

———. 1997. "Dynamics of Households' Income, Debt, and Attitudes Toward Credit, 1983–1989." *Journal of Consumer Affairs* 31 (2): 303–25.

Goffman, Erving. 1951. "Symbols of Class Status." *British Journal of Sociology* 2: 294–304.

Goldberg, Herb, and Robert Lewis. 1978. *Money Madness: The Psychology of Saving, Spending, Loving, and Hating Money*. New York: Morrow.

Goldring, Luin. 1998. "The Power of Status in Transnational Social Fields." In *Transnationalism from Below*, edited by Michael Peter Smith and Luis Eduardo Guarnizo, 165–95. New Brunswick, NJ: Transaction.

———. 2003. "Gender, Status, and the State in Transnational Spaces." In *Gender and U.S. Immigration: Contemporary Trends*, edited by Pierrette Hondagneu-Sotelo, 341–58. Berkeley: University of California Press.

Gornick, Janet C., and Markus Jantii. 2011. "Child Poverty in Comparative Perspective: Assessing the Role of Family Structure and Parental Education and Employment." Luxemburg Income Study Working Paper Series #570.

Gouldner, Alvin W. 1960. "The Norm of Reciprocity: A Preliminary Statement." *American Sociological Review* 25 (2): 161–78.

Goux, Jean-Joseph. 1990. "General Economics and Postmodern Capitalism." *Yale French Studies* 78 (1): 206–24.

Gradin, Greg. 2010. *Empire's Workshop: Latin America, the United States, and the Rise of the New Imperialism*. New York: Holt.

Granovetter, Mark S. 1985. "Economic Action and Social Structure: The Problem of Embeddedness." *American Journal of Sociology* 91 (3): 481–510.

Grasmuck, Sherri, and Patricia Pessar. 1991. *Between Two Islands: Dominican International Migration*. Berkeley: University of California Press.

Guarnizo, Luis E. 2003. "The Economics of Transnational Living." *International Migration Review* 37 (3): 666–99.

Guarnizo, Luis E., and Michael Peter Smith. 1998. "The Location of Transnationalism." In *Transnationalism from Below*, edited by Michael Peter Smith and Luis Eduardo Guarnizo, 3–34. New Brunswick, NJ: Transaction.

Harms, Erik. 2011. "Material Symbolism on Saigon's Edge: The Political-Economic and Symbolic Transformation of Ho Chi Minh City's Periurban Zones." *Pacific Affairs* 84 (3): 455–73.

Harvey, David. 1995. "Globalization in Question." *Rethinking Marxism* 8 (4): 1–17.

———. 1996. *Justice, Nature, and the Geography of Difference*. Oxford: Blackwell Publishers.

———. 2005. *The New Imperialism*. Oxford: Oxford University Press.

———. 2010. *The Enigma of Capital*. London: Profile Books.

Heilbroner, Robert L. 1956. *The Quest for Wealth: A Study of Acquisitive Man*. New York: Simon and Schuster.

Heintz, James, and Radhika Balakrishnan. 2012. "Debt, Power, and Crisis: Social Stratification and the Inequitable Governance of Financial Markets." *American Quarterly* 64 (3): 387–409.

Hekman, Susan J. 1983. "Weber's Ideal Type: A Contemporary Reassessment." *Polity* 16 (1): 119–37.

Hiebert, Murray. 1996. *Chasing the Tigers: A Portrait of the New Vietnam.* New York: Kodansha International Publishers.

Hirschman, Elizabeth C. 1979. "Differences in Consumer Purchase Behavior by Credit Card Payment System." *Journal of Consumer Research* 6 (1): 58–66.

Hirschman, Elizabeth, and Morris B. Holbrook. 1982. "Hedonic Consumption: Emerging Concepts, Methods, and Propositions." *Journal of Marketing* 46 (3): 92–101.

Hoang, Kimberly Kay. 2010. "Economies of Emotion, Familiarity, Fantasy, and Desire: Emotional Labor in Ho Chi Minh City's Sex Industry." *Sexualities* 13 (2): 255–72.

———. 2011. "'She's Not a Low-Class Dirty Girl': Sex Work in Ho Chi Minh City." *Journal of Contemporary Ethnography* 40 (4): 367–96.

———. Forthcoming. *Chasing the Tiger: Sex and Finance in the New Global Economy.* Berkeley: University of California Press.

Hoang, Lan Anh. 2011. "Gendered Networks and Migration Decision-Making in Northern Vietnam." *Social and Cultural Geography* 12 (5): 419–34.

Hochschild, Arlie Russell. 1994. "The Commercial Spirit of Intimate Life and the Abduction of Feminism: Signs from Women's Advice Books." *Theory, Culture, and Society* 11 (2): 1–24.

———. 2000. "The Commodity Frontier." In *Self, Social Structure, and Beliefs,* edited by Jeffrey C. Alexander, Gary T. Marx and Christine L. Williams, 38–56. Berkeley: University of California Press.

———. 2002. "Love and Gold." In *Global Woman: Nannies, Maids, and Sex Workers in the New Economy,* edited by Barbara Ehrenreich and Arlie Russell Hochschild, 15–30. New York: Metropolitan Books.

Hochschild, Jennifer L. 1995. *Facing Up to the American Dream.* Princeton, NJ: Princeton University Press.

Holbrook, Morris B. 1986. "Emotion in the Consumption Experience: Towards a New Model of the Human Consumer." In *The Role of Affect in Consumer Behavior: Emerging Theories and Applications,* edited by Robert A. Peterson, Wayne D. Hoyer, and William R. Wilson, 17–52. New York: Lexington Books.

Hollands, Robert. 2002. "Divisions in the Dark: Youth Cultures, Transitions, and Segmented Consumption Spaces in the Night-time Economy." *Journal of Youth Studies* 5 (2): 153–71.

Homlong, Nathalie, and Elisabeth Springler. 2012. "Is Vietnam the New Asian Tiger? Scoreboard and Macroeconomic Evaluation of the Attractiveness for Foreign Investment." *International Journal of Economics and Finance Studies* 4 (2): 175–84.

Hondagneu-Sotelo, Pierrette. 1994. *Gendered Transitions: Mexican Experiences of Immigration.* Berkeley: University of California Press.

———. 2001. *Domestica: Immigrant Workers Cleaning and Caring in the Shadows of Affluence.* Los Angeles: University of California Press.

Hondagneu-Sotelo, Pierrette, and Ernestine Avila. 1997. "'I'm Here, but I'm There': The Meanings of Latina Transnational Motherhood." *Gender and Society* 11 (5): 548–71.

Hoyt, Elizabeth E. 1956. "The Impact of a Money Economy on Consumption Patterns." *Annals of the American Academy of Political and Social Science* 305 (May): 12–22.

Huang, Shirlena, Brenda S. A. Yeoh, and Theodora Lam. 2008. "Asian Transnational Families in Transition: The Liminality of Simultaneity." *International Migration* 46 (4): 3–13.

Hugo, Graeme. 2005. "Asian Experiences with Remittances." In *Beyond Small Change: Making Migrant Remittances Count*, edited by Donald F. Terry and Steven R. Wilson, 341–74. Washington, DC: Inter-American Development Bank.

Hyman, Louis. 2012a. *Borrow: The American Way of Debt*. New York: Vintage Books.

———. 2012b. "The Politics of Consumer Debt: U.S. State Policy and the Rise of Investment in Consumer Credit, 1920–2008." *Annals of the American Academy of Political and Social Science* 644 (1): 40–49.

Ingham, Geoffrey. 1996. "Money as a Social Relation." *Review of Social Economy* 54 (4): 508–29.

Itzigsohn, Jose. 1995. "Migrant Remittances, Labor Markets, and Household Strategies: A Comparative Analysis of Low-Income Household Strategies in the Caribbean Basin." *Social Forces* 74 (2): 633–55.

Itzigsohn, Jose, Carlos Dore Cabral, Esther Hernandez Medina, and Obed Vazquez. 1999. "Mapping Dominican Transnationalism: Narrow and Broad Transnational Practices." *Ethnic and Racial Studies* 22 (2): 316–421.

James, William. [1890] 1950. *The Principles of Psychology*. New York: Dover.

Jantzen, Christian, and Per Ostergaard. 1999. "The Rationality of 'Irrational Behavior': Georges Bataille on Consuming Extremities." In *Romancing the Market*, edited by Stephen Brown, Bill Clarke, and Anne Marie Doherty, 125–36. New York: Routledge.

Johnson, Heather Beth. 2006. *The American Dream and the Power of Wealth: Choosing Schools and Inheriting Inequality in the Land of Opportunity*. New York: Routledge.

Johnson, Phyllis J. 2003. "Financial Responsibility for the Family: The Case of Southeast Asian Refugees in Canada." *Journal of Family and Economic Issues* 24 (2): 121–42.

Jones, Huw, and Alan Findlay. 1998. "Regional Economic Integration and the Emergence of the East Asian International Migration System." *Geoforum* 29 (1): 87–104.

Juan, Karin Aguilar-San. 2009. *Little Saigons: Staying Vietnamese in America*. Minneapolis: University of Minnesota Press.

Kasinitz, Philip, John H. Mollenkopf, Mary C. Waters, and Jennifer Holdaway. 2008. *Inheriting the City: The Children of Immigrants Come of Age*. New York: Russell Sage Foundation.

Kasser, Tim. 2012. *The High Price of Materialism*. Cambridge, MA: Bradford Books.

Katrak, Ketu. 1996. "South Asian American Writers: Geography and Memory." *Amerasia Journal* 22 (3): 121–38.

Keely, Charles B., and Bao Nga Tran. 1989. "Remittances from Labour Migration: Evaluations, Performance, and Implications." *International Migration Review* 23 (3): 500–25.

Kelly, Gail Paradise. 1977. *From Vietnam to America: A Chronicle of the Vietnamese Immigration to the United States*. Boulder, CO: Westview Press.

Kenney, Catherine T. 2006. "The Power of the Purse: Allocative Systems and Inequality in Couple Households." *Gender and Society* 20 (3): 354–81.

Khairullah, Durriya Z., and Zahid Y. Khairullah. 1999. "Behavioral Acculturation and Demographic Characteristics of Asian-Indian Immigrants in the United States of America." *International Journal of Sociology and Social Policy* 19 (1/2): 57–80.

Kibria, Nazli. 1990. "Power, Patriarchy, and Gender Conflict in the Vietnamese Immigrant Community." *Gender and Society* 4 (1): 9–24.

———. 1993. *Family Tightrope: The Changing Lives of Vietnamese Americans*. Princeton, NJ: Princeton University Press.

———. 1994. "Household Structure and Family Ideologies: The Dynamics of Immigrant Economic Adaptation among Vietnamese Refugees." *Social Problems* 41 (1): 81–96.

———. 1997. "The Construction of 'Asian American': Reflections on Intermarriage and Ethnic Identity among Second-Generation Chinese and Korean Americans." *Ethnic and Racial Studies* 20 (3): 523–43.

———. 2002. *Becoming Asian American: Second-Generation Chinese and Korean American Identities*. Baltimore: Johns Hopkins University Press.

Kim, Ji-hoon Jamie. 2010. "Transnational Identity Formation of Second-Generation Korean-Americans Living in Korea." *Torch Trinity Journal* 13 (1): 70–82.

Kim, Kwang Chung, Won Moo Hurh, and Shin Kim. 1993. "Generation Differences in Korean Immigrants' Life Conditions in the United States." *Sociological Perspectives* 36 (3): 257–70.

Kitano, Harry H. L., and Stanley Sue. 1973. "The Model Minorities." *Journal of Social Issues* 29 (2): 1–9.

Klineberg, Eric. 2012. *Going Solo: The Extraordinary Rise and Surprising Appeal of Living Alone*. New York: Penguin Press.

Knight, James. 1968. *For the Love of Money: Human Behavior and Money*. New York: Lippincott.

Knodel, John, Jed Friedman, Truong Si Anh, and Bui The Cuong. 2000. "Intergenerational Exchanges in Vietnam: Family Size, Sex Composition, and the Location of Children." *Population Studies* 54 (1): 89–104.

Kohn, Melvin. 1987. "Cross-National Research as an Analytic Strategy." *American Sociological Review* 52 (6): 713–31.

Kokko, Ari. 1998. "Vietnam Ready for Doi Moi II?" *ASEAN Economic Bulletin* 15 (3): 319–27.

Kolb, Holger, and Henrik Egbert. 2008. *Migrants and Markets: Perspectives from Economics and the Other Social Sciences*. Amsterdam: Amsterdam University Press.

Kurien, Prema A. 2002. *Kaleidoscopic Ethnicity: International Migration and the Reconstruction of Community Identities*. New Brunswick, NJ: Rutgers University Press.

Kuroda, Akinobu. 2008. "What Is the Complementarity among Monies?" *Financial History Review* 15 (1): 7–15.

Lam, Andrew. 2005. *Perfume Dreams: Reflections on the Vietnamese Diaspora*. Berkeley: Heyday Books.

Lamb, David. 1997. "Viet Kieu: A Bridge between Two Worlds." *Los Angeles Times*, November 4.

Lamont, Michele. 1992. *Money, Morals, and Manners: The Culture of the French and the American Upper-Middle Class*. Chicago: University of Chicago Press.

———. 2000. *The Dignity of Working Men: Morality and the Boundaries of Race, Class, and Immigration*. New York: Russell Sage Foundation.

Larmer, Brook. 2000. "You Can Go Home Again: Returning 'Viet Kieu' Add a Strong Dash of America." *Newsweek*, November 27, 52.

Lascu, Dana-Nicoleta, Lalita A. Manrai, and Ajay K. Manrai. 1994. "Status Concern and Consumer Purchase in Romania: From the Legacies of Prescribed Consumption to the Fantasies of Desired Acquisition." In *Consumption in Marketizing Economies*, edited by Clifford J. Shultz, Russell W. Belk, and Guliz Ger, 80–122. New York: JAI Press.

Lea, Stephen E. G., Paul Webley, and Catherine M. Walker. 1995. "Psychological Factors in Consumer Debt: Money Management, Economic Socialization, and Credit Use." *Journal of Economic Psychology* 16 (4): 681–701.

Lee, Jennifer. 2002. *Civility in the City: Blacks, Jews, and Koreans in Urban America*. Cambridge, MA: Harvard University Press.

Levi-Strauss, Claude. 1965. "The Principle of Reciprocity." In *Sociological Theory: A Book of Readings*, edited by Lewis A. Coser and Bernard Rosenberg, 74–84. New York: Macmillan.

Levine, Joshua. 1997. "Liberte, Fraternite: But to Hell with Egalite." *Forbes*, Issue 11, 80–89.

Levinger, Benjamin, Marques Benton, and Stephan Meier. 2011. "The Cost of Not Knowing the Score: Self-Estimated Credit Scores and Financial Outcomes." *Journal of Family and Economic Issues* 32 (4): 566–85.

Levitt, Peggy. 1998. "Social Remittances: Migration Driven Local-Level Forms of Cultural Diffusion." *International Migration Review* 32 (4): 926–48.

———. 2001a. "Transnational Migration: Taking Stock and Future Directions." *Global Networks* 1 (3): 195–216.

———. 2001b. *The Transnational Villagers*. Berkeley: University of California Press.

Levitt, Peggy, and Nina Glick Schiller. 2004. "Conceptualizing Simultaneity: A Transnational Social Field Perspective on Society." *International Migration Review* 38 (3): 1002–39.

Leyshon, Andrew, and Nigel Thrift. 1995. "Geographies of Financial Exclusion: Financial Abandonment in Britain and the United States." *Transactions of the Institute of British Geographers* 3 (3): 312–41.

Lima, Fernando Herrera. 2001. "Transnational Families: Institutions of Transnational Social Space." In *New Transnational Social Spaces: International Migration and Transnational Companies in the Early Twenty-First Century*, edited by Ludger Pries, 77–93. London and New York: Routledge.

Lin, Jan. 1998. "Globalization and the Revalorizing of Ethnic Places in Immigration Gateway Cities." *Urban Affairs Review* 34 (2): 313–39.

Lindgren, Henry Clay. 1980. *Great Expectations: The Psychology of Money*. Los Altos, CA: William Kaufmann.

Lindley, Anna. 2010. *The Early Morning Phonecall: Somali Refugees' Remittances*. New York: Berghahn.

Lipsitz, George. 1995. "The Possessive Investment in Whiteness; Racialized Social Democracy and the 'White' Problem in American Studies." *American Quarterly* 47 (3): 369–87.

Lipton, Michael. 1980. "Migration from Rural Areas of Poor Countries: The Impact on Rural Productivity and Income Distribution." *World Development* 8 (1): 1–24.

Littwin, Angela K. 2007. "Beyond Usury: A Study of Credit Card Use and Preference among Low-Income Consumers." Harvard Law School Faculty Scholarship Series #8. Cambridge, MA: Harvard Law School.

Liu, William T., Maryanne Lamanna, and Alice Murata. 1979. *Transition to Nowhere: Vietnamese Refugees in America*. Nashville, TN: Charter House.

Livingstone, Sonia M., and Peter L. Lunt. 1992. "Predicting Personal Debt and Debt Repayment: Psychological, Social, and Economic Determinants." *Journal of Economic Psychology* 13 (1): 111–34.

Long, Lynellyn D. 2004. "Viet Kieu on a Fast Track Back." In *Coming Home? Refugees,*

Migrants, and Those Who Stayed Behind, edited by Ellen Oxfeld and Lynellyn D. Long, 65–89. Philadelphia: University of Pennsylvania Press.

Louie, Vivian. 2012. *Keeping the Immigrant Bargain: The Costs and Rewards of Success in America*. New York: Russell Sage Foundation.

Lowe, Lisa. 1996. *Immigrant Acts: On Asian American Cultural Politics*. London: Duke University Press.

Lucas, Robert E. B., and Oded Stark. 1985. "Motivations to Remit: Evidence from Botswana." *Journal of Political Economy* 93 (5): 901–18.

Lundberg, Shelly, and Robert A. Pollack. 1993. "Separate Spheres Bargaining and the Marriage Market." *Journal of Political Economy* 101 (6): 988–1010.

Lynd, Robert S., and Helen Merrell Lynd. 1937. *Middletown in Transition: A Study of Cultural Conflicts*. New York: Harcourt, Brace.

Ma, Eric Kit-wai. 2001. "Consuming Satellite Modernities." *Cultural Studies* 15 (3–4): 444–63.

Mahler, Sarah J. 1995. *American Dreaming: Immigrant Life on the Margins*. Princeton, NJ: Princeton University Press.

———. 2001. "Transnational Relationships: The Struggle to Communicate across Borders." *Identities* 7 (4): 583–619.

Mai, Nguyen Thi Tuyet, Kwon Jung, Garold Lantz, and Sandra G. Loeb. 2001. "An Exploratory Investigation into Impulse Buying Behavior in a Transitional Economy: A Study of Urban Consumers in Vietnam." *Journal of International Marketing* 11 (2): 13–35.

Mai, Nguyen Thi Tuyet, and Kirk Smith. 2011. "The Impact of Status Orientations on Purchase Preferences for Foreign Products in Vietnam and Implications for Policy and Society." *Journal of Macromarketing* 32 (1): 52–60.

Mai, Nguyen Thi Tuyet, and Siok Kuan Tambyah. 2011. "Antecedents and Consequences of Status Consumption among Urban Vietnamese Consumers." *Organizations and Markets in Emerging Economies* 2 (1): 75–98.

Malinowski, Bronislaw. 1932. *Argonauts of the Western Pacific*. London: Routledge and Kegan Paul.

Manning, Robert D. 2000. *Credit Card Nation: The Consequences of America's Addiction to Credit*. New York: Basic Books.

Martin, Philip. 1991. "Labor Migration and Economic Development." In *Determinants of Emigration from Mexico, Central America, and the Caribbean*, edited by Sergio Diaz-Briquets and Sidney Weintraub, 241–58. Boulder: Westview Press.

Maruyama, Masayoshi, and Le Viet Trung. 2007. "Supermarkets in Vietnam: Opportunities and Obstacles." *Asian Economic Journal* 21 (1): 19–46.

Marx, Karl, and Frederick Engels. 1988. *Economic and Philosophic Manuscripts of 1844* and *The Communist Manifesto*. Translated by Martin Milligan. New York: Prometheus Books.

Massey, Douglas S., and Deborah S. Hirst. 1998. "From Escalator to Hourglass: Changes in the U.S. Occupational Wage Structure 1949–1989." *Social Science Research* 27 (1): 51–71.

Mauss, Marcel. 2000. *The Gift: The Form and Reason for Exchange in Archaic Societies*. New York: W. W. Norton.

McCall, Leslie. 2001. "Sources of Racial Wage Inequality in Metropolitan Labor Markets: Racial, Ethnic, and Gender Differences." *American Sociological Review* 66 (4): 520–41.

McCracken, Grant. 1986. "Culture and Consumption: A Theoretical Account of the Structure and Meaning of Consumer Goods." *Journal of Consumer Research* 13 (1): 71–84.

———. 1988. *Culture and Consumption: New Approaches to the Symbolic Character of Consumer Goods and Activities*. Bloomington: Indiana University Press.

McKay, Deirdre. 2007. "'Sending Dollars Shows Feelings': Emotions and Economies in Filipino Migration." *Mobilities* 2 (2): 175–94.

McKenzie, Sean, and Cecilia Menjívar. 2011. "The Meanings of Migration, Remittances, and Gifts: Views of Honduran Women Who Stay." *Global Networks* 11 (1): 63–81.

Medoff, James, and Andrew Harless. 1996. *The Indebted Society: Anatomy of an Ongoing Disaster*. Boston: Little, Brown.

Meeus, Bruno. 2012. "How to 'Catch' Floating Populations? Research and the Fixing of Migration in Space and Time." *Ethnic and Racial Studies* 35 (10): 1775–93.

Migheli, Matteo. 2012. "Do the Vietnamese Support the Economic Doi Moi?" *Journal of Development Studies* 48 (7): 939–68.

Miller, Daniel. 1995. "Consumption Studies as the Transformation of Anthropology." In *Acknowledging Consumption: A Review of New Studies*, edited by Daniel Miller, 264–95. New York: Routledge.

———. 1998a. *Material Cultures*. Chicago: University of Chicago Press.

———. 1998b. *A Theory of Shopping*. Ithaca, NY: Cornell University Press.

Miller, Daniel, Peter Jackson, Nigel Thrift, Beverley Holbrook, and Michael Rowlands. 1998. *Shopping, Place, and Identity*. London and New York: Routledge.

Mishel, Lawrence, Jared Bivens, Elise Gould, and Heidi Shierholz. 2012. *The State of Working America*. Ithaca, NY: Institute of Labor Relations/Cornell University Press.

Montero, Darrel. 1979. *Vietnamese Americans: Patterns of Resettlement and Socioeconomic Adaptation in the United States*. Boulder, CO: Westview Press.

Morey, Nancy C., and Fred Luthans. 1984. "An Emic Perspective and Ethnoscience Methods for Organizational Research." *Academy of Management Review* 9 (1): 27–36.

Munger, Frank. 2007. *Laboring below the Line: The New Ethnography of Poverty, Low-Wage Work, and Survival in the Global Economy*. New York: Russell Sage Foundation.

Newman, Katherine S. 1993. *Declining Fortunes: The Withering of the American Dream*. New York: Basic Books.

———. 1999. *Falling from Grace: Downward Mobility in the Age of Affluence*. Berkeley: University of California Press.

Newman, Katherine S., and Victor Tan Chen. 2008. *The Missing Class: Portraits of the Near Poor in America*. Boston: Beacon.

Nghiep, Le Thanh, and Le Huu Quy. 2000. "Measuring the Impact of Doi Moi on Vietnam's Gross Domestic Product." *Asian Economic Journal* 14 (3): 317–33.

Nguyen, Hong. 2002. "Viet Kieu Remittances Set to Top $2 Billion Target." *Vietnam Investment Review*, December 9, 9.

Nguyen, Mimi Thi. 2012. *The Gift of Freedom: War, Debt, and Other Refugee Passages*. Durham. NC: Duke University Press.

Nguyen-Marshall, Van, Lisa B. Welch Drummond, and Daniele Belanger. 2012. *The Reinvention of Distinction: Modernity and the Middle Class in Urban Vietnam*. London and New York: Springer.

Nhat, Hong. 1999. "Hankering for 'Viet Kieu' Money." *Vietnam Economic News*, December 9, 12.

Nocera, Joseph. 1994. *A Piece of the Nation: How the Middle Class Joined the Money Class*. New York: Simon and Schuster.

Nurkse, Robert. 1957. *Problems of Capital Formation in Underdeveloped Countries*. New York: Basil Blackwell.

Ogbu, John U. 1987. "Variability in Minority School Performance: A Problem in Search of an Explanation." *Anthropology and Education Quarterly* 18 (4): 312–34.

Ogbu, John U., and Herbert D. Simons. 1998. "Voluntary and Involuntary Minorities: A Cultural-Ecological Theory of School Performance with Some Implications for Education." *Anthropology and Education Quarterly* 29 (2): 155–88.

Ohno, Kenichi. 2009. "Avoiding the Middle-Income Trap." *Renovating Industrial Policy Formulation in Vietnam* 26 (1): 25–43.

Ordabayeva, Nailya. 2011. "Getting Ahead of the Joneses: When Equality Increases Conspicuous Consumption among Bottom-Tier Consumers." *Journal of Consumer Research* 38 (1): 27–41.

Orellana, Marjorie Faulstich. 2001. "The Work Kids Do: Mexican and Central American Immigrant Children's Contributions to Households and Schools in California." *Harvard Educational Review* 71 (3): 366–90.

Orozco, Manuel. 2002. "Globalization and Migration: The Impact of Family Remittances in Latin America." *Latin American Politics and Society* 44 (2): 41–66.

Osella, Filippo, and Caroline Osella. 2000. "Migration, Money, and Masculinity in Kerala." *Journal of the Royal Anthropological Institute* 6 (1): 117–33.

Packard, Le Anh Tu. 1999. "Asian American Economic Engagement: Vietnam Case Study." In *Across the Pacific: Asian Americans and Globalization*, edited by Evelyn Hu-Dehart, 79–108. Philadelphia: Temple University Press.

Pahl, Jan. 2000. "The Gendering of Spending within Households." *Journal of Radical Statistics* 75 (August): 38–48.

Park, Kyeyoung. 1997. *The Korean American Dream: Immigrants and Small Business in New York City*. Ithaca, NY: Cornell University Press.

Park, Lisa Sun-Hee. 2005. *Consuming Citizenship: Children of Asian Immigrant Entrepreneurs*. Stanford: Stanford University Press.

Parrenas, Rhacel Salazar. 2001a. "Mothering from a Distance: Emotions, Gender, and Intergenerational Relations in Filipino Transnational Families." *Feminist Studies* 27 (2): 361–90.

———. 2001b. *Servants of Globalization: Women, Migration, and Domestic Work*. Stanford: Stanford University Press.

———. 2005. *Children of Global Migration*. Stanford: Stanford University Press.

Parrenas, Rhacel Salazar, and Eileen Boris. 2010. *Intimate Labors: Cultures, Technologies, and the Politics of Care*. Stanford: Stanford University Press.

Parry, Jonathan, and Maurice Bloch. 1989. "Introduction: Money and the Morality of Exchange." In *Money and the Morality of Exchange*, edited by Jonathan Parry and Maurice Bloch, 1–32. Cambridge, UK: Cambridge University Press.

Pellerin, Lisa A., and Elizabeth Stearns. 2001. "Status Honor and the Valuing of Cultural and Material Capital." *Poetics* 29 (1): 1–24.

Pels, Dick, Kevin Hetherington, and Frederic Vandenberghe. 2002. "The Status of the Object." *Theory, Culture, and Society* 19 (5/6): 1–21.

Pelto, Pertti J. 1970. *Anthropological Research: The Structure of Inquiry*. New York: Harper and Row.

Pelzer, Kristin. 1993. "Socio-Cultural Dimensions of Renovation in Vietnam: Doi Moi as Dialogue and Transformation in Gender Relations." In *Reinventing Vietnamese Socialism: Doi Moi in Comparative Perspective*, edited by William S. Turley and Mark Selden, 309–36. Boulder, CO: Westview Press.

Pertierra, Raul. 1992. *Remittances and Returnees: The Cultural Economy of Migration in Ilocos*. Ilocos Quezon City: New Day Publishers.

Peter, Kankonde Bukasa. 2010. "Transnational Family Ties, Remittance Motives, and Social Death among Congolese Migrants: A Socio-Anthropological Analysis." *Journal of Comparative Family Studies* 41 (2): 225–44.

Peterson, Christopher. 2003. *Taming the Sharks: Towards a Cure for the High-Cost Credit Market*. Akron, OH: University of Akron Press.

Pew Social and Demographic Trends Research Group. 2012. The Rise of Asian Americans. Washington, DC: Pew Research Center.

Pfau, Wade Donald, and Long Thanh Giang. 2009. "Determinants and Impacts of International Remittances on Household Welfare." *International Social Sciences Journal* 60 (197/198): 431–43.

Pham, Vu Hong. 2002. "Beyond and Before Boat People: Vietnamese American History before 1975." Ph.D. diss., Cornell University.

Phillips, Joan, and Robert B. Potter. 2009. "Questions of Friendship and Degrees of Transnationality among Second-Generation Return Migrants to Barbados." *Journal of Ethnic and Migration Studies* 35 (4): 669–88.

Pickles, John, and Adrian Smith. 1998. *Theorizing Transition: The Political Economy of Post-Communist Transformations*. New York: Routledge.

Pluiss, Caroline, and Chan Kwok-Bun. 2012. *Living Intersections: Transnational Migrant Identifications in Asia*. New York: Springer.

Poon, Jessie P. H., Diep T. Thai, and Deborah Naybor. 2012. "Social Capital and Female Entrepreneurship in Rural Regions: Evidence from Vietnam." *Applied Geography* 35 (1–2): 308–15.

Portes, Alejandro, and Ruben G. Rumbaut. 2001. *Legacies: The Story of the Immigrant Second Generation*. Berkeley: University of California Press.

Portes, Alejandro, and Julia Sensenbrenner. 1993. "Embeddedness and Immigration: Notes on the Social Determinants of Economic Action." *American Journal of Sociology* 98 (6): 1320–50.

Portes, Alejandro, and Min Zhou. 1992. "Gaining the Upper Hand: Economic Mobility among Immigrants and Domestic Minorities." *Ethnic and Racial Studies* 15 (4): 491–521.

———. 1993. "The New Second Generation: Segmented Assimilation and Its Variants." *Annals of the American Academy of Political and Social Science* 530 (1): 74–96.

Preparata, Guido Giacomo. 2008. "Un(for)giving: Bataille, Derrida, and the Postmodern Denial of the Gift." *Catholic Social Science Review* 13 (1): 169–200.

Pribilsky, Jason. 2012. "Consumption Dilemmas: Tracking Masculinity, Money, and Transnational Fatherhood between the Ecuadorian Andes and New York City." *Journal of Ethnic and Migration Studies* 38 (2): 323–43.

Prince, Melvin. 1992. "Women, Men, and Money Styles." *Journal of Economic Psychology* 14 (1): 175–82.

———. 1993. "Self Concept, Money Beliefs, and Values." *Journal of Economic Psychology* 14 (1): 161–73.

Pugh, Allison J. 2009. *Longing and Belonging: Parents, Children, and Consumer Culture.* Berkeley: University of California Press.

Radhakrishnan, Smitha. 2011. *Appropriately Indian: Gender and Culture in a New Transnational Class.* Durham, NC: Duke University Press.

Rainwater, Lee. 1974. *What Money Buys.* New York: Basic Books.

Rainwater, Lee, and Timothy M. Smeeding. 2005. *Poor Kids in a Rich Country: America's Children in Comparative Perspective.* New York: Russell Sage Foundation.

Ramstad, Yngve. 1998. "Veblen's Propensity for Emulation: Is It Passe?" In *Thorstein Veblen in the Twenty-First Century*, edited by Doug Brown, 3–27. Aldershot: Edward Elgar.

Ratha, Dilip, Sanket Mohapatra, and Ani Silwa. 2011. *Migration and Remittances Factbook 2011.* Washington, DC: World Bank.

Reichert, Joshua. 1981. "The Migrant Syndrome: Seasonal U.S. Wage Labor and Rural Development in Central Mexico." *Human Organization* 40 (1): 56–66.

———. 1982. "A Town Divided: Economic Stratification and Social Relations in a Mexican Migrant Community." *Social Problems* 29 (4): 413–23.

Reisman, David. 2012. *The Social Economics of Thorstein Veblen.* Northampton, MA: Edward Elgar.

Rivlin, Gary. 2011. *Broke, USA: From Pawnshops to Poverty, Inc.: How the Working Poor Became Big Business.* New York: HarperCollins.

Roberts, James A. 2011. *Shiny Objects: Why We Spend Money We Don't Have in Search of Happiness We Can't Buy.* New York: HarperOne.

Roitman, Janet. 2005. *Fiscal Disobedience: An Anthropology of Economic Regulation in Central Africa.* Princeton, NJ: Princeton University Press.

Rouse, Roger. 1991. "Mexican Migration and the Social Space of Postmodernism." *Diaspora* 1 (1): 8–23.

Rubin, Beth A. 2012. "Shifting Social Contracts and the Sociological Imagination." *Social Forces* 91 (2): 1–20.

Rubin, Lillian Breslow. 1976. *Worlds of Pain: Life in the Working-Class Family.* New York: Basic Books.

———. 1985. *Just Friends: The Role of Friendship in Our Lives.* New York: Harper and Row.

Rudmin, Floyd Webster. 1992. "Cross-Cultural Correlates of the Ownership of Private Property." *Social Science Research* 21 (1): 57–83.

Russell, Sharon Stanton. 1986. "Remittances from International Migration: A Review in Perspective." *World Development* 14 (6): 677–96.

Rutledge, Paul James. 1992. *The Vietnamese Experience in America.* Bloomington: Indiana University Press.

Sacks, Karen Brodkin. 1989. "Toward a Theory of Class, Race, and Gender." *American Ethnologist* 16 (3): 534–50.

Safri, Maliha, and Julie Graham. 2010. "The Global Household: Toward a Feminist Post-capitalist International Political Economy." *Signs: Journal of Women in Culture and Society* 36 (1): 99–121.

Said, Edward W. 1979. *Orientalism*. New York: Vintage Books.

Sampson, Helen. 2003. "Transnational Drifters or Hyperspace Dwellers: An Exploration of the Lives of Filipino Seafarers Abroad and Ashore." *Journal of Ethnic and Racial Studies* 26 (2): 253–77.

Sana, Mariano. 2005. "Buying Membership in the Transnational Community: Migrant Remittances, Social Status, and Assimilation." *Population Research and Policy Review* 24 (3): 231–61.

Sassen, Saskia. 1988. *The Mobility of Labor and Capital: A Study in International Investment and Labor*. New York: Cambridge University Press.

———. 1989a. "America's Immigration Problems." *World Policy Journal* 6 (4): 811–32.

———. 1989b. "New York City's Informal Economy." In *The Informal Economy: Studies in Advanced and Less Developed Countries*, edited by Alejandro Portes, Manuel Castells, and Lauren A. Benton, 60–77. Baltimore and London: Johns Hopkins University Press.

———. 1993. "The Impact of Economic Internationalization on Immigration: Comparing the U.S. and Japan." *International Migration Review* 31 (1): 73–99.

———. 1994. *Cities in a World Economy*. Thousand Oaks, CA: Pine Forge Press.

———. 1995. "Immigration and Local Labor Markets." In *The Economic Sociology of Immigration: Essays in Networks, Ethnicity, and Entrepreneurship*, edited by Alejandro Portes, 87–127. New York: Russell Sage Foundation.

———. 1996a. "New Employment Regimes in Cities: The Impact on Immigrant Workers." *New Community* 22 (4): 579–94.

———. 1996b. "Whose City Is It? Globalization and the Formation of New Claims." *Public Culture* 8 (2): 205–23.

———. 1998. *Globalization and Its Discontents: Essays on the New Mobility of People and Money*. New York: New Press.

———. 2001. *The Global City: New York, London, Tokyo*. Princeton, NJ: Princeton University Press.

———. 2002. "Deconstructing Labor Demand in Today's Advanced Economies: Implications for Low-Wage Employment." In *Laboring Below the Line: The New Ethnography of Poverty, Low-Wage Work, and Survival in the Global Economy*, edited by Frank Munger, 73–93. New York: Russell Sage Foundation.

Sassen-Koob, Saskia. 1981. "Towards a Conceptualization of Immigrant Labor." *Social Problems* 29 (1): 65–85.

Schiller, Nina Glick. 1999. "Transmigrants and Nation-States: Something Old and Something New in the U.S. Immigrant Experience." In *The Handbook of International Migration*, edited by Charles Hirschman, Josh DeWind, and Philip Kasinitz, 94–119. New York: Russell Sage Foundation.

———. 2005. "Transnational Social Fields and Imperialism: Bringing a Theory of Power to Transnational Studies." *Anthropological Theory* 5 (4): 439–63.

Schiller, Nina Glick, Linda Basch, and Cristina Blanc-Szanton. 1992. "Transnationalism: A New Analytic Framework for Understanding Migration." *Annals of the New York Academy of Sciences* 645 (1): 1–24.

Schiller, Nina Glick, Linda Basch, and Cristina Szanton Blanc. 1995. "From Immigrant to Transmigrant: Theorizing Transnational Migration." *Anthropological Quarterly* 68 (1): 48–63.

Schmalzbauer, Leah. 2004. "Searching for Wages and Mothering from Afar: The Case of Honduran Transnational Families." *Journal of Marriage and Family* 66 (5): 1317–31.

———. 2005a. *Striving and Surviving: A Daily Life Analysis of Honduran Transnational Families.* New York: Routledge.

———. 2005b. "Transamerican Dreamers: The Relationship of Honduran Transmigrants to the American Dream and Consumer Society." *Berkeley Journal of Sociology* 49 (1): 3–31.

———. 2008. "Family Divided: The Class Formation of Honduran Transnational Families." *Global Networks* 8 (3): 329–46.

Schor, Juliet B. 1998. *The Overspent American: Why We Want What We Don't Need.* New York: HarperCollins.

———. 2004. *Born to Buy: The Commercialized Child and the New Consumer Culture.* New York: Scribner.

Schwartz, Alex F. 2006. *Housing Policy in the United States.* New York: Routledge.

Schwenkel, Christina. 2009. *The American War in Contemporary Vietnam: Transnational Remembrance and Representation.* Bloomington: Indiana University Press.

Scitovsky, Tibor. 1969. *Money and the Balance of Payments.* London: Unwin.

Seshan, Ganesh, and Dean Yang. 2012. "Transnational Household Finance: A Field Experiment on the Cross-Border Impacts of Financial Education for Migrant Workers." Working Paper, Department of Economics, University of Michigan, Ann Arbor.

Seskin, Eugene P., and Shelly Smith. 2011. *Annual Revision of the National Income and Product Accounts.* Washington, DC: U.S. Department of Commerce, Bureau of Economic Analysis.

Shen, Hsiu-Hua. 2008. "The Purchase of Transnational Intimacy: Women's Bodies, Transnational Masculine Privileges in Chinese Economic Zones." *Asian Studies Review* 32 (1): 57–75.

Shipler, David K. 2004. *The Working Poor: Invisible in America.* New York: Alfred A. Knopf.

Shohet, Merav. 2010. "Silence and Sacrifice: Intergenerational Displays of Virtue and Devotion in Central Vietnam." Ph.D. diss., University of California, Los Angeles.

Shove, Elizabeth. 2003. *Comfort, Cleanliness, and Convenience: The Social Organization of Normality.* New York: Berg.

Shultz, Clifford, Nguyen Xuan Que, Anthony Pecotich, and William Ardrey. 1998. "Vietnam: Market Socialism, Marketing, and Consumer Behavior." In *Marketing and Consumer Behavior in East and South-East Asia*, edited by Anthony Pecotich and Clifford Shultz, 715–43. New South Wales, Australia: McGraw-Hill.

Simmel, Georg. 1904. "Fashion." *American Journal of Sociology* 62 (May): 541–58.

———. 1950. "The Metropolis and Mental Life." In *The Sociology of Georg Simmel*, edited by Kurt H. Wolff, 409–24. New York: Free Press.

———. [1900] 2004. *The Philosophy of Money.* Translated by Tom Bottomore and David Frisby. New York: Routledge.

Singh, Supriya. 1997. *Marriage Money: The Social Shaping of Money in Marriage and Banking.* St. Leonards, Australia: Allen and Unwin.

———. 2006. "Towards a Sociology of Money and Family in the India Diaspora." *Contributions to Indian Sociology* 40 (3):375–98.

———. 2009. "Mobile Remittances: Design for Financial Inclusion." *Internationalization, Design, and Global Development* 5263 (1): 515–24.

Singh, Supriya, Anuja Cabraal, and Shanthi Robertson. 2010. "Remittances as a Currency of Care: A Focus on 'Twice Migrants' among the Indian Diaspora in Australia." *Journal of Comparative Family Studies* 41 (2): 245–63.

Singh, Supriya, Shanthi Robertson, and Anuja Cabraal. 2012. "Transnational Family Money: Remittances, Gifts, and Inheritance." *Journal of Intercultural Studies* 33 (5): 475–92.

Skrbis, Zlatko. 2008. "Transnational Families: Theorising Migration, Emotions, and Belonging." *Journal of Intercultural Studies* 29 (3): 231–46.

Small, Ivan. 2012a. "Embodied Economies: Vietnamese Transnational Migration and Return Regimes." *Sojourn: Journal of Social Issues in Southeast Asia* 27 (2): 234–59.

———. 2012b. "Over There: Imaginative Displacements in Vietnamese Remittance Gift Economies." *Journal of Vietnamese Studies* 7 (3): 157–83.

Smelt, Simon. 1980. "Money's Place in Society." *British Journal of Sociology* 31 (2): 204–23.

Smith, Robert Courtney. 2006. *Mexican New York: Transnational Lives of New Immigrants.* Berkeley: University of California Press.

———. 2008. "Horatio Alger Lives in Brooklyn: Extra Family Support, Intrafamily Dynamics, and Socially Neutral Operating Identities in Exceptional Mobility among Children of Mexican Immigrants." *Annals of the American Academy of Political and Social Science* 620 (1): 270–90.

Song, Miri. 1999. *Helping Out: Children's Labor in Ethnic Businesses.* Philadelphia: Temple University Press.

Spivak, Gayatri Chakravorty. 1996. "Diasporas Old and New: Women in the Transnational World." *Textual Practice* 10 (2): 245–69.

Stark, Oded. 1986. "Remittances and Inequality." *Economic Journal* 96 (383): 722–40.

Stark, Oded, and Robert E. B. Lucas. 1988. "Migration, Remittances, and the Family." *Economic Development and Cultural Change* 36 (3): 465–81.

Strauss, Anselm, and Juliet Corbin. 1997. *Grounded Theory in Practice.* Thousand Oaks, CA: Sage.

Suksomboon, Panitee. 2008. "Remittances and 'Social Remittances': Their Impact on Livelihoods of Thai Women in the Netherlands and Non-Migrants in Thailand." *Gender, Technology, and Development* 12 (3): 461–82.

Sullivan, Teresa, Elizabeth Warren, and Jay Lawrence Westbrook. 1989. *As We Forgive Our Debtors: Bankruptcy and Consumer Credit in America.* New York: Oxford University Press.

———. 2000. *The Fragile Middle Class.* New Haven, CT: Yale University Press.

Suro, Roberto. 2003. *Remittance Senders and Receivers: Tracking the Transnational Channels.* Annual report by the director of the Multilateral Investment Fund and the Pew Hispanic Center, Washington, DC.

Tang, Eric. 2000. "Collateral Damage: Southeast Asian Poverty in the United States." *Social Text* 18 (1): 55–79.

Taylor, J. Edward. 1999. "The New Economics of Labour Migration and the Role of Remittances in the Migration Process." *International Migration* 37 (1): 63–88.

Teigen, Karl Halvor, Marina V. G. Olsen, and Odd Egil Solas. 2005. "Giver-Receiver Asymmetries in Gift Preferences." *British Journal of Social Psychology* 44 (1): 125–44.

Terry, Donald F., and Steven R. Wilson. 2005. *Beyond Small Change: Making Migrant Remittances Count*. Washington, DC: Inter-American Development Bank.

Thai, Hung Cam. 2006. "Money and Masculinity among Low Wage Vietnamese Immigrants in Transnational Families." *International Journal of Sociology of the Family* 32 (2): 247–71.

———. 2008. *For Better or for Worse: Vietnamese International Marriages in the New Global Economy*. New Brunswick, NJ: Rutgers University Press.

———. 2009. "The Legacy of Doi Moi, the Legacy of Immigration: Overseas Vietnamese Grooms Come Home to Vietnam." In *Reconfiguring Families in Contemporary Vietnam*, edited by Magali Barbieri and Daniele Belanger, 237–62. Stanford: Stanford University Press.

———. 2011. "Homeland Visits: Transnational Magnified Moments among Low-Wage Immigrant Men." In *At the Heart of Work and Family: Engaging the Ideas of Arlie Hochschild*, edited by Anita Ilta Garey and Karen V. Hansen, 250–61. New Brunswick, NJ: Rutgers University Press.

———. 2012a. "The Dual Roles of Transnational Daughters and Transnational Wives: Monetary Intentions, Expectations, and Dilemmas." *Global Networks* 12 (2): 216–32.

———. 2012b. "Low-Wage Vietnamese Immigrants, Social Class, and Masculinity in the Homeland." In *Men and Masculinities in Southeast Asia*, edited by Michele Ford and Lenore Lyons, 56–67. New York: Routledge.

———. Forthcoming. "Special Money in the Vietnamese Diaspora." In *Transpacific Studies*, edited by Janet Hopkins and Viet Thanh Nguyen. Honolulu: University of Hawaii Press.

Thao, Nguyen Minh. 2009. Migration, Remittances, and Economic Development: Case of Vietnam. Working Paper, Central Institute for Economic Management, Hanoi.

Thomas, Mandy. 1997. "Crossing Over: The Relationship between Overseas Vietnamese and Their Homeland." *Journal of Intercultural Studies* 18 (2): 153–76.

———. 1999a. "Dislocations of Desire: The Transnational Movement of Gifts within the Vietnamese Diaspora." *Anthropological Forum* 9 (2): 145–61.

———. 1999b. *Dreams in the Shadows: Vietnamese-Australian Lives in Transition*. Sydney: Allen and Unwin.

———. 2001. "Public Spaces/Public Disgraces: Crowds and the State in Contemporary Vietnam." *Sojourn* 16 (2): 306–30.

Thorne, Barrie. 1992. "Feminism and the Family: Two Decades of Thought." In *Rethinking the Family: Some Feminist Questions*, edited by Barrie Thorne with Marilyn Yalom, 3–30. Boston: Northeastern University Press.

Thorne, Barrie, and Marilyn Yalom. 1992. *Rethinking the Family: Some Feminist Questions*. Boston: Northeastern University Press.

Thu, Truong Thien, and Ranjith Perera. 2011. "Consequences of the Two-Price System for Land and Housing Market in Ho Chi Minh City, Vietnam." *Habitat International* 35 (1): 30–39.

Thu-Huong, Nguyen-Vo. 2008. *The Ironies of Freedom: Sex, Culture, and Neoliberal Governance in Vietnam*. Seattle: University of Washington Press.

Tingvold, Laila, Anne-Lise Middelthon, James Allen, and Edvard Hauff. 2012. "Parents and

Children Only? Acculturation and the Influence of Extended Family Members among Vietnamese Refugees." *International Journal of Intercultural Relations* 36 (2): 260–70.

Tran, Tini. 2000. "Business Opportunities Draw Viet Kieu Back to Vietnam." *AsianWeek* 21 (36): 14–16.

Trigg, Andrew B. 2001. "Veblen, Bourdieu, and Conspicuous Consumption." *Journal of Economic Issues* 35 (1): 99–115.

Truitt, Allison. 2006. "Big Money, New Money, and ATMs: Valuing Vietnamese Currency in Ho Chi Minh City." *Research in Economic Anthropology* 24 (1): 283–308.

———. 2008. "On the Back of a Motorbike: Middle Class Mobility in Ho Chi Minh City, Vietnam." *American Ethnologist* 35 (1): 3–19.

———. 2013. *Dreaming of Money in Ho Chi Minh City*. Seattle: University of Washington Press.

Turner, Sarah, and Phuong An Nguyen. 2005. "Young Entrepreneurs, Social Capital, and Doi Moi in Hanoi, Vietnam." *Urban Studies* 42 (10): 1693–1710.

Twitchell, James B. 2003. *Living It Up: America's Love Affair with Luxury*. New York: Simon and Schuster.

U.S. Census Bureau. 2012. *Labor Force, Employment, and Earnings, Table 652: Federal and State Minimum Wage Rates, 1940–2011*. Washington, DC: U.S. Census Bureau Statistical Abstract of the United States.

Urry, John. 2010. "Consuming the Planet in Excess." *Theory, Culture, and Society* 27 (2–3): 191–212.

Ustuner, Tuba, and Douglas B. Holt. 2010. "Toward a Theory of Status Consumption in Less Industrialized Countries." *Journal of Consumer Research* 37 (1): 37–56.

Valenta, Marko, and Zan Strabac. 2011. "Transnational Ties and Transnational Exchange." In *The Bosnian Diaspora: Integration in Transnational Communities*, edited by Marko Valenta and Sabrina P. Ramet, 163–84. Surrey: Ashgate.

Valenzuela, Jr., Abel. 1999. "Gender Roles and Settlement Activities among Children and Their Immigrant Families." *American Behavioral Scientist* 42 (4): 720–42.

Valverde, Kieu-Linh Caroline. 2012. *Transnationalizing Vietnam: Community, Culture, and Politics in the Diaspora*. Philadelphia: Temple University Press.

Vanwey, Leah K. 2004. "Altruistic and Contractual Remittances between Male and Female Migrants and Households in Rural Thailand." *Demography* 41 (4): 739–56.

Veblen, Thorstein. [1899] 1994. *The Theory of the Leisure Class*. New York: Penguin.

Vietnam News. 2002. "First Viet Kieu to Receive Property Certificate." *Vietnam News*, March 28, 2.

Waldinger, Roger, and Cynthia Feliciano. 2004. "Will the New Second Generation Experience 'Downward Assimilation'? Segmented Assimilation Re-assessed." *Ethnic and Racial Studies* 27 (3): 376–402.

Waldman, Michael. 2003. "Durable Goods Theory for Real World Markets." *Journal of Economic Perspectives* 17 (1): 131–54.

Waller, Spencer Weber, and Lan Cao. 1997. "Law Reform in Vietnam: The Uneven Legacy of Doi Moi." *International Law and Politics* 29:555–76.

Wallerstein, Immanuel Maurice. 1974. *The Modern World-System*. New York: Academic Press.

Warren, Elizabeth, and Amelia Warren Tyagi. 2003. *The Two-Income Trap*. New York: Basic Books.

Wasem, Ruth Ellen. 2010. *U.S. Immigration Policy on Permanent Admissions*. Congressional Research Service Report for Congress. Washington, DC: Congressional Research Service.

Waters, Mary. 1994. "Ethnic and Racial Identities of Second Generation Black Immigrants in New York City." *International Migration Review* 28 (4): 795–820.

———. 1999. *Black Identities: West Indian Immigrant Dreams and American Realities*. Cambridge, MA: Harvard University Press.

Watson, Matthew. 2012. "Desperately Seeking Social Approval: Adam Smith, Thorstein Veblen, and the Moral Limits of Capitalist Culture." *British Journal of Sociology* 63 (3): 491–512.

Weber, Max. 1947. *The Theory of Social and Economic Organization*. Translated by A. M. Henderson and Talcott Parsons. New York: Free Press.

———. [1922] 1978. *Economy and Society*. Berkeley: University of California Press.

Webley, Paul, and Richenda Wilson. 1989. "Social Relationships and the Unacceptability of Money as a Gift." *Journal of Social Psychology* 129 (1): 85–91.

Weiss, Robert Stuart. 1995. *Learning from Strangers: The Art and Method of Qualitative Interview Studies*. New York: Free Press.

Werner, Jayne, and Daniele Belanger. 2002. *Gender, Household, State: Doi Moi in Vietnam*. Ithaca, NY: Cornell University Southeast Asia Program Publications.

Wilson, Patricia, and Ray Pahl. 2011. "The Changing Sociological Construct of the Family." *Sociological Review* 36 (2): 233–66.

Wilson, William Julius. 1987. *The Truly Disadvantaged: The Inner City, the Underclass, and Public Policy*. Chicago: University of Chicago Press.

———. 1996. *When Work Disappears: The World of the New Urban Poor*. New York: Vintage Books.

Wimmer, Andreas, and Nina Glick Schiller. 2002. "Methodological Nationalism and Beyond: Nation-State Building, Migration, and the Social Sciences." *Global Networks* 2 (4): 301–34.

———. 2003. "Methodological Nationalism, the Social Sciences, and the Study of Migration: An Essay in Historical Epistemology." *International Migration Review* 37:556–610.

Woods, Walter. 1960. "Psychological Dimensions of Consumer Decision." *Journal of Marketing* 24 (3): 15–19.

World Bank. 2007. "Remittance Flows to Developing Countries to Exceed $200 Billion in 2006." Migration and Development Brief #2. Washington, DC: Migration and Remittances Team.

———. 2011. *Gross National Income per Capita 2010, Atlas Method and Purchasing Power Parity*, edited by World Development Indicators. Washington, DC: World Bank.

———. 2012a. "Remittances to Developing Countries Will Surpass $400 Billion in 2012." Migration and Development Brief #19. Washington, DC: World Bank.

———. 2012b. *Well Begun, Not Yet Done: Vietnam's Remarkable Progress on Poverty Reduction and the Emerging Challenges*, edited by World Bank Hanoi. Hanoi: World Bank.

Wright, Eric Olin. 1997. *Class Counts: Comparative Studies in Class Analysis*. Cambridge, UK: Cambridge University Press.

Wucker, Michele. 2004. "Remittances: The Perpetual Migration Machine." *World Policy Journal* 21 (2): 37–46.

Yablonsky, Lewis. 1991. *The Emotional Meaning of Money*. New York: Gardner Press.

Yamane, Linus. 2012. "Labor Market Discrimination: Vietnamese Immigrants." *Journal of Southeast Asian American Education and Advancement* 7 (1): 1–25.

Yeates, Nicola. 2004. "A Dialogue with 'Global Care Chain' Analysis: Nurse Migration in the Irish Context." *Feminist Review* 77 (1): 75–95.

Yeoh, Brenda, and Noor Abdul Rahman. 2005. *Asian Women as Transnational Domestic Workers*. Singapore: Marshall Cavendish International.

Young, Ken. 1999. "Consumption, Social Differentiation, and Self-Definition of the New Rich." In *Privilege in Capitalist Asia*, edited by Michael Pinches, 56–85. London: Routledge.

Yu, Elena S. H. 1979. "Family Life and Overseas Remittances in Southeastern China." *Journal of Comparative Family Studies* 10 (3): 445–54.

Zarate-Hoyos, German A. 2004. "Consumption and Remittances in Migrant Households: Toward a Productive Use of Remittances." *Contemporary Economic Policy* 22 (4): 555–65.

Zelizer, Viviana A. 1989. "The Social Meaning of Money: 'Special Monies.'" *American Journal of Sociology* 95 (2): 342–77.

———. 1994. *The Social Meaning of Money: Pin Money, Paychecks, Poor Relief, and Other Currencies*. New York: Basic Books.

———. 1996. "Payment and Social Ties." *Sociological Forum* 11 (3): 481–95.

———. 1997. *The Social Meaning of Money: Pin Money, Paychecks, Poor Relief, and Other Currencies*. Princeton, NJ: Princeton University Press.

———. 1998. "How People Talk about Money." *American Behavioral Scientist* 41 (10): 1373–83.

———. 2000. "The Purchase of Intimacy." *Law and Social Inquiry* 25 (3): 817–48.

———. 2005. *The Purchase of Intimacy*. Princeton, NJ: Princeton University Press.

———. 2012. "How I Became a Relational Economic Sociologist: What Does That Mean?" *Politics and Society* 40 (2): 145–74.

Zentgraf, Kristine M., and Norma Stoltz Chinchilla. 2012. "Transnational Family Separation: A Framework for Analysis." *Journal of Ethnic and Migration Studies* 38 (2): 345–66.

Zhou, Min, and Carl L. Bankston. 1998. *Growing Up American: How Vietnamese Children Adapt to Life in the United States*. New York: Russell Sage Foundation.

Zia, Helen. 2000. *Asian American Dreams: The Emergence of an American People*. New York: Farrar, Straus, and Giroux.

Zinn, Maxine Baca. 1994. "Feminist Rethinking from Racial-Ethnic Families." In *Women of Color in U.S. Society*, edited by Maxine Baca Zinn and Bonnie Thornton Dill, 303–14. Philadelphia: Temple University Press.

INDEX

Made in the USA
Las Vegas, NV
20 January 2022

41871823R00178